ENRIQUE GRANADOS

Enrique Granados.
Photo Courtesy of Douglas Riva.

ENRIQUE GRANADOS

A Bio-Bibliography

Carol A. Hess

Bio-Bibliographies in Music, Number 42
Donald L. Hixon, Series Adviser

GREENWOOD PRESS
New York • Westport, Connecticut • London

Library of Congress Cataloging-in-Publication Data

Hess, Carol A.
Enrique Granados : a bio-bibliography / Carol A. Hess.
p. cm.—(Bio-bibliographies in music, ISSN 0742-6968 ; no. 42)
Discography
Includes index.
ISBN 0-313-27384-7 (alk. paper)
1. Granados, Enrique, 1867-1916—Bibliography. 2. Granados, Enrique, 1867-1916—Discography. I. Title. II. Series.
ML134.G79H5 1991
016.78'092—dc20 91-32585

British Library Cataloguing in Publication Data is available.

Library of Congress Catalog Card Number: 91-32585
ISBN: 0-313-27384-7
ISSN: 0742-6968

First published in 1991

Greenwood Press, 88 Post Road West, Westport, CT 06881
An imprint of Greenwood Publishing Group, Inc.

Printed in the United States of America

The paper used in this book complies with the Permanent Paper Standard issued by the National Information Standards Organization (Z39.48-1984).

10 9 8 7 6 5 4 3 2 1

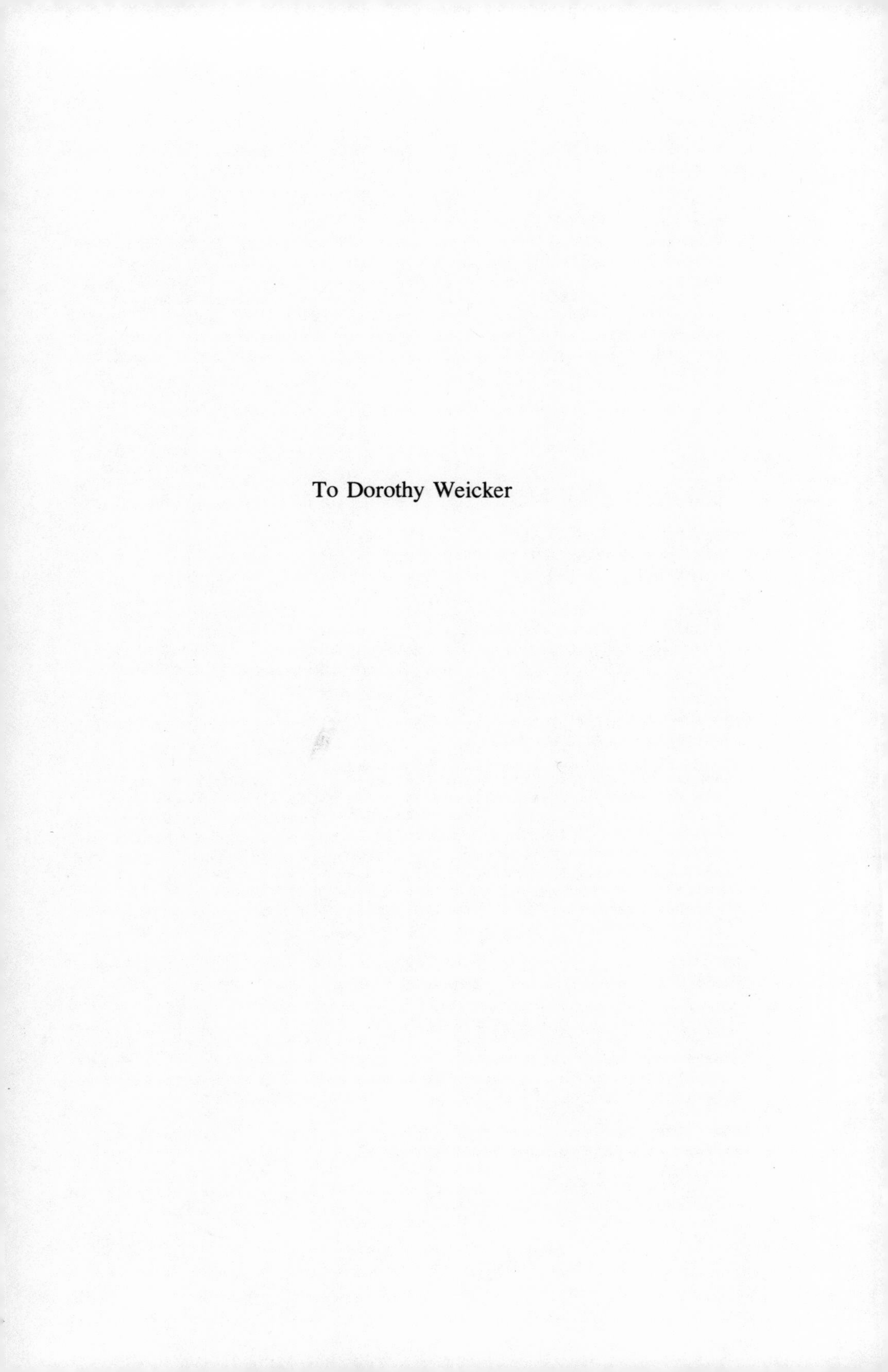

To Dorothy Weicker

Contents

Introduction 1

1. Biography 5

2. Bibliography 37

3. Works and Performances 111

4. Discography 133

Appendix 1. Listing of Original Works by Scoring 175

Appendix 2. Chronology of Important Events During Granados's Lifetime 179

Index 185

ENRIQUE GRANADOS

Introduction

At present, there exists neither a comprehensive bibliographic study nor an English-language treatment of the life and works of the Spanish composer Enrique Granados. This study, therefore, contains a short biography of the composer, an annotated bibliography of selected materials, a catalog of his works, a discography, and two appendices.

Granados's style is rooted in the late-Romantic idiom (with occasional integration of Spanish folk elements); compared with his contemporaries, Manuel de Falla and Isaac Albéniz, Granados seems conservative. Nonetheless, he lived and worked during a forward-looking period for the arts in Spain, particularly evident in Barcelona, where he spent his adult life. It was the height of the movement known as Catalan modernism, one that embraced all areas of artistic endeavor. In painting, Ramon Casas and Santiago Rusiñol adapted the techniques of French Impressionism and Art Nouveau (Picasso's early exhibits were held in Barcelona); in architecture, Antoní Gaudí drew upon Gothic elements, curvilinear shapes, and Art Nouveau's predilection for stained glass, brick, and mosaic. A newly founded Catalan-language press, including journals like *Pel & Ploma* and *Joventut*, engaged Barcelona's intellectuals in lively debate on political, literary, and artistic subjects.

Musical life in turn-of-the-century Barcelona also flourished, a renaissance due in large part to the efforts of musicologist, critic, teacher, and composer Felip Pedrell. His 1891 manifesto, *Por nuestra música*, for example, exhorted Spanish composers to seek inspiration in native musical traditions. Another strong influence was Wagner (the first Barcelona performance of *Lohengrin* in 1882 had created a great stir) and composers Granados, Albéniz, Enric Morera, Joaquín Nin, Joan Gay, Antoní Nicolau, Jaime Pahissa, and Amadeu Vives were variously influenced by that composer's aesthetic. Wagnerian ideals were particularly evident in efforts to establish a Catalan school of lyric theater, an enterprise that prompted much experimentation and discussion. In addition, works by the Franco-Belgian school of Franck and d'Indy figured on many concert programs during this period. Choral singing also enjoyed great popularity at this time, which spurred the founding of vocal ensembles like the Orfeó Catalá and Catalunya Nova. Finally, pianistic virtuosity reached an unprecedented level of excellence, as the careers of Granados, Albéniz, Nin, Joaquím Malats, and Ricardo Viñes all attest.

Granados was active in all of the above areas. A pianist of international reputation, he composed mainly for the keyboard; his works range from the unpretentious salon pieces of his youth to the justly renowned *Goyescas* suite. As Spain's first modern piano pedagogue, he authored one of the earliest treatments of pedaling; Granados also founded a musical academy that numbers pianist Alicia de Larrocha and soprano Conchita Badia among its graduates. Less known than his piano works are his chamber and orchestral works, among them a symphonic poem based on the *Divina Commedia*. Granados was intensely interested in lyric drama; in addition to his settings of Spanish libretti (*María del Carmen*, *Goyescas*), he also collaborated with more than one Catalan librettist in an effort to promote sung Catalan on the stage. Undoubtedly the high point of his career was his United States tour in 1916, during which several of his works received their American premieres. Granados's death at age forty-eight abruptly ended a career still full of promise.

Procedure: For a preliminary overview of source materials, the *Music Index* and the *RILM Abstracts of Music Literature* were consulted. Since few books and articles devoted solely to Granados exist, sources on or by individuals closely associated with the composer (Pedrell, Casals, Frank Marshall) have been examined. It quickly became clear, however, that many books and articles on Granados were filled with inaccuracies; therefore, contemporary articles from newspapers and artistic journals form the basis of this study.

In Chapter 1, **Biography**, only the more significant discrepancies between sources have been noted; citing every inaccuracy in dating would have been unprofitable and cumbersome. The **Bibliography**, Chapter 2, encompasses books, journal articles, selected dictionary and encyclopedia entries, theses and dissertations, program notes, and newspaper articles on Granados. Untitled reviews are arranged chronologically. The Music Division of the New York Public Library maintains a clipping file on the composer; these entries are cited with the abbreviation NYPL since many of the short articles and reviews on file do not give complete bibliographic details. The final section of the **Bibliography** includes selected correspondence to, from, or about Granados arranged chronologically; in lieu of the occasional missing date or place of writing, the archive source is cited.

Works, Chapter 3, also posed certain difficulties. First, Granados's works have an extremely uneven publication history; first performances sometimes took place up to two decades before the music was published. Second, many works were published posthumously, and then with arbitrary opus numbers, some of which have been maintained by biographers. Granados's own working habits further complicate attempts to establish a chronology of his output. His correspondence reveals that he frequently reworked earlier compositions that he had absent-mindedly or hastily sold (often under financial pressure) in unrevised form; therefore, only broad chronological categories can be established. Here, works have been arranged alphabetically (a listing by scoring appears in **Appendix 1**). Conflicting opus numbers have been noted and publication information and manuscript locations given when possible. Also, since many of Granados's works are widely known through arrangements by other composers, a representative sampling of these arrangements is given at the end of the **Works** section. For further information on arrangements, many of which are cited in the **Discography**, the reader is advised to consult *Classical Guitar Music in Print* (Philadelphia: Musicdata, 1989),

Music for More Than One Piano (Bloomington: Indiana University Press, 1983), and similar references.

Finally, since I have had limited access to the Granados family archives it was not always possible for me to update the efforts of two earlier catalogers, Iglesias and Tarazona (both of whom tend to cite unpublished works without giving manuscript information). A work for which no location was available to me is therefore listed with its references in either Iglesias or Tarazona, and can be assumed to be part of the family archive. Listings of publishers is by no means all-inclusive. Granados's unpublished pedagogical writings are cited by Boladeres Ibern.

Chapter 4, **Discography**, is a selective list of recordings currently available or of historical interest. **Appendix 2** is a chronology of musical, artistic, literary, and political events during Granados's lifetime, with emphasis on developments in Spanish music.

Unless otherwise specified, all translations are my own. In general, given the choice of Catalan or Castilian spellings, the more familiar usage has prevailed, e.g., "Enrique" rather than "Enric," but "Palau de la Música Catalana" rather than "Palacio." In potentially ambiguous cases, both Castilian and Catalan are given. Standardization of written Catalan did not occur until years after Granados's death; also, a change in Castilian accentuation took place during the 1950s. Both of these factors, in addition to inconsistencies in Granados's written French, have caused the author to transcribe all citations as they appeared in the original source, with no attempt at correction.

The author thanks Intersection for the Arts (San Francisco) for a grant contributing to her work in the United States. A research and travel grant generously provided by the Generalitat de Catalunya through the Institut d'Estudis Catalans (Barcelona) was essential for the collection of data in several institutions in Barcelona. It is also a pleasure to acknowledge the willing assistance of several individuals: Francesc Bonastre (Universitat Autònoma de Barcelona) for his support and advice; William Meredith (San Jose State University) for encouragement from the project's outset; Professor Emeritus Joaquín Nin-Culmell (University of California at Berkeley) for many valuable suggestions; Jaume Sobrequés (Universitat Autònoma de Barcelona), Maria Gloria Porrini, and Maria Dolores Millet for facilitating my work in Barcelona; the staff of the Biblioteca de l'Orfeó Català and of the Centre de Documentació Musical; Carlotta Garriga of the Marshall Academy, Barcelona; Milton Azevedo (University of California, Berkeley) for advice on Catalan translations; J. Rigbie Turner of the Pierpont Morgan Library in New York City; and Walter Clark (University of California, Los Angeles) for information on the manuscript of *María del Carmen*. I am also especially grateful to Alejandro Planchart (University of California, Santa Barbara) for reading the manuscript in its final stages.

Douglas Riva's generosity in providing materials from his own collection on the composer cannot be overstated; Mrs. Janos Scholz of the Schelling Archive in New York City gave graciously of her time and energy to make available important items of Granados's correspondence. In addition to Florence Myer's and Barbara DeMarco's editorial scrutiny, the interest and assistance of Greenwood's editorial staff are particularly appreciated, as is the clerical assistance of Pat Vercruyssen. Finally, special thanks to Dorothy Weicker, to whom this volume is warmly dedicated.

1

Biography

Youth

Pantaleón Enrique Joaquin Granados y Campiña was born on July 27, 1867, in Lleida (Lérida), Carrer Tallada, No. 1.[1] His mother, Enriqueta Elvira Campiña, was from Santander and his father, Calixto Granados Armenteros (an army captain in the Navarra Regiment), had been born in Cuba, still a Spanish colony. After a short assignment in Lleida, he was stationed as Military Governor in Santa Cruz de Tenerife for three and a half years. Granados states in his diary that the family moved to Barcelona around 1874 to take up residence in the Carrer Fenosa and later in the Passeig de Gracia.[2] Here, young Granados began to study solfège and piano with a family friend and musical dilettante, Captain José Junqueda.[3]

In 1879 he began to study piano at Barcelona's Escolania de la Mercé with Francesc Jurnet, a teacher of limited abilities; nonetheless Granados performed for Peter II, the deposed Emperor of Brazil, during the latter's tour of Europe in the late 1870s.[4] During 1879-80 Granados's musical studies were interrupted by a short stay in Olot (130 kilometers from Barcelona), where his older brother, also in the military, was stationed. Back in Barcelona, Granados was advised to study with Joan Baptista Pujol (1835-1898), then considered the best piano teacher in Barcelona. A graduate of the Paris Conservatory and a composer of brilliant opera paraphrases, Pujol authored a piano method, *Nuevo mecanismo del piano* (A New Approach to Piano Technique), and trained a generation of Catalan pianists, including Granados, Isaac

---

[1] *Libro de bautizos* no. 365 (folio 1), *Archivo Castrense del Ministerio del Ejército*, Parish Church of Lleida Cathedral, July 29, 1867. Several biographers cite July 29, 1868, as Granados's date of birth, probably because the composer's son Victor incorrectly gave the latter date.

[2] B365: 50.

[3] Variant spellings include "Junceda" and "Junquero." Granados's diary also states that these lessons began in Barcelona, not earlier in Lleida, as some biographers have suggested (see B365: 51-56).

[4] B304: 10. Tarazona incorrectly identifies the Emperor as Peter I.

Albéniz (1860-1909), Carles Vidiella (1856-1915), and Joaquím Malats (1872-1912). Pujol's contribution to the foundation of the so-called Catalan Piano School has been characterized by "[emphasis upon] clarity, color, and a mastery of the secrets of the pedals . . . an improvisatory style of playing, with all its attendant felicities of elaboration and embellishment."[5]

Granados began studies with Pujol in 1880; in 1883 he won an academy -sponsored contest, the Concurs Pujol, in which he performed Schumann's Sonata in G Minor and sight-read a commissioned work by Martínez-Imbert. Granados's later comment that the Schumann sonata was "the first decent work" he studied gives some idea of the level of his previous training.[6] Besides Albéniz, the Concurs Pujol jury included Felip Pedrell (1841-1922); apparently this occasion was Granados's first contact with the important critic, musicologist, teacher, and composer. The following year he began harmony and composition studies with Pedrell.

Although these studies laid the foundations for Granados's mature style, Pedrell's influence on the younger composer is ambiguous. Largely self-taught, Pedrell has been attacked for failure to provide his many students with a secure technical foundation. A common criticism of Granados that can presumably be traced to Pedrell, for example, is lack of finesse with larger forms; ever under the spell of Wagner, Pedrell made several attempts to imitate Wagnerian grandiosity, as in his vast, unsuccessful operatic trilogy, *Els Pirineus*. In a positive vein, however, Pedrell is justly credited for having initiated the nineteenth-century "Spanish musical renaissance," primarily through his transcriptions of hundreds of regional folk tunes and his desire to expose his students to this rich heritage. All were encouraged to embrace Spanish musical nationalism in their own fashion, as evidenced in the sharply defined personalities of Granados, Albéniz, and Falla. Granados, for example, displayed somewhat less inclination towards the nationalist tendencies Pedrell espoused, for aside from isolated instances of *andalucismo* (the *Twelve Spanish Dances* or *Seis piezas sobre cantos populares españoles*), the occasional use of traditional Spanish melodies (*Goyescas*), or the Catalan dance motifs of the op. 37 *Sardana*, Granados remained drawn to Central European models. Thus, although they differed in orientation, Granados was always quick to acknowledge Pedrell's influence in his artistic and philosophical development, and despite a short-lived public controversy in 1907 the two maintained consistently cordial relations.

Lessons with Pedrell may have ended because of financial strain brought about by the death of Granados's father earlier. In January of 1886 it was decided that Granados would work as a café-pianist to help support the large family, and soon he was employed five hours daily at the Café de las Delicias. The setting for Narcís Oller's novel *La Bogeria*, the Delicias was once one of Barcelona's best cafés, but by the time of Granados's brief tenure there, the atmosphere had deteriorated markedly. The management's tastes leaned towards opera pastiches laden with cheap pianistic flourishes (*efectos*) which Granados found himself incapable of producing; as a result of his artistic scruples, he soon found himself out of work. By this time, Granados's needs had come to

---

5 B182: n.p. (liner notes).

6 B365: 57.

the attention of Catalan entrepreneur Eduard Condé. Condé, who had already underwritten some of Granados's educational expenses, promptly engaged Granados to teach his own children for the then exorbitant rate of one hundred pesetas a month. Granados also made his first semipublic appearances at this time, including a performance April 9, 1886, at the Barcelona Athenaeum where he performed Gottschalk's two-piano *Tarantella* with Francisco Viñas in addition to García Robles's *Fantasía for Two Pianos, Harmonium, and String Quartet*.

Despite the prestige of being the best-paid piano teacher in Barcelona, however, Granados realized that a complete musical education was impossible in Spain, and with Condé's support, his goal of studying in Paris became feasible. To defray some of his expenses Granados again found café work, this time--with no illusions--at the Café Filipino. Although by the turn of the century café and cabaret life in Barcelona would reach a level comparable to Montmartre's Auberge du Clou, such sophistication was not apparent during Granados's two-month stint at the Filipino, where, in addition to improvising on popular melodies, he was expected to accompany patrons of dubious musical gifts, an activity he later engagingly described in his diary. In September 1887 Granados was finally able to leave for Paris.[7]

Paris

His goal was to enter the Conservatory, but a long bout with typhoid fever prevented him from taking the entrance exams, and by the time he recovered he had passed the age limit for admission.[8] Granados then decided to study piano privately with Charles Wilfrid de Bériot (1833-1914), son of violinist Charles August de Bériot and singer García-Malibran; de Bériot had co-authored with his father two manuals on accompaniment (*Méthode d'accompagnement pour piano et violon* and *L'Art de l'accompagnement appliqué au piano*) and had joined the Conservatory faculty in 1887 after serving at the Ecole Niedermeyer. It has been said that "de Bériot empathized more with the Spanish students than did Louis Diémer, the other prominent pedagogue at the Conservatoire."[9] Other students in de Bériot's class included a young Maurice Ravel (1875-1937) and the above-mentioned Viñes (1875-1943), also from Lleida, with whom Granados shared living quarters at the Hotel de Cologne et d'Espagne, Rue de Trévise. Viñes later recalled this period in his

---

[7] There is some disagreement as to the dates of Granados's stay in Paris. Although most sources give 1887 (B45: 175; B147, v. 1: 171; B304: 14;), others say that he departed in 1888. The matter is complicated by Granados's recollection in his diary (B365: 68) of having left for Paris at age seventeen-and-a-half, i.e. January 1885. According to Elaine Brody (B34: 170), Ricardo Viñes's diary states that when Viñes arrived in Paris October 13, 1887, "Enrique Granados . . . was already there . . . studying with Charles de Bériot."

[8] Illness is the reason usually given for Granados's decision to study privately rather than through the Conservatory. In 1887 the age limit for admission was twenty-two (Granados would have just turned twenty); in 1888 a quota of two foreign students per class was imposed. The length of his illness is not known.

[9] B34: 171.

unpublished diary and in memorial articles on Granados.[10] The future pioneer of modern piano music, Viñes would eventually perform Granados's more important works, in addition to those of Albéniz, Falla, Debussy, and Ravel.

As a piano student in Paris, Granados was routinely exposed to de Bériot's insistence on extreme refinement in tone production; his subsequent interest in pedal technique is also attributed to his teacher's influence. Another area de Bériot emphasized was improvisation. Although the practice of preluding (i.e. preparing the audience for an ensuing recital by improvising a short introduction) had largely died out by the late nineteenth century, improvisation still figured in many of Granados's performances (see B274). Already highly skilled as an improviser, his work with de Bériot only reinforced this natural ability.

Paris's impact on Granados the young composer is less clear.[11] French music was then at a point of transition: although the influence of the Franco-Belgian school, led by César Franck (1822-1890) and Vincent d'Indy (1851-1931), was beginning to wane, "Impressionism" was not yet a significant musical force. (Debussy, for example, had composed little but early "Wagnerian" songs and the *Two Arabesques* for piano.) Granados seems to have established contacts in more conservative French musical circles, such as his associations with d'Indy and the Schola Cantorum. Indeed, although Granados maintained ties with Paris throughout his career, the modern French idiom never attracted him as it did Albéniz; rather, his mature style reflects the late-Romantic propensity for meandering chromaticism, virtuosic flourishes, and thematic reminiscence. Nevertheless, it has been claimed that his juxtaposition of modal and tonal writing and his use of the augmented triad, "which he frequently used in a coloristic way rather than as a means of obscuring the tonality" can be attributed to French influence.[12] A record of Granados's development as a composer during the Paris years is found in the recently discovered *Album: Paris, 1888*, a collection of nearly forty piano miniatures and sketches. According to an early biographer, Henri Collet, the *Jota* for *Miel de la Alcarria* (dedicated to Viñes) was also conceived in Paris[13] as were many of the *Twelve Spanish Dances*.

After two years abroad and several unsuccessful attempts to interest Parisian publishers in his music, Granados returned to Barcelona on July 14, 1889.

---

[10] See B370. There is confusion among biographers regarding Granados's association with this important figure; Iglesias, for example, claims (with no apparent justification) that Granados lodged with Catalan tenor Francesc Viñas.

[11] Several biographers state that Granados studied with Massenet, an assertion that seems to be unfounded.

[12] B153: 18.

[13] B45: 177-78.

Early Career: Barcelona and Madrid

Upon his return, Granados negotiated the publication of his *Twelve Spanish Dances* with Barcelona's Casa Dotesio. Published individually in the early 1890s, the *Spanish Dances* were the first works by which Granados gained international recognition, for Cui, Massenet, Saint-Saëns and Grieg all praised them. On April 20, 1890, Granados made his official debut at Barcelona's Teatre Líric[14] where he premiered several original compositions: the early *Arabesca*, selected *Spanish Dances*, and the now-lost *Serenata española* (often confused with Albéniz's composition of the same title). The concert typified that era's tastes in programming; in addition to the above, Granados performed Saint-Saëns's *Allegro appassionato*, Bizet's Minuet from *L'Arlesienne*, Mendelssohn's *Capriccio brillante*, a substantial Chopin group, and Beethoven's Trio op. 1 no. 1 with members of a sextet that performed the *Sinfonia* from Mozart's *Zauberflöte*, transcriptions of a Schubert *Moment Musical*, *Souvenir de Tannhäuser*, and yet another Mozart arrangement. The press greeted Granados's compositions enthusiastically, and one reviewer emphasized the new depth the young composer's style had acquired in Paris:

> As a pianist, he is of the refined and elegant type. . . As a composer, the work we were favored with, the *Serenata española*, reveals that [Granados's] genius--which seems even greater when compared with his more modest, earlier creations--is growing from day to day.[15]

The *Spanish Dances* proved to be among Granados's most popular works. At the Palace of Sciences on July 31, 1892, he performed several of the *Dances* with the newly founded Orfeó Català (Granados's involvement in this organization's initial stages is described below). On October 29, 1892, Granados returned to the Líric to perform *Spanish Dance* no. 3, "Fandango," in a concert honoring Catalan composer and conductor Antoní Nicolau (1858-1933). Several of the *Spanish Dances* were eventually orchestrated (by Joan Lamote de Grignon and Rafael Ferrer); the earliest orchestration, however, seems to be that by García Farià, who presented three orchestrated *Dances* on April 10, 1892, in a concert by the Perez Cabrero Orchestra at the Líric. The concert also included a Passacaglia by García Farià and Granados's interpretation of the Grieg Concerto in A Minor, Schumann's *Variations on the Name ABEGG*, and several shorter piano works.

In 1891 Granados participated in the founding of one of Barcelona's most visible musical symbols, the Orfeó Català. Enthusiasm for Catalan language and literature sparked by the mid-century movement known as the *Renaixança* had long since entered musical life, and Barcelona's composers were quick to express Catalanist sentiments through new arrangements of traditional folk songs. Several choruses, each with its particular slant, were founded in the last decades of the century to perform either folk repertory, new works by Catalan composers, standard

---

[14] Fernández-Cid incorrectly gives 1889 as the date of Granados's debut at the Líric (see B101: 49).

[15] "Como pianista es el tipo de la elegancia y del sentimiento. . . . Como compositor, la *Serenata española*, obra suya que nos dejó oír, revela que va creciendo de día en día el génio que se manifestó ya con gran pujanza al apuntar las modestas producciones de que hablamos antes". B64: 5076.

classical repertory, or some combination of the above. The founding of the most influential of these choruses, the Orfeó Català, is generally attributed to Amadeu Vives (1871-1932) and Lluís Millet (1867-1941). Granados's diary, however, sheds a different light on the organization's beginnings: "With Amadeo Vives . . . and Luis Millet, fervent enthusiast of choral singing . . . we founded in 1891 the Orfeó Català. Another friend, Enrique [*sic*] Morera, lent us his assistance."[16]

It appears, however, that the Orfeó soon acquired political overtones that were distasteful to Granados. Of the "musical Catalanists," often unreceptive to Castilian or Andalusian musical traditions, Granados commented:

> They want to impart to the Orfeó a Catalanist political tone with which I am not in sympathy, for it seems to me that art has nothing to do with politics. . . . This matter has caused me more unpleasantness, to the point of receiving criticisms and anonymous letters in which I have been accused of writing Andalusian dances! As if this were a sin. . . . I consider myself as much a Catalan as anyone, but in my music I want to express what I feel, what I admire, what seems right to me, be it Andalusian or Chinese.[17]

Nevertheless, over the course of his career Granados maintained cordial ties with the Orfeó and founders Vives, Millet, and Morera (1865-1942). For example, he gave a benefit concert dedicated "to the choristers of the Orfeó Català" May 2, 1902; more important, he engaged the group for the premiere of his two most ambitious vocal works, *Cant de les estrelles* (1911) and *Elegía eterna* (1914). But although Granados set to original music numerous Catalan texts, both in theater and art song, arranging traditional Catalan folk-songs, the route to local recognition for many of Barcelona's composers, never seems to have attracted him.

In 1892 Granados met Amparo Gal y Lloberas, daughter of Valencian businessman Francesc Gal; as of November of the same year Granados's name disappears from extant records of Barcelonese musical life. This hiatus from 1892-95 (which some biographers call "the long silence") is often attributed to his courtship and subsequent marriage, for in 1893 the couple was married in Barcelona's fashionable Iglesia de la Merced. In July 1894 their first child, Eduardo, was born; five other children --Solita, Enrique, Victor, Francisco, and Natalia--would eventually follow.

Granados was in fact quite active during this period. He spent part of 1894-95 in Madrid, where besides trying to publish his music he sought

---

16 "Con Amadeo Vives . . . y Luis Millet, fogoso entusiasta de las masas corales . . . hemos fundado (1891) el Orfeó Català. Nos ayuda mucho otro compañero que se llama Enrique Morera". B365: 78.

17 "Al Orfeó se le quiere dar un color político catalanista, y en eso no estoy conforme. A mi me parece que el arte no tiene nada que ver con la política . . . ¡Esto me ha causado algunos disgustos, llegando a recibir desprecios y anónimos en que se me acusa de escribir danzas andaluzas! Como si fuera un pecado. . . . Yo me considero tan catalán como el que más, pero en mi música quiero expresar lo que siento, lo que admiro y lo que me parezca bien sea andaluz o chino". Ibid.

a Chair in piano on the faculty of the Madrid Conservatory. As in Paris, however, he fell ill and was unable to present himself for the required public exams (*oposiciones*); besides, according to one biographer the jury was rigged in favor of Pilar Fernández de la Mora, then a favorite with Madrid's audiences.[18] Granados also presented concerts of his own works at the Salón Romero. For example, on February 15, 1895, he performed the Piano Trio (completed in January of the previous year), the Quintet in G Minor, and several piano works: *Spanish Dances* nos. 1-3, a now lost *Balada*, the *Valses poéticos*, and an Impromptu. Assisting Granados were Mssrs. Francés, Peraita, Cuenca, and a promising young cellist, Pablo Casals (1876-1973).

By October 1895 Granados was back in Barcelona, where he performed d'Indy's *Symphony on a French Mountain Air* under the auspices of the Catalan Concert Society (Societat Catalana de Concerts) a subscription series founded by Nicolau. On November 14 of the same year Granados performed Albéniz's *Rhapsodie espagnole*, with the composer conducting. Between December 1896 and May 1897 Granados gave seven chamber music concerts with the Catalan Concert Society, often with the Belgian violinist Mathieu Crickboom (1871-1947), who had moved to Barcelona in 1895. Other performances included Granados's January 17, 1897, appearance with Catalunya Nova, the choral group founded by Morera. Here Granados gave the first Barcelona performance of his Impromptu, which, judging from concert reviews, was overshadowed by the premiere of Morera's *Plany*.

When the Catalan Concert Society dissolved during the summer of 1897, Crickboom founded the Philharmonic Society (Societat Filharmonica), with the goal of promoting chamber music in the essentially opera-oriented Barcelonese musical environment. Granados's first appearance with the new society took place November 9, 1897, at the Sala Estela, where he played Lekeu's Sonata for Violin and Piano with Crickboom, and Beethoven's Trio in D Major, op. 70 no. 1 with Crickboom and Casals. In the next seven years, Granados performed with the Philharmonic Society on more than twenty-five occasions, often with Casals and occasionally giving the Barcelona premiere of new works from France, like Saint-Saëns's Violin Sonata, op. 75 on December 28, 1902. He also continued to compose, although none of his own chamber works (such as those completed earlier in Madrid) figures on Philharmonic Society programs. At this time Granados also tried his hand at orchestral composition, and on October 31, 1899, conductor Joan Lamote de Grignon of the Musical Society of Barcelona (Societat Musical de Barcelona) premiered the *Suite sobre cantos gallegos* and the *Marcha de los vencidos*. On December 4 Granados gave what seems to have been the first Barcelona performance of the *Valses poéticos*, which were warmly if not perceptively received:

> The *Valses poéticos* of maestro Granados, which so aptly justify their title, were played by the composer and aroused the enthusiasm of the select audience.[19]

---

[18] B300: 3.

[19] "Los *Valses poéticos* del maestro Granados, que tan bien justifican su título, ejecutados por su autor, despertaron el entusiasmo de la selecta concurrencia". B332: 13498.

In mid-1898 Granados returned to Madrid to premiere his first stage work, the *zarzuela María del Carmen*. During the winter of 1896 he had seen the play of the same title by Josep Feliu y Codina (1845-1897), a successful work that the novelist Clarín praised after one of its many revivals. The idea of composing a *zarzuela* (loosely defined as a Spanish version of *singspiel*, in which spoken dialogue substitutes for recitative) may well have beckoned commercial success to Granados, since the lightweight *zarzuelas* of Chueca and Chapí were then extremely popular. Granados had already composed incidental music for Feliu y Codina's *Miel de la Alcarria*, a work in a similar vein,[20] and was thus familiar with the playwright's style. Like *Miel de la Alcarria*, *María del Carmen* concerns violent passions, this time in the orchards of Murcia. According to one account, playwright and composer spent several weeks in that province, presumably in search of authenticity: "Poet and musician moved to Murcia and lived in the orchards, generously subsidized by the Count of Roche."[21]

María del Carmen opened on November 12, 1898, at Madrid's Teatro de Parish,[22] with Marina Gurina as María. Other singers included Navarro, Puiggener, and Simonetti; the composer conducted (Casals had rehearsed the orchestra). The work was a qualified success, with most favorable responses directed towards Granados's deft incorporation of popular elements. The libretto, however, provoked negative reactions:

> It is unnecessary to analyze in any detail the reasons why [*María del Carmen*'s] success was not as warm and decisive as might have been expected. The main reason is the libretto, written in a form that makes lyric declamation impossible. And, being used by a composer constantly eager to declaim, its pedestrian quality was thus accentuated, rather than attenuated or suppressed.[23]

Other critics mentioned lack of receptivity to Granados's departures from more familiar zarzuela formulae, especially evident in his frequent use of the orchestra as protagonist rather than as mere accompaniment. Since the lyric season at the Parish featured more conventional works like "classic" zarzuelas *Dolores* (Bretón) and the immensely popular *Jugar con fuego* (Barbieri), the commentary of critic Eduardo Bustillo is not surprising: "Some of the motifs and dramatic situations are

---

[20] Marquez Villanueva points out the double meaning in the title: "La Alcarria, a region in central Spain, is famous for its excellent honey, and the title is quite a sarcastic one, as the drama is a bitter and most brutal portrait of Spanish rural life." See B175: 4.

[21] "Poeta y músico trasladaronse á Murcia, vivieron en la huerta espléndidamente asistidos y obsequiados por el conde de Roche". See B198: 2.

[22] The name of the theater is often incorrectly given as "Price," another *zarzuela* theater in Madrid.

[23] "No es menester analizar mucho para dar con la causa de que el éxito no fuera tan decisivo y caluroso como había derecho á esperar. La principal está en el libretto, escrito en una forma que hace imposible la declamación lírica y servido por el músico, en su afán de declamar siempre, de un modo que evidencia los prosaismos en lugar de atenuarlos, de suprimirlos". B198: 2.

treated in too elevated a fashion for the typical 'ignorant zarzuelist', whose powerful tastes rule and will always rule popular theater."[24]

Between the November 1898 premiere and January 9, 1899, *María del Carmen* received a total of nineteen performances. On December 8 and 17, 1898, Granados and baritone Puiggener gave benefit recitals at the Teatro Parish, the second one for the Madrid Press Association. Most important, *María del Carmen* attracted the attention of the Queen Regent María Cristina, who decorated the composer with the Cross of Carlos III.

In Barcelona, the press prepared the public for the musical aspects of *María del Carmen* by reporting sarcastically on Madrid's reception of the work:

> "Informed specialists" believe that the work is hardly musical; they miss a duo or a *romanza* of the old school and believe that Granados has abused [the concept of] sung dialogues, the specialty of Wagner.[25]

Granados conducted the Barcelona premiere on May 31, 1899, at the Teatre Tívoli. Critics praised the orchestration and the composer's dramatic sense, with particular accolades for the second act. The advance publicity in combination with political sentiments may have contributed to the presence of opening night claques (see B310), for by departing from the formulae of the convention-bound zarzuela Granados was certain to disappoint the more musically conservative public; by employing overtly non-Catalan subject matter and musical materials he was sure to arouse the ire of Catalanist advocates of a theatrical tradition removed from the influence of the essentially Castilian zarzuela. The suggestion of reviewer "M.J.B." that the claques were politically motivated therefore has credence. Addressing the main character herself, "M.J.B." makes a vague gesture of reconciliation: "How welcome you are, gentle maid of the orchards, cloaked in the garb of a *murciana*--but with the soul of a Catalan."[26]

Again, despite a generally positive reaction to the work, Granados was urged to seek libretti worthy of his talent. A reviewer for the popular Catalan journal *La Esquella de la Torratxa* declared:

> And now I will say that if *María del Carmen* does not enjoy the same fate as her French counterpart [Bizet's *Carmen*], it will not be Granados's fault as a composer . . . rather for having applied his

---

[24] "Algunos motivos y situaciones están tratados por el gran maestro demasiado alto y brillantemente para el 'vulgo zarzuelero', cuyo gusto dominante impera e imperará siempre en aquel popular teatro". Quoted by Angel Sagardia in B268: (n. p.).

[25] "Los hombres del oficio creen que . . . la obra es poco musical [y] echan de menos algun duo y alguna romanza de la antigua escuela y opinan que el señor Granados ha abusado de los diálogos cantados, que son la especialidad de Wagner". B254: 12618.

[26] "Bienvenida seas, gentil huertana; vas vestida de murciana y tienes el alma catalana". B310: 5.

> music to such a deficient, unmusical, and undramatic libretto. . . [with] ordinary, pedestrian recitatives written in prose.[27]

In June 1899 *María del Carmen* received eleven performances at the Tívoli in addition to several brief revivals throughout the year, including one in December at the Teatre Principal. It was also performed in Valencia. Although Granados always considered María del Carmen his best stage work, it was not revived again in Barcelona until December 1935 (see B174).

Catalan Lyric Theater Works

Throughout the remainder of 1899 Granados continued his chamber music performances with the Philharmonic Society. He also gave a two-piano recital with Malats at the Teatre de Novetats on June 9. *María del Carmen* seems to have piqued his interest in the stage, however; like Albéniz, he remained drawn to the theater throughout his career and put great effort in the production of his dramatic works. Granados's half-dozen settings of Catalan libretti are considered below, while his last opera, *Goyescas*, is discussed on pp. 25-32.

In 1899 the Catalan poet Adrià Gual (1872-1943) founded the Teatre Intim, an experimental company that presented original works by Catalan authors and modern theater works (e.g. Ibsen, Hauptmann, Maeterlinck) in Catalan translation. One of the new company's first productions was Gual's *Blancaflor*, a lyric drama based on Catalan folk legends. Gual had originally commissioned Albéniz to provide a score; however, due to the production of that composer's opera *Arthur*, Albéniz had to abandon *Blancaflor* and Granados was called in at the last minute. Along with Maeterlinck's *Interior*, *Blancaflor* premiered with doubtful success at the Teatre Líric on January 30, 1899. In his memoirs, Gual describes the premiere's adverse circumstances; these included an unduly long intermission due to scene change complications and the unexplained absence of three orchestra players. Reviews were sympathetic to Gual's conception but bluntly noted his lack of technical expertise:

> To fully describe the impression [*Blancaflor*] made on the public . . . it would be necessary to fill many pages, and there is no time for that. May they [the Teatre Intim] continue in their worthy endeavor: perhaps someday they will achieve the success that eluded them last night.[28]

Granados collaborated with Gual in only one other project, a Vetllades Artístiques presentation (a theater series sponsored by a shopkeepers' organization) that took place June 6, 1906. It consisted of Granados's

---

27 "Y ara diré que si á *María del Carmen* no li passa lo mateix que á sa famosa tocaya francesa [*Carmen* de Bizet] la culpa no será d'en Granados com à autor de la música . . . sino per haver-la aplicada á un llibre tan deficient, tan poch musical, tan poch dramátich . . . [amb] recitats vulgars, pedestres y escrits en prosa". B60: 362-63.

28 "Para decir *toda* la impresión que causó al público . . . sería preciso llenar muchas cuartillas . . . [y] no hay tiempo para ello. Sigan adelante en su noble empresa: quizás otro día alcanzarán la victoria, que anoche no lograron". B309: 673.

conducting of Grieg's *Letzter Frühling* (*L'ultima primavera*) while the actors improvised movements; in the second part Granados improvised at the piano as a background to a recitation of Alfred de Musset's poem *La nuit d'octobre*.

Although Granados's next lyric production, *Petrarca*, was never performed, it marks the beginning of his collaboration with Catalan poet and dramatist Apel.les Mestres (1854-1936). Granados was only a child when he first met Mestres; presumably during this first visit Mestres requested that Granados set his poem *El cavaller s'en va a la guerra*. (This would have been Granados's first attempt at vocal music; the song is now lost, however.) According to literary scholar Marquez Villanueva,

> Mestres was incredibly prolific as a poet, showing a late-Romantic, post-Becquerian personality, much indebted to Heine and to Northern European topics . . . prone to indulge into extremes of both stale Romanticism and a tart, biting humor.[29]

While some scholars have given the date of *Petrarca* as 1901, the recently discovered manuscript is dated 1899 (see B261). It consists of a series of *tableaux* that dramatize the fourteenth-century poet's love for Laura. Commentary based on the manuscript compares *Petrarca* to Granados's subsequent collaborations with Mestres: "In the first place, [*Petrarca*] is more extended and reveals more markedly the influence of Wagner . . . the music is more ambitious than that of the other [stage] works."[30]

The second Mestres collaboration, *Picarol*, was premiered February 28, 1901, at the Tívoli. The one-act piece about a medieval jester who falls in love with a princess was Granados's most assured theatrical success to date. *Picarol* is also significant in that it helped launch a new venture, the Teatre Líric Català. Begun in January 1901 to produce Catalan theater works, the Teatre Líric Català was one of many efforts to overcome the dominance of Italian opera in the city's musical life, a repertory especially prominent in the productions of Barcelona's main opera house, the Liceu. Fondness for Italian opera (in addition to continued enthusiasm for zarzuela) stimulated Catalan dramatists and musicians to create original works with the goal of preserving cultural identity. Critics and intellectuals authored numerous polemics on the viability and purpose of Catalan theater; these themes figured in reviews of the Catalan lyric dramas of Granados and his contemporaries.

Because of its brevity, *Picarol* appeared alongside a new production by Catalan artist and *litterateur* Santiago Rusiñol (1861-1931), *Cigales y formigues* (Grasshoppers and Ants). Music of the latter was by Morera (both works were conducted by C. Sadurní, music director of the Teatre Líric Català). The pairing of these works appears to have been a liability for Granados, as can be seen in a review in the newly founded arts magazine *Joventut* by Joaquím Pena (1873-1944), one of the few critics of the period who refused to submerge his critical sense in a welter

---

[29] B175: 5.

[30] "En primer lloc, és més extensa i acusa de forma notable la influència de Wagner . . . és una música més ambiciosa que la de les altres obres". Mark Larrad, quoted in B251: 496.

of exaggerated, politically slanted accolades. Of the joint production Pena declared:

> *Cigales y formigues* is as weak as most of the works that have been put forth this season. . . . The music of *Cigales y formigues* is the worst Morera has produced to date, due to the fact that in no sense does it reflect the libretto.[31]

In comparing *Cigales y formigues* to *Picarol*, however, Pena took a more encouraging tone:

> In setting music to *Picarol*, Granados has acquitted himself more admirably. We find that the principal merit lies in the fact that the composer has read the libretto . . . and has illustrated it with notes more in harmony with its spirit. He has not always shown great originality in doing so, however.[32]

Pena, himself a leader in fostering Wagnerian opera in Barcelona, attributed this lack of originality to an attempt to imitate the German master. Despite his praise for numerous aspects of *Picarol* (such as the introductory chorus and the two baritone airs) and his insistence that the ovation Granados received was "one of few of the season that was truly deserved," Pena warned both Granados and Morera against the dangers of epigonism: "One can imitate the masters and follow them in terms of procedure, of form, but never is it possible to appropriate the *essence* of their compositions."[33]

The reviewer for *Catalunya artística* was more impressed with *Picarol* than Pena, particularly with the work's conclusion:

> The end of the work is filled with delicate sentiments. Everyone goes away, to the sound of the wedding march, everyone departs . . . leaving the poor *Picarol* all alone, whose presence is felt only in moments of *spleen*.[34]

Although the season closed with only a few performances of *Picarol*, the work received some thirty performances (with Morera and Rusiñol's popular *L'Alegria que passa*) in a 1906 revival by another theatrical enterprise, the Espectacles Graner.

---

31 "*Cigales y formigues* es tan dolenta com la majoria de las que'ns ha offert en aquesta temporada. . . . La música de *Cigales y formigues* es de lo pitjor qu'ha fet en Morera, perque en ella no trobém cap assimilació del llibre". B236: 166.

32 "En Granados ha estat un xich millor al posar música a . . . *Picarol*. El mérit principal li trobém en demostrar qu'ha llegit l'obra literaria, y l'ha ilustrada buscant las notas més en armonia ab l'esperit de la mateixa. No sempre ha mostrat gran originalitat". Ibid.

33 "Als mestres pot imitárselos y seguirlos en els procidiments, en la forma: peró may arribar á appropriarse'l fondo de sas composicions". Ibid.

34 "El final de la obra es d'un sentiment delicadíssim. Tothóm se'n va al so de la marxa nupcial, tothóm se'n va . . . ben sol al pobre *Picarol*; que no més se'l busca en els moments de *spleen*". B311: 109.

In conjunction with his new interest in setting Catalan, Granados participated in a 1902 concert of original Catalan songs. The Musical Association of Barcelona (one of the more durable concert series of that period) sponsored the February 13 performance at the Sala Chaissagne. In addition to new songs by Vives, Millet, Nicolau, Borràs de Palau, and Lamote de Grignon, Marina Cañizares performed Granados's *La boira*. The importance of the event was stressed by the press, even if, according to one reviewer, *La boira* "received considerably less applause than it deserved" (see B334).

Although Granados's and Mestres's third collaboration, *Follet*, was performed April 4, 1903, the manuscript indicates that Granados began the score as early as 1901 (*Catalunya artística* also published fragments of the score the same year). An opera in three acts, *Follet* concerns the adventures of a romantic bard. A failure, the April 4 performance for a private audience at the Liceu seems to have taken place under difficult circumstances. Frustrated with the narrow-mindedness of the Liceu's upper-middle-class patrons, the critic for the journal *Pel & Ploma*, Rafael Moragas, wryly observed:

> We are certain that if the artists had been better endowed vocally, that if the orchestra had not been short-changed of rehearsals, and that if the organizers had denied entry to all the members of the Liceu (or to anyone who presented himself *only* with only these meager qualifications) that the resulting *Follet* would have been completely different.[35]

On the question of staging Catalan theater works in this uncongenial environment Moragas added:

> We believe the following an indispensable condition: now that the "ridiculous" question of theater in Catalan has been put forth (and undertaken by the likes of a master such as Granados) works must be judged by those dedicated to true Art, *not* by small-minded business-men.[36]

After this initial private hearing, *Follet* seems to have disappeared from the active repertory. (Curiously, neither was it among the Mestres operas discovered in the Salabert Archives in Paris in 1989 [see B251].) The Prelude to Act III was performed February 29, 1904, at the Principal, although as the final work in a lengthy symphonic program that included Beethoven's Fifth Symphony, two entire cello concertos, and four shorter works it may have been insufficiently appreciated. Critics, however, referred to the "deeply felt melody" and the "brilliance of the orches-

---

[35] "Estem segurs que si els intérpretes que'ns la van fer sentir haguessin estat adornats de millors facultats artístiques, si no haguessin mancat els ensaigs a l'orquesta i que'ls organisadors neguessin l'entrada a tot propietari del Liceu o a tot aquell que's presentés *solament* ab aquest titol, el resultat de *Follet* fora totalment diferent". B193: 143.

[36] "Creyém condició indispensable que ja que's posa la ridícola prova d'una ópera catalana, encara que vingui aquesta de les mans d'un artista de la talla d'en Granados, lo trevall d'aquest te d'esser judicat per gent que's consagri al veritable Art, pero no per senyors de balansos". Ibid.

tration" (see B336). The *Follet* Prelude was also performed in Mallorca in 1905. In 1906 the Teatre Bosch announced public rehearsals and a premiere of the opera; before the end of the season, however, it was mysteriously dropped and two other works were announced in its place (see B307).

The next Mestres collaboration, *Gaziel*, was more successful. A one-act piece with only three characters, *Gaziel* ran for some thirty performances, opening October 27, 1906, at the Principal under the auspices of Espectacles Graner. Marquez Villanueva describes the *dramatis personae*: "a poet, his beloved lady, and the Gaziel, a clever and heartless neo-Mephistopheles who plays with the poet's dreams of love and glory."[37] Performers included Josep Santpere and Assumpció Paricio; the set-design team Moragas and Alarma also collaborated. Reviewers commented that although Mestres's poem was not "eminently theatrical," Granados's score had risen to the occasion:

> Gaziel's song in the first tableau is an agreeable melody, as evidenced by the applause that resulted here as well as in the pact scene in the second tableau. Here, the maestro has written a duo carefully fashioned within a strict waltz rhythm, [although] possibly its proportions are somewhat distorted.[38]

According to the *Diario de Barcelona*, the admiring audience called Granados to the stage at the end of the second tableau. Similar enthusiasm greeted the premiere of *Liliana*, which took place July 9, 1911, at Barcelona's Palacio de Bellas Artes. Jaime Pahissa (1880-1969), who premiered his own *Estudio sinfónica* during the program's first half, conducted *Liliana*, a tale of animals and imaginary beings. Liliana was the final large-scale collaboration between Granados and Mestres, who had published his poem of the same title five years earlier. Lloró, Puiggarí, Capdevila, Balot, and Santpere (of *Gaziel*) sang against the backdrop of Moragas and Alarma's attractive sets. Mestres, also a painter, had designed some of the tableaux. Although again the press expressed reservations about the suitability of the poem for lyric declamation (see B218, 253), Granados's "picturesque orchestration" was upheld as especially noteworthy. Granados himself was also very pleased with *Liliana*, as he confessed at length in a letter to a French colleague (see B382). A song from *Liliana* (*Canço*) was later extracted as a concert work; Conchita Badia premiered this version in a 1915 recital.

More than any other part of his output, these lyric theater works represent Granados's involvement in Catalan modernism, the turn-of-the-century artistic movement whose manifestations encompass the architecture of Antoní Gaudí (1852-1926) and certain early works of Picasso (1881-1973). The extent of Granados's sympathy with this movement is difficult to determine, since most of his music is firmly rooted in nineteenth-century idioms. Certain modernist activities attracted his interest, however. For example, in 1893 he attended the second of the five "Modernist Festivals" (Festes Modernistes) at Sitges, a coastal town

---

[37] B175: 5.

[38] "La cancion de Gaziel en el cuadro primero, es de una melodía agradable, como tambien se hizo aplaudir el brindis del segundo cuadro. En éste ha escrito el maestro un duo, en ritmo de vals muy bien cuidado, pero al que quizás perjudican sus dimensiones". B339: 12341.

south of Barcelona where Catalan and foreign intellectuals gathered at the artistic colony known as the Cau Ferrat (see Appendix 2). This second festival featured a concert of works by Franck and Morera and a performance in Catalan translation of Maeterlinck's *L'Intruse*. In 1897 Granados heard the premiere of Morera's "Wagnerian fairy opera," *La fada*, at the fourth Festa Modernista, also at Sitges, and in June 1899 he performed excerpts of *María del Carmen* at the Cau Ferrat in an informal gathering attended by Ernest Chausson (1855-1899). Another site of modernist activity was the café Els Quatre Gats, Barcelona's deliberate copy of Montmartre's Auberge du Clou. In addition to dramatic readings, meetings of the Wagner Association (founded 1901), and art exhibitions, the Quatre Gats organized concerts by Albéniz; Malats; Cuban composer, pianist, and musicologist Joaquín Nin (1879-1949); and Granados himself.

Administrator and Teacher

In 1900 Granados founded the Society of Classical Concerts (Societat de Concerts Clàssics) a subscription series for the promotion of symphonic and chamber music in Barcelona. During the politically troubled early years of the century, many subscription series or "academies" were begun only to disappear within a few seasons. Granados himself had participated in some of these short-lived enterprises; for example, he is listed among "members and benefactors" of the Catalan Concert Society. He also served as administrator of piano and chamber music activities of Crickboom's Philharmonic Society.

Despite these failed earlier ventures, Granados had reason to hope that the Society of Classical Concerts would survive. First, his reputation was carrying increasing weight in international musical circles and he may have believed that his name would lend credibility to the enterprise. Second, the Society was founded on a well-organized platform. Granados's first act was to distribute to the musical community and its patrons a circular describing the organization's goal: the performance of symphonic music through the establishment of a proficient, well-rehearsed string ensemble. Eventually woodwinds, brass, and percussion would be added in order to program works for full orchestra. The circular also described a schedule of concerts, each of which would include one "popular" (i.e. nonsymphonic) violin or piano work. Of practical interest is Granados's insistence that players receive fixed salaries in return for their punctual attendance at rehearsals and concerts.

Granados's project evidently attracted needed financial support, and the Society's first concert took place May 15, 1900, at the Teatre Líric. Granados conducted Grieg's "Hohlberg" Suite (a first performance in Barcelona), Cramer's Andante for Flute and String Orchestra, a Handel Minuet, and his own orchestral transcription of a Bach fugue from the *Well-Tempered Clavier*. Guest pianist Joaquím Malats performed several Chopin works and the Bach Keyboard Concerto in D Minor. Press reaction was generally encouraging, although critic F. Suarez Bravo doubted the ensemble's potential: "An artist with the stature of Granados, founder and director . . . [is] obliged to present an ensemble that, if not perfect (not possible at first), is at least on its way to perfection."[39]

---

[39] "Un artista como Granados, fundador y director . . . [está] obligado á presentar un conjunto, si no perfecto, que ésto no puede lograrse desde el primer momento, sí en vias de perfeccionamiento". B296: 5896.

Pena also recognized the limitations of the ensemble and the lack of a symphonic or chamber music tradition in Barcelona at this time: "In all fairness to Granados, we must recognize that what he has attempted is serious Art . . . this fine intention we sincerely applaud."[40]

Whatever the opinions of the press, the concert ended with an ovation. The second concert took place June 16, also at the Líric. Even Pena was satisfied, presumably due to the participation of Pablo Casals, who performed the Saint-Saëns Cello Concerto, op. 33, and two solo cello works. Again Granados conducted, opening the concert with a Mozart Serenade and closing with the "Hohlberg" Suite. The third concert a week later minimizes the role of the orchestra: short cello and piano works by Handel, Fauré, and Boellman played by Casals and Granados, and again, the Saint-Saëns concerto and the Mozart Serenade. A fourth concert, in collaboration with (Joaquím) Cassadó's choral group Capella Catalana,[41] took place November 4, 1900, at the Teatre de Novetats. In addition to then unusual programming of choral works by Bach, Palestrina, and Durante, Leon Moreau conducted his *Sur la mer fontaine*. Granados conducted two *Norwegian Dances* (Grieg) and Beethoven's Fourth Symphony. Pena had grave reservations, especially about the Beethoven:

> [The Fourth Symphony] was executed in a mediocre fashion: despite the fact that maestro Granados conducted with an appropriate sense of tempo, he was unable to communicate to an orchestra (made up of extremely deficient members) the necessary expression . . . the monotonous interpretation showed a lack of rehearsal and an absence of authority.[42]

The concert of November 11, 1900, billed as a "concierto extraordinario," featured Granados, Malats, and Vidiella in solo and multiple keyboard works. Domínguez Sánchez conducted the orchestral numbers, including the Paderewski Concerto in F Minor (Malats) and the Bach Concerto for Three Harpsichords. Granados's new orchestration of Chopin's Concerto in F Minor, op. 21 (first movement) was premiered on this occasion and greeted with exaggerated enthusiasm by at least one anonymous critic (see B333), who also praised all the pianos used in the Bach, calling them "instruments that glorify the national industry." Pena's comments contrast with the empty bombast just cited:

> The Estela pianos . . . were four boiler-tanks without a single virtue. And it is irksome that they should ruin an otherwise decent performance. Is it possible that an artist like Granados has no ear for this? We have no ill-will towards the Estela firm . . . but

---

[40]"Hem de fer á en Granados la justicia de regoneixer que ha intentat fer Art serio . . . per tota aquest bona voluntat applaudim de cor al mestre Granados". See B231: 237.

[41] Organist and composer Joaquím Cassadó (1867-1926) should not be confused with his cellist son, Gaspar (1897-1966).

[42] "[La Quarta Sinfonia] fou molt mitjanament executada, puig si be'l mestre Granados la va conduhir ab justesa de temps, no sapigué communicar á la orquesta (formada ab elements molt deficients), la expressió que aquells requereixen . . . la interpretació pecá de monótona y revelá falta d'ensajos, trobantse a faltar energia en la batuta". B232: 638.

> what causes us artistic pain is that their detestable products continue to intrude in places where serious art is being produced. And the great majority of the public seems to share this opinion.[43]

Despite a large audience and a positive review from the *Diario de Barcelona*, the December 9, 1900, performance at the Novetats was the last by the Society of Classical Concerts. The program consisted mainly of recycled repertory from earlier programs. According to Pena, the entity planned to merge with another arts organization, the Circle of Painters and Sculptors; at this point, however, Granados seems to have dissociated himself from the organization. Pena offers a cryptic explanation for the demise of the Society of Classical Concerts, discounting the possibility of financial problems:

> It is unfortunate that a Society with such hopeful beginnings has disappeared--such good fortune is not easy to come by. From the financial success obtained at all the concerts and from the signatures on the circular we received, we can deduce that the Society did not end for want of monetary support rather, for lack . . . of other means.[44]

Pena then suggests that the Society suffered from a lack of both clearly defined goals and experienced personnel to carry them out.[45] Certainly the absence of a symphonic tradition in Barcelona would have contributed to the Society's demise as well.

Granados, meanwhile, was involved in other community enterprises. In 1901 he assisted Pena with the founding of the Wagner Association, an organization dedicated to the study of Wagnerian scores and translation of Wagner into Catalan. (Since the 1882 production of *Lohengrin* at the Liceu, Wagner's orientation towards folk legends and sensitivity to natural speech inflection had served as a model for Barcelona's composers.) The Association also presented lectures and recitals; Granados appeared in February and June of 1904 with all-Chopin and all-Schumann programs respectively. He also continued to promote chamber and symphonic music through the Chamber Music Association of Barcelona (Associació de Música da Camera), serving intermittently as that organization's artistic director (see B18). Other activities

---

[43] "[Els pianos Estela] . . . foren quatre calderas sense una sola condició recomenable. Y es realment molest que l'instrument vingui á espatllar la bona execució d'una obra. ¿Es que no té orellas que com en Granados es tot un artista de piano? Nosaltres no sentim cap animadversio contra la casa Estela . . . peró'ns molesta que *artisticament* siguin imposats sos detestables productes en llochs ahont se vol fer art serio. Y d'aquesta opinió es la inmensa majoria del publich". Ibid.

[44] "Es trist que desaparegui una Societat qu'havia comensat ab una sort que no á tothóm es fácil conseguir. Del éxit pecuniari obtingut en tots els concerts y de las firmas que suscriuhen la Circular qu'hem rebut, podém deduhir que no ha mort dita Societat precisament per falta de medis materials (com succeheix ordinariament) sinó per falta . . . dels altres". B234: 53.

[45] "Es menester, ademés, *entendre* en lo que's vol fer, ó quan manys assessorarse de personas péritas". Ibid.

included participating in a jury for a Catalan Music Festival sponsored by the Orfeó Català (see B102), presiding over a committee to resolve problems surrounding the directorship of the Municipal Band, and supervising memorial events after Albéniz's death in 1909, all of which reflect Granados's commitment to Barcelona's musical community.

In addition, the state of music education in Spain greatly concerned Granados. Despite rather pathetic advertisements in the *Diario de Barcelona* announcing his availability to teach music classes "especially for young ladies," Granados was seriously interested in pedagogy, although his habitually straitened circumstances forced him to teach more than he wished. Joaquín Nin describes the effect of constant teaching on the composer: "Granados was fighting tooth and nail to earn a living teaching. He lived modestly, heroically resigned."[46]

Granados kept written records of his students' progress, notes that resulted in three pedagogical essays: *Breves consideraciones sobre el ligado*, *Ornamentos*, and *Método teórico práctico para el uso de los pedales del piano*. The first two studies are unpublished; the pedaling study, however (published 1954, Madrid), has been applied by the composer's followers to intermediate-level Romantic works. Of his pedaling method, Granados is said to have claimed: "My method has the merit of having been the first," an assertion that is more or less true, since in England Tobias Matthay (1858-1945) was also writing on modern pedaling technique in a similar degree of detail.[47] Granados, however, was the first Spaniard to take a systematic interest not only in pedaling but in pedagogical problems in general.

His teaching philosophy appears to be based on recollections of his own teacher Pujol. Granados's diary recalls with some distaste Pujol's authoritarian stance and meditates on the importance of cultivating the individual student's musical personality (see B365: 57); in 1901 Granados founded a small academy based on these ideals, in which instruction in piano, solfège, beginning harmony, voice, and several string instruments was offered. Perhaps influenced by experimentation in general educational methods at this time in Catalonia (the secular and coeducational Escoles modernes were established in 1901) the Granados Academy was quick to incorporate new trends in musical education, such as Emile-Jacques Dalcroze's method of cultivating musical sensitivity through body movement. Concert series then considered novel, like the 1907 Beethoven piano sonata cycle by Eduard Risler (1873-1929), were also organized by the Academy for the general public as well as lectures such as Pedrell's "On National Music" (1902) and "The Origin of Musical Forms" (1905-1906).

After the donation of new facilities in 1912 by one of Granados's early patrons, pharmacist Dr. Salvador Andreu i Grau, the Academy moved to Avenue Tibidabo, where the school's concert hall was known as the Sala Granados. In keeping with Granados's interest in chamber music,

---

[46] "Granados vivait alors aux prises avec les griffes tenaces de l'enseignement; il vivait modestement, héroiquement résigné". Quoted in B45: 179.

[47] See Section V, "As to Pedalling and the Element of Duration," in Matthay's *Musical Interpretation*, 3d ed. (Boston: Boston Music Company, 1913), 125-47.

the Granados Academy organized a series of chamber music evenings, Cap-Vespres Musicals, with another small conservatory, the Ainaud Academy, in 1914. In addition a "Trio Granados" (Granados, violinist Perelló, and cellist Raventós) was founded in 1909, although this ensemble does not appear to have performed regularly.

Since its founding the Granados Academy has graduated a number of professional and semiprofessional musicians; the three best known should be mentioned here. Frank Marshall, born in Mataró in 1883 of English parents, had been a prize-winning student of Buyé's at the Liceu Conservatory when he first heard Granados in recital. Immediately Marshall sought admission to the Academy; Granados accepted him on the condition that he relearn piano technique from the beginning to better grasp Granados's method. After becoming Granados's teaching assistant, copyist, and secretary, Marshall directed the Academy after Granados's death. (The school bears Marshall's name today.) The Academy's "star pupil," pianist Alicia de Larrocha, presently serves as nominal Director. A third Academy graduate, singer Conchita Badia (1897-1975), who premiered the *Tonadillas* and the *Canciones amatorias* and later sang in the Barcelona revival of *María del Carmen*, studied with Granados himself. It is believed that Badia, who was active as a teacher, has transmitted a "Granados tradition" of interpretation to numerous singers and pianists.

Another of Granados's piano students was composer Roberto Gerhardt (1896-1970), although his work with Granados was limited, dating from 1915, the year before Granados died.

Since at no point did Granados give up composing or concertizing, his schedule must have been extremely taxing. From a 1905 letter to the composer by Risler, it can be surmised that he even considered giving up his concert career, for Risler admonishes him: "It would be unpardonable on your part if you were to give up working and [no longer] see yourself as a pianist."[48]

Artistic Maturity

In the first decade of the twentieth century, the Spanish "musical renaissance" manifested itself in Spain and France. In Paris, Albéniz began his *Iberia* suite, twelve "impressions" for solo piano in which he combined his own harmonic syntax with unprecedented technical demands. Falla's *La vida breve* attracted international notice; in Barcelona, the foundation stone was laid for the Palau de la Música Catalana, the brick, glass, and mosaic structure conceived by Catalan architect Domènech i Muntaner (1850-1923) in pure modernist spirit. Granados likewise achieved wider recognition and greater professional stability at the beginning of the new century. An outline of some of his more important activities follows.

In 1903 the director of the Madrid Conservatory, Tomás Bretón, announced a contest in which a faculty jury would award a cash prize to the composer of an *Allegro de concierto*. The piece would also serve as an examination piece for graduating piano students. Twenty-four composers submitted *Allegros de concierto*, and after reviewing the three

---

48 "Seria imperdonable de vostra part deixar de treballar y no fervos sentir com pianista". B259: 109.

finalists--José Guervós, Vicente Zurrón, and Granados--the jury decided in Granados's favor with an almost unanimous vote. (The young de Falla won honorable mention.) Its Lisztian virtuosity and sophisticated pedal technique have made *Allegro de concierto* one of Granados's more enduring works.

On June 21, 1903, Granados's *Melodía* for violin and piano was premiered at the Teatre de Catalunya; on May 27, 1904, Granados began his association with Belgian violinist Eugène Ysaye (1858-1931) with a performance at Barcelona's Teatre de les Arts of Brahms's Sonata in D Minor, op. 108 and several paraphrases. Granados's *Escenas románticas*, the series of piano miniatures whose voluptuous textures and vocal style foreshadow *Goyescas*, appears to have received its first performance on November 20 of the same year. (For Granados's two Wagner Association concerts and the premiere of the Prelude to Act III, *Follet*, also in 1904, see B20, 21, 336.)

His first Paris appearance as a mature artist took place March 31, 1905, when he and Crickboom performed at the Salle Pleyel; on this occasion Granados introduced several previously unpublished Scarlatti keyboard sonatas that he had transcribed himself from original manuscripts, incorporating Romantic flourishes typical of the late nineteenth century. In April of the same year Granados conducted three orchestral programs at the Círculo de Bellas Artes; the programs included various excerpts from Wagnerian operas and works by Bizet, Saint-Saëns, and Thomàs.

In 1906 the young pianist Mieczyslaw Horszowski was touring Spain; in January, Granados conducted his performance of Mozart's Concerto in D Minor, K. 466, Beethoven's G Major Concerto, op. 58, and Chopin's *Andante spianato and Grande Polonaise Brilliante*. In the spring of that year Granados made a short tour of Valencia, Madrid, San Sebastian, Pamplona, and Saragossa. In preparation, he gave two concerts on March 1 and 3 at the Principal under sponsorship of the Espectacles Audicions Graner; both programs are typical of his repertory: Sonata in F, K. 332 (Mozart), Sonatas 9 and 15 (Scarlatti-Granados), Sonata in B Minor, op. 58 (Chopin), *Lyric Pieces*, op. 47 (Grieg), and *Hungarian Rhapsodie* no. 8 (Liszt). The second concert consisted of Sonatas 1, 4, and 14 (Scarlatti-Granados), "Waldstein" Sonata in C Major, op. 53 (Beethoven), a Chopin group that included the *Ballade* in A-flat, a Schumann group, and the *Grand Polonaise* in E-flat (Liszt). Barcelona's critics reacted enthusiastically, especially to the Scarlatti transcriptions:

> A novelty was offered us by these concerts: the harpsichord Sonatas of Scarlatti written for the Spanish Court in the eighteenth century and arranged for the modern piano by Granados himself. The compositions are lovely and the interpretation was no less so.[49]

Granados was back in Barcelona by the end of April, where he gave two concerts with Eduard Risler, both at the Principal. The first, on April 28, included Chabrier's *Valses romantiques*; at the second (April 30) Granados and Risler performed Mozart's Concerto in E-flat for Two

---

[49] "Una novetat ens van oferir aquests concerts: les Sonates de Scarlatti escrites pera clavicordi en segle XVIII, pera la Cort d'Espanya, y modernament arreglades pera piano pel mateix Granados. Les composicions són hermoses y la interpretació no va desmeréixer". B31: 154.

Pianos, K. 365. Two conducting engagements in May appear to be Granados's last appearances of that year. He performed relatively little in 1907; in 1908, however, the Liceu sponsored a Grieg Festival at which he performed the A Minor Concerto. Saint-Saëns came to Barcelona in spring of the same year; on April 2 the Musical Association of Barcelona presented a concert dedicated to the French composer's works. Here Granados performed the Concerto in F Minor, op. 130 and the two-piano transcription of Chopin's Sonata in B-flat Minor, op. 35, with Saint-Saëns himself.

An important event occurred in June 1908, when two movements of Granados's symphonic poem *Dante* ("Dante e virgilio" and "Paolo e Francesca") premiered at the newly completed Palau de la Música Catalana.[50] According to the composer, Rosetti's drawings furnished inspiration for Dante; the work calls for full orchestra and mezzo-soprano soloist and was Granados's most ambitious work to date. This first performance (after which the composer made several revisions) took place before a private audience. Granados presented *Dante* again during a Lenten concert series of 1910; despite further revisions and another performance by the Madrid Symphony on May 25, 1915, critics still had reservations about the score's vast proportions (see B295).

On November 8, 1908, Granados gave his first performance with French violinist Jacques Thibaud (1880-1953). They performed Beethoven's Sonata for Violin and Piano op. 47 (the "Kreutzer") in a Musical Association Concert at the Liceu; the following year Granados returned to Paris to perform with Thibaud on June 2 and 9 at the Salle des Agricultures. This visit took place in conjunction with Granados's adjudicating for the prestigious Diémer competition, a triennial contest for pianists sponsored by the Paris Conservatory. Among the adjudicators were Moritz Moszkowski, Moritz Rosenthal, Harold Bauer, and Gabriel Fauré (then Conservatory Director); the Barcelona press made much of Granados's nomination to the jury. On the same trip Granados visited Albéniz on his deathbed at Cambó-les-Bains, where, in accordance with her husband's wishes, Rosina Albéniz presented to Granados the unfinished manuscript of Albéniz's piano piece *Azulejos* for completion.

He returned to Barcelona shortly before the spate of workers' riots later known as the Setmana Trágica (Tragic Week) had "left Barcelona like a dead city."[51] In a letter to Malats dated August 26, 1909, Granados vaguely refers to the violent events of the Setmana Trágica as having "deprived [him] of many things." Nonetheless the earliest extant sketches for his masterwork, *Goyescas*, date from this period.

Goyescas

During his 1898 stay in Madrid, Granados viewed for the first time the work of the Aragonese painter Francisco Goya (1746-1828), whose canvasses in the Prado museum so impressed the young composer that he immediately began to explore their musical potential. Later, in a 1915 interview Granados explained:

---

50 Some scholars have incorrectly given 1907 as the date of the *Dante* premiere.

51 B38: 3.

About seventeen years ago I put forth a work which failed. It doubtless deserved failure; nevertheless, I was broken-hearted over the matter. Whatever may have been its faults as a whole, I felt convinced of the value of certain portions of it and these I carefully preserved. In 1909 I took them up once more, and reshaped them into a suite for piano.[52]

The bulk of his reworking of these early sketches took place over the course of 1909-10. Granados described the results in a letter to Malats dated August 31 of that year: "And this summer I have composed a collection of *Goyescas*, works of great sweep and difficulty."[53]

Rafael Moragas describes a private performance of *Goyescas* (Book One) that took place in Barcelona that summer. Joaquím Pena and Isolda Wagner were among the guests; in addition to *Goyescas* Granados performed Liszt's Sonata in B Minor.[54] By the winter of 1910 Granados had not yet approached a publisher with *Goyescas*; given his composing habits it can be assumed that he was reworking the score. (See B388. Dotesio published the work in 1912.) The public premiere of *Goyescas* took place March 11, 1911, in an all-Granados concert at the Palau de Música Catalana. The first half consisted of the *Valses poéticos*, the Albéniz-Granados *Azulejos*, a Scarlatti-Granados transcription, and the *Allegro de concierto*. For the second half Granados performed Book One (nos. 1-4) of Goyescas and, with the Orfeó Català, a work Granados considered "very important,"[55] the *Cant de les estrelles* (Hymn of the Stars) for chorus, piano, and organ. He also played his favorite encore, the *Jota valenciana* from the *Twelve Spanish Dances*.

Press reactions ranged from encomia on the virtues of Iberian music to more critical views, especially with regard to *Cant de les estrelles*, whose instrumentation was described as turgid. *Goyescas* made an extremely favorable impression, however, and the composer was praised for the richness of melodic invention and the modernity of the harmonies, particularly in "Coloquio en la reja" (see B107, 225, 299).

Granados appears to have spent the remainder of 1911 in relative isolation from public life. In May he performed in Lleida with Ricardo Viñes, and in a Musical Association of Barcelona concert on June 22, Carme Mendival premiered the song (which Granados referred to as a lied), *L'Ocell profeta*. Earlier that spring, Lamote de Grignon had led the orchestra of the Orfeó in his own orchestration of three *Spanish Dances*: "Orientale," "Andaluza," and "Rondalla aragonesa."

---

52 B239: 3.

53 "Y he escrito este verano una colección de *Goyescas*, obras de gran vuelo y dificultad". B380. In Tarazona's quoting of the same letter there are minor changes in the text that obscure the time frame in which *Goyescas* was composed (see B304: 42).

54 B194:8. Tarazona, on the other hand, complicates the occurrence of this first performance by misquoting Falla on a reading Granados gave of the opera *Goyescas* years later in Paris at the home of Joaquín Nin. See B304: 43, and source cited in B255 (Falla, Manuel de. *Escritos sobre la música* [Madrid: Espasa-Calpe, 1950]: 25).

55 B388.

On February 4, 1912, Granados gave a solo recital in honor of Dr. Andreu i Grau, donor of the Sala Granados, and later that month presented a demanding program with Thibaud at the Palau. In April he played Book One of *Goyescas* at Madrid's Comedia and on July 7 *Elisenda*, the suite for chamber orchestra, piano, and voice, premiered at the Sala Granados.[56] An important association began in November 1912 when Granados met American pianist Ernest Schelling (1876-1939), who gave four concerts at the Principal and later an unscheduled appearance at the Granados Academy on November 17.

Schelling's role in promoting Granados's music cannot be exaggerated. First, he acted as Granados's agent and translator in negotiations with the New York publisher G. Schirmer, resulting in a two-year contract with yearly advance royalties of 6,000 (French) francs, an arrangement Granados initially found highly satisfactory. (Later Schelling would try to reconcile differences between Granados and Schirmer.) Second, Schelling sought professional contacts for Granados. In 1912 he introduced him to baritone Emilio Gorgoza, the first singer of international fame to interpret the *Tonadillas*. (Schelling also acted as middleman when Gorgoza requested a male version of "La maja dolorosa." See B169).

Third, and most important, Schelling actively promoted performances of Granados's music. In December of 1913, for example, Schelling gave the London premier of *Goyescas* (his New York performances of Granados's works are cited below). Schelling also approached British conductor Sir Henry J. Wood, director of the Queen's Hall Orchestra, with *Dante*, and the work was scheduled for September 8, 1914, as part of that orchestra's Promenade series. (See B397. The work does not appear to have been reviewed.) By early 1913, when Granados was converting the piano suite *Goyescas* into an opera of the same name, Schelling suggested a performance to the Chicago Grand Opera company; director Campanini, however, showed no immediate interest. Eventually Schelling's contacts with New York's Metropolitan Opera's Giulio Gatti-Casazza brought about the 1916 New York premiere of *Goyescas*.[57]

In early 1913, however, the opera *Goyescas* was still in its early stages. In a February 3 letter to Schelling Granados describes his progress on a related work, the song collection *Tonadillas*, which the composer viewed as "[preparatory] essays for *Goyescas*." At the same time he was working on a *sainete*, which, as he confessed to Schelling, was a work "for the public," one which he hoped might enable him to concentrate upon *Goyescas* without financial preoccupations.[58] He had already selected a librettist, Fernando Periquet, a bank employee with literary ambitions[59] (a choice that was later roundly criticized).

---

[56] Reviews of *Elisenda* are based on its second performance on January 26, 1913.

[57] Initially Granados wished to entitle the opera *Goyesca: Literas y Calesas* to distinguish it from the piano suite. Almost immediately after the opera premiered, however, the press began referring to the work as *Goyescas* (see B169: 98).

[58] A *sainete* is a dramatic work, usually in one act, of light, popular character.

[59] B69: 6.

In May 1913 Granados, Periquet, and Linares Rivas gave a presentation on the history of the *tonadilla* at the Madrid Athenaeum, the pseudo-political organization known as "a stronghold of liberalism" during the wave of conservatism in early twentieth-century Spain. According to his correspondence, Granados considered visiting Schelling at his summer home in Céligny, Switzerland; it seems that illness prevented such a visit, however, since in a letter to Schelling dated "Barcelona, July 18," Granados complains of an inflammation. Nonetheless he spent part of the summer on the Mediterranean, working on *Goyescas* in a makeshift summer cottage.

Ill health continued to plague the composer and his next several letters refer to weight loss and continued *malaise* throughout the fall. He seems to have given only two concerts during that period: one on October 8 at Madrid's Teatro Real in honor of the President of the French Republic and a chamber music concert at the Sala Granados on December 21. In the ensuing months he dedicated himself to the preparation of an all-Granados concert for Paris's Salle Pleyel, scheduled for April 4, 1914. At this highly successful performance, Granados introduced to Paris both books of *Goyescas*, two *Spanish Dances*, the Serenade for Two Violins and Piano (with Mssrs. Costa and Zighera), and the *Tonadillas* (with Mme. Polack); for this appearance he was awarded the Medal of the Legion of Honor.[60] During the same visit Granados heard concert versions of *The Rite of Spring* and *Petrouchka* conducted by Monteux, and in an interview with composer and scholar Jacques Pillois he described the impression Stravinsky's scores had made on him (see B243: 4).

On June 27 Conchita Badia's Barcelona premiere of the *Tonadillas* took place at the Palau, with Ricart Vives as her accompanist.[61] By this time Granados had already left for his second visit to Paris that year, where he was to give a private audition for the "gentlemen of the Opera."[62] By the end of June the Paris Opera Committee had accepted *Goyescas* for the coming season, at which time Granados went to see Schelling at Céligny. Upon the outbreak of World War I, however, he returned to Spain accompanied by his daughter Solita. By this time, financial difficulties of the Paris Opera had caused the premature retirement of its managerial team, Mssrs. Messager and Broussan (although their successor, Rouché, declared that he would pay debts out of his own pocket if this were necessary to keep the opera solvent). These financial problems in combination with the war rendered a Paris premiere of *Goyescas* impossible.

With Schelling continuing to help him seek a performance for *Goyescas*, Granados resumed his normal routine in Barcelona, including a benefit performance March 1, 1915, for the French Red Cross, the Barcelona premiere of two cello pieces, *Trova* and *Madrigal*, with (Gaspar) Cassadó May 2, and a solo recital May 30. In addition, his *Elegía eterna* had

---

[60] This concert is often incorrectly cited as the Paris premiere of *Goyescas*; in fact, Montoriol-Tarres had performed it at the Salle Erard early in 1914.

[61] Badia and Granados had given a semiprivate performance of the *Tonadillas* June 10 at the Granados Academy. Granados left Barcelona the following day.

[62] B398.

received favorable notices in London, where María Barrientos performed it during the Orfeó's 1914 tour of Britain. Eventually negotiations were settled with the Metropolitan Opera of New York for a January 1916 premiere of *Goyescas*, to be attended by the composer and his wife. Granados, therefore, spent most of the summer of 1915 isolated in his Mediterranean cottage finishing details of orchestration. In the fall of 1915 he gave only one public performance (his last in Barcelona), playing on November 14 the Grieg A Minor Concerto, the work that had helped launch his career as a pianist over twenty years earlier. On November 16 Granados and Periquet signed a contract for the rights to *Goyescas*; at Cádiz on November 30 Granados and Amparo boarded the *Montevideo* of the Compañia Transatlántica Española. Fear of sea travel and the threat of warfare did not contribute to Granados's peace of mind; after a rough crossing, during which the vessel was searched twice, the couple arrived in New York City on December 15.

Granados's music was not completely unknown to New York audiences, for Percy Grainger, Ernest Schelling, and George Copeland had recently performed various *Goyescas* and *Spanish Dances*. Performances of selected *Tonadillas* by Gorgoza and by mezzo-soprano Rosa Culmell also preceded Granados's arrival, and in November the Chicago Symphony had given the American premiere of *Dante* with soloist Sophie Braslau, a contralto from the Metropolitan Opera Company. Shortly before opening night Granados performed with Casals at the Ritz-Carlton Hotel in a concert sponsored by the fledgling society, The New York Friends of Music. Granados played four *Goyescas* (including "El Pelele"), the *Valses poéticos*, *Jota valenciana*, and *Danza árabe*; with Casals he performed the *Trova* serenade, *Madrigal*, and an arrangement of *Danza andaluza*. There was unanimity among critics as to Granados's brilliant pianism; regarding his compositions, however, there was a greater range of opinion. According to Richard Aldrich of the *New York Times*:

> The *Goyescas*, which are the best known of Mr. Granados's music in New York, seemed the best, the most original and substantial of what was heard yesterday. The *Valses poéticos* grazed closely the line of salon music, and sometimes broke through it. They also have much less of the Spanish national coloring than the rest of this music; salons are cosmopolitan. The *Trova serenade* . . . is of much introspective charm, with the character of an improvisation. The madrigal betrays its period in certain modal characteristics which Mr. Granados has preserved.[63]

Aldrich concluded with a description of Granados's piano playing:

> Mr. Granados's own playing was a surprise to many on account of its easy command of the very considerable difficulties he has scattered through these compositions. A "composer's technique" is a well-recognized effect in music. Mr. Granados has a technique of a very different sort. He played with brilliancy and power; there were also the languor, the smoldering fire, the tenderness and passion which belong in this music, by which it is marked with Spanish character even more than the rhythms and certain of the melodic traits that run through it.[64]

---

63 B10: 494.

64 Ibid. 495.

The press gave ample notice of "New York's first Spanish opera" and Granados granted several interviews during his stay.[65] When in rehearsal it became clear that more time was needed for a scene change, Granados immediately composed the popular Intermezzo; the press also publicized this accomplishment. Another last-minute concern was a change in cast, for director Gatti-Casazza had originally intended to cast Lucrezia Bori as the noblewoman Rosario. When Bori fell ill, Anna Fitziu, a singer in musical theater, hastily learned Spanish diction for her Metropolitan debut. Giovanni Martinelli was cast as Fernando, Rosario's jealous lover, Flora Perini as the *maja*, Pepa, and Guiseppe de Luca as the toreador, Paquiro. As he had done twenty years earlier for the Madrid run of *María del Carmen*, Casals conducted open rehearsals of *Goyescas*; the last of these included Mrs. Richard Aldrich, Mrs. Otto Kahn, and Mrs. Vincent Astor in the "enormous gathering [that] applauded each act almost in the manner of a first night audience."[66]

Enthusiasm was sustained through opening night, January 28, when there was "ecstatic applause after each of the first two tableaux and more at the end of the opera,"[67] in addition to curtain calls for cast, for conductor Gaetano Bavagnoli, and for composer and librettist. (Critics suggested that the opening night enthusiasm was due to the presence of a close-knit "Spanish colony.") Yet despite the warm reception, *Goyescas* received only four more performances before it was dropped from the Metropolitan repertory.

There are several reasons for the subsequent neglect of *Goyescas*. First, critics commented on the weakness of the libretto: "The dramatic quality of *Goyescas* is not of outstanding value. The drama is scarcely more than a sketch; there is little action; the development of motive is inadequate, hardly more than indicated."[68]

Other reviewers commented that in addition to an intrinsically deficient libretto, the relation of the score to the dramatic action was poorly timed:

> The fact that the plot is obvious is not against it, for *Carmen* is obvious from the beginning. . . . No composer has the right to take his audience through two brisk incidents in which his plot is being developed and then lead it into a love scene where the heroine sings of heartbeats and nightingales for half an hour.[69]

In general, however, critics praised the purely musical content of *Goyescas*:

---

[65] *Goyescas* may be more accurately described as "New York City's first Spanish-*language* opera," since two operas by Manuel Garcia, *L'Amante astuto* and *La figlia dell'aria*, were performed in Italian translation at the Park Theater in 1825.

[66] B252: 13.

[67] B10: 495.

[68] Ibid.: 497.

[69] B201: 11.

> Mr. Granados has a rich and unconventional harmonic feeling, though he does not follow those who are most conspicuous in the exploitation of "modern harmony." . . . This music has haunting power. It would be too much to say that the opera is a great contribution to modern art, or even that it approaches greatness; but it is genuine and vital.[70]

Another factor was production expense. Each *tableau* of *Goyescas* requires a scene change (the lavish Metropolitan sets were some of the most expensive in the company's history); moreover, since the work lasts just over an hour, *Goyescas* must be paired with another work, requiring yet a fourth set.

Even Granados himself was not completely satisfied with *Goyescas*, as numerous pencilled emendations to his manuscript of the piano reduction attest. Despite the mixed reviews the opera received, however, other opportunities presented themselves, including a successful joint concert with Anna Fitziu on February 22 at Aeolian Hall. Granados also recorded several *Spanish Dances*, two *Goyescas*, and two "Improvisations" for the Duo-Art piano roll company, in addition to furnishing music for the American debut of the Spanish dancer "La Argentina." On January 19 the Hispanic Society of America made Granados a member, presenting him with a silver medal; in addition, Schelling collected donations for a "loving cup" to be presented to the composer upon his departure. The cup contained a draft for the equivalent in pesetas of $4,100; contributors included Spanish ambassador Riaño y Gayangos, Chairman of the Board of Directors of the Metropolitan Opera Otto Kahn, Fritz Kreisler, Ignaz Paderewski, and ambassador Robert Bliss and his wife. This sum, in addition to the opera proceeds of about $4,000 must have eased Granados's financial anxieties considerably.

Granados was also invited to perform at a March 15 benefit concert "for the musicians of the Paris Conservatoire, sufferers of the war." An invitation for a performance at the White House, however, changed his plans. President Wilson was a great music lover (during World War I he declared music "a national need"); his daughter, Margaret, a semi-professional singer, engaged Granados and Dutch singer Julia Culp for the White House's "musicale" series. In addition to accompaniments for Miss Culp, Granados performed a group of his Scarlatti transcriptions, a Chopin *Nocturne*, "Jota valenciana," *Allegro de concierto*, and "El Pelele."

The unexpected command performance meant rebooking passage back to Spain. Riaño y Gayangos advised sailing on the "Antonio Lopez," a Spanish (i.e. neutral) vessel that went directly from New York to Barcelona without stopping on the continent; however Granados had already made arrangements to leave New York on March 11 on the Holland-America S.S. *Rotterdam*. (From Falmouth, England, the couple would take the British mail-boat S.S. *Sussex* across the Channel.) Since Granados was unable to change the reservation without losing his money, he and Amparo returned promptly to New York and sailed March 11.[71]

---

[70] B10: 497.

[71] The printed programs for the March 15 benefit concert include Granados's name, a fact that has led some biographers to believe that he participated in this concert. His travel dates contradict this pos-

They spent a few days in London as guests of Catalan sculptor Ismael Smith, who wished to pursue the question of a London performance of *Goyescas*; on March 24 the couple boarded the *Sussex* from Folkestone. While crossing the Channel at midafternoon, the vessel was torpedoed by a German submarine, the UB-29. Both Granados and Amparo were immediately drowned.

Death and Aftermath

Biographers give conflicting versions of the tragedy, although all base their descriptions on the testimony of witnesses. Many claim that Granados, safely in a lifeboat, saw Amparo struggling in the waves and leapt in to save her; others say that it was Amparo, an accomplished swimmer, who tried to save her husband. Yet another account claims (incorrectly) that of all the *Sussex*'s passengers and attendants, Granados and Amparo were the only ones lost.[72] The following outline of the torpedoing, extracted from a contemporary report in the *Diario de Barcelona* (B303), seems to be the most objective account:

The UB-29, commanded by a Lieutenant Pustkuchen, struck only part of the *Sussex*; therefore her telegraph machines remained functional. In the call for aid, however, the telegraph operator gave the ship's location incorrectly, thus it was with difficulty that only one French torpedo boat and several British destroyers were able to locate the vessel. Given that these vessels took 40 passengers to Folkestone and another 198 to Boulogne, it seems likely that Granados and Amparo drowned in the earliest stages of the disaster. Approximately 50 persons remained unaccounted for, however, and for several weeks rumors circulated that Granados and Amparo had been found aboard a hospital ship. Thus, official confirmation of the composer's death was received relatively slowly.

The *Sussex* incident caused a small international scandal, especially since the UB-29 was the first submarine to defy the Channel blockade then in effect. President Wilson's letter of April 19 to the German government protested submarine war and vowed that the United States would no longer tolerate such attacks.[73] Germany declared that the attack on the poorly equipped *Sussex* had been intentional; presumably Field Marshall Hindenburg was pleased that the submarine had "combatted the enemy so effectively."[74] It has even been suggested that the British government purposely exposed the *Sussex* to provoke a German attack and thereby draw the United States into the war, for the vessel was unarmed, had only one funnel, and, being painted entirely in black, displayed no insignia. Moreover the ship travelled without escort and failed to

---

sibility, as does the absence of his name from reviews of the concert. His correspondence from the Hotel Wellington (postmarked New York City) confirms his whereabouts on the dates in question.

72 B163: 61.

73 B249: n.p.

74 "Nous nous réjouissons que l'ennemi soit combatu par nos marins avec succés!" Quoted in B249.

follow the route prescribed for merchant ships.[75] International pressure and petitions from musical organizations, however, convinced the German government to pay an indemnity of 666,000 pesetas to the Granados orphans; in January 1917 an official apology by Foreign Minister von Jagow "expressed regret for the death of the composer in . . . 1916."

The Spanish king Alfonso XIII took up a collection to benefit the Granados children, and proceeds from several memorial concerts also helped ease their plight. In Madrid the Italian pianist Stefaniani organized a concert which took place on April 15, 1916, and was attended by the *Infanta* Isabel. The National Society for Music sponsored a concert May 31, 1916, that featured performances by pianist Federico Longàs, Conchita Badia, and members of the Madrid Philharmonic in some of Granados's lesser-known works, like *Elisenda* and *Navidad*. A Barcelona memorial concert featured former students: Badia, Longàs, Fernando Via, and Mercedes Maner; on June 30, 1916, Paris honored the composer's memory in a performance at the *Comédie Française*.

In London Sir Thomas Beecham raised 4,000 duros for the orphans with a performance of Mozart's *Abduction from the Seraglio*. This benefit, which was attended by ambassadors from several countries, had distinctly political overtones, for in the weeks before, concert organizers circulated an explicitly anti-German pamphlet. Probably the most lucrative memorial concert, however, was the New York concert organized by Schelling for May 7, 1916. In his autobiography, Casals gives a moving description of the sold-out concert at the Metropolitan Opera House:

> Walter Damrosch conducted, and Paderewski, Kreisler and I played the Beethoven Trio in B-flat. The famous singers Maria Barrientos, Julia Culp, and John McCormack also took part. . . . Towards the end of the concert all the lights were turned out. A candle was placed on the piano. Then--with that solitary flame flickering on the stage in the great hall--Paderewski played Chopin's "Funeral March."[76]

Even after the composer's death, Schelling mediated in Granados's heirs' dealings with Schirmer. Eduardo, the oldest son, insisted that Schirmer had owed the composer a quarterly payment, while Schirmer claimed that Granados owed the publisher $2,800 "for sums advanced." On July 25, 1916, therefore, Eduardo authorized Schelling to withdraw "all of the manuscripts of [Granados's] musical works in Schirmer's power," thus appointing himself sole custodian of his father's scores. While it is impossible to know how this decision affected subsequent dissemination of Granados's music, it would seem that terminating relations with one of North America's more prestigious publishers was not entirely desirable; undoubtedly, financial and psychological pressures caused Granados's heirs to make hasty decisions which ultimately affected

---

[75]See H. C. Peterson, *Propaganda for War: The Campaign for American Neutrality 1914-1917* (Norman, Okla., 1939) and Samuel F. Bemis, *A Diplomatic History of the United States* (New York, 1936). Bemis describes "the *Sussex* . . . lumbering along . . . through a sea littered with the wreckage of recently torpedoed vessels" (610).

[76] B40: 149. Casals did *not*, however, organize the concert, as his autobiography suggests; rather, Schelling had to persuade Casals (who favored soliciting individual donations) to support the idea.

the fate of their father's music. Eduardo's sale of the five Mestres operas to Salabert is discussed elsewhere (see B195: 251); he may also have been as absent-minded as his father (see **Introduction**), for in the letter of July 25 he confesses to having left one manuscript in a Parisian taxi.

Eduardo also assumed the directorship of the Granados Academy, which took up its normal class schedule after a hiatus in the spring of 1916. Frank Marshall directed the piano classes, Mas i Serracant solfège and theory, and Granados's eldest daughter, Solita, taught elementary classes. Pedrell seems to have held an honorary directorship, and in this capacity he initiated the publication of a musical journal for a general readership, *Musiciana*. Within a year Eduardo turned over the directorship to Marshall.

What did Granados leave unfinished? According to one source, he had completed negotiations for a Buenos Aires performance of *Goyescas* for June 1916 and had planned to travel there after spending April in Barcelona.[77] Of greater interest are the sketches for a Symphony in E Minor, composed between 1904 and 1910 (see B190). Riva's recent sketchbook study discusses some of Granados's unrealized plans for vocal music (see B263); in addition Riva has illuminated the many sources of discrepancies in the piano music: annotations in Granados's own manuscripts, in Frank Marshall's scores, errors in published editions, and Granados's own digressions as found in his recordings. A complete edition based on the sources cited above, however, has yet to be produced.

We may wonder why Granados's music has not been more widely performed. During his lifetime his piano works were conspicuously absent from virtually every recital program in Barcelona other than his own and those of his students.[78] Despite Granados's popularity in Paris, it was not until the publication of the piano suite *Goyescas* that pianists of international reputation began to program his works. (For example, when Schelling played in Barcelona in November 1912, he played Albéniz but not Granados.) In addition, Granados does not seem to have actively promoted his own chamber music in his numerous appearances with the Philharmonic Society, nor did he program his own symphonic works when he conducted. In his three orchestral concerts in April 1905, for example, he could have programmed the *Marcha de los vencidos*, the *Suite sobre cantos gallegos*, or the *Follet* prelude; in his own series, the Society of Classical Concerts, he would have enjoyed even greater authority in programming. Attempts to establish reasons for Granados's lack of self-promotion degenerate into speculation; however, as late as 1933 Casals declared that Granados's music was still "practically unknown" in Spain.

Certainly the critical point in the supervision of Granados's music occurred in the decade after his death (Eduardo died in 1928). Moreover, the horrors of the Spanish Civil War (1936-39) contributed to the loss of manuscripts and biographical documents, although ironically it was in the midst of that dire period that the only revivals in Spain of

---

[77] B82: 53.

[78] A single exception seems to be the performance of a *Spanish Dance* by Leon Moreau in Barcelona in 1910.

María del Carmen and *Goyescas* occurred--the latter chosen to celebrate the reopening of the Liceu months after Franco's victory.

A letter to Vives from America shows that in the last year of his life, Granados saw himself on the threshold of new accomplishments, although his optimism was tempered by a certain bitterness about past struggles:

> At last I have seen the realization of my dreams. It's true that my hair is turning white, [yet] that one could say that I am *beginning* my work, that I am filled with confidence and enthusiasm to work more and more. . . . I am a Spaniard; alas, no other Spaniard has begun any earlier. I am a survivor of the sterile battle to which the ignorance and indifference of our country subjects us. . . . I am dreaming of Paris, and I have a world of ideas.[79]

Granados was Spain's only bona fide Romantic composer; his most fruitful period occurred, paradoxically, while Falla and Albéniz were pushing Spanish music to the brink of modernity. One can only conjecture the "world of ideas" he envisioned.

---

[79] "Per fi he vist els meus somnis realitzats. Es veritat que tinc el cap ple de cabells blancs i que es dir que ara començo la meva obra, mes estic ple de confiança i d'entusiasme per treballar més i més. . . . Soc espanyol i ja mai cap espanyol ha començat abans. Soc un supervivent de la lluita estèril a que ens sotmet la ignorancia i la indiferencia de la nostra patria. . . . Somnío amb París, i tinc un món de projectes." B371: 182.

2

Bibliography

B1. "Academia Granados." *Diario de Barcelona*, April 6, 1915, p. 4298.

A review of Conchita Badia's April 5 premiere of the three songs, "Mañanica era," "Mira que soy niña," and "Descubre el pensamiento," in addition to "Canço," from *Liliana*. "De los antiguos romanceros y cancioneros castellanos ha sacado . . . esa curiosa mezcla de sencillez, de ingenuidad popular, y de discreto retórico. Las quatro canciones . . . son originales, con un sabor que no puede llamarse arcaico, porque tienen mucho de muy moderno". (From old *romanceros* and song collections [Granados] has extracted . . . that curious mixture of simplicity, ingenuous appeal, and discreet rhetoric. The four songs are original, with a flavor that one could hardly call archaic, since there is much in them that is very modern.)

B2. "Academia Granados." *Revista Musical Catalana* 1 (1904): 151.

A review of the June 6, 1904, performance in the concert hall of the Granados Academy of *La nuit d'octobre* (on a text by Alfred de Musset) with "scenic dialogue" ("diàlech escènich") by Marie Monros and Pierre Rettmeyer, and improvisations by Granados. The same concert also featured Adrià Gual's scenic representation of Grieg's *Ultima primavera* (*Letzter Frühling*) with members of the Teatre Intim. The actors improvised movements while a string orchestra, directed by Granados, played. "Els invitats sortiren molt complaguts de la vetllada". (The guests left well pleased with the events of the evening.)

B3. "Abandon Hope for *Goyescas* Composer: Sñr. and Sra. Granados Lost in "Sussex" Disaster, Friends Fear. No Trace of Either." *Morning Telegraph*, March 27, 1916, NYPL.

"When last seen Señor and Señora Granados were clinging to a small raft. . . . It is thought the light raft was unable to weather the heavy seas or the couple was washed overboard to drown." Gives Granados's departure date from the United States (incorrectly) as March 3.

B4. Abbado, Michelangelo. "Le prime rappresentazioni al Teatro alla Scala: *Goyescas*." *Rassegna della instruzione artistica* 8 (1938): 116-20

Synopsis of the opera and incidental details of Granados's career. Singers for the 1938 performance were Maria Carbone, Paolo Civil, Afro Poli, Cloe Elmo. "Le scene, dipinte da Alberto Scaioli su bozzetti di Giuseppe Sert, non si sono scostate dai canoni tradizionali." (The set, painted by Alberto Scaioli from sketches by Guiseppe Sert, did not stray from the traditional canon.)

B5. "Act of Barbarism: Professor Baldwin's Story of the *Sussex*, Spain, and the Outrage." *London Times*, March 30, 1916, p. 5.

An American professor's account of the torpedoing of the *Sussex*. From Madrid it is reported that Alfonso XIII is inquiring of Spanish ambassadors in Paris and London as to Granados's fate; Professor Baldwin also reports that "the catastrophe is causing considerable feeling throughout Spain."

B6. "Aeolian Hall: Concierto de Maestro Granados." *Las Novedades*, February 24, 1916, p. 5.

A review of Granados's February 22, 1916, premiere of selected piano and vocal works. "Críticos hay . . . para quienes la ópera [*Goyescas*] se resiente de su origen pianístico. No lo creemos: la vida y el movimiento de los dos primeros cuadros nos obligan a recordar que Granados habia compuesto ya tres obras teatrales antes de *Goyescas*". (There are critics who would argue that the opera is weakened by its pianistic origins. We are not of this opinion, however, for the life and movement of the two first books [of the piano suite] force us to recall that Granados had already written three stage works before *Goyescas*.) In fact, the composer had written over half a dozen stage works prior to *Goyescas*.

B7. "Aid for Granados Children: Spanish Ambassador Issues Appeal for Orphans of Composer." *New York Times*, May 6, 1916, p. 11.

The Spanish Consul General of New York, F. Javier Salas, has issued an international appeal in the name of the Spanish ambassador "on behalf of the [six] orphaned children of Professor Granados."

B8. Alaveda, Joan. *Conxita* [*sic*] *Badia: una vida artística*. Barcelona: Editorial Pòrtic, 1975.

A commemorative volume on Conchita Badia (1897-1975), the most authoritative interpreter of Granados's vocal music, to whom he dedicated several *Tonadillas* and *Canciones amatorias*. Several references to Granados that center mainly around life at the Granados Academy.

B9. Albet, Montserrat. "Concert d'Homenatge a Enric Granados." Program notes for a piano recital at the Sala Vila, Barcelona, June 17, 1987.

For a recital by Catalan pianist Carlotta Garriga. Albet gives a biographical outline in which the author explains the background of *La cieguecita de Belén*, and dwells at somewhat greater length than other sources on the collaboration between Granados and Gabriel Miró.

B10. Aldrich, Richard. "Friends of Music Society, Enrique Granados, Pablo Casals," and "*Goyescas*." In *Concert Life in New York: 1902-1923*, 494-500. New York: G. P. Putnam's Sons, 1941.

A collection of reviews (arranged by season) by New York's most prominent critic during the first two decades of the twentieth century. Perceptive commentary on two of Granados's 1916 New York appearances (see **Biography**, p. 29 for citation).

B11. Alier, Roger. "Musical Life in Barcelona, 1888-1936." In *Homage to Barcelona: The City and Its Art (1888-1936)*, ed. Michael Raeburn, 277-85. London: Thames and Hudson, 1985.

In a discussion of opera and musical life in Barcelona the author compares Granados, classified as a *Renaixança* composer, with Morera, a modernist. Rich in photographs and reproductions from these two periods.

B12. "American Pianist Aids Orphans of Spanish Composer." Press release from Press Department, Metropolitan Musical Bureau, 1502 Aeolian Hall, New York City, [1917?]. Schelling Archive, New York.

"The 'loving cup' [presented to Granados by Schelling and various New York contributors] went down . . . on the torpedoed 'S.S. Sussex' And since the draft on the Fifth Avenue Bank for four thousand dollars has never been presented for collection, it is presumed that it went down also. Fortunately, Mr. Schelling . . . preserved a duplicate of the draft, and after certain formalities were complied with, the Granados children . . . received the money. A large sum that the composer of *Goyescas* carried in gold was lost altogether, however."

B13. Anglès, Higini, and Joaquín [Joaquím] Pena, eds. "Granados, Enrique." *Diccionario de la Música Labor* 1: 1123-25. Barcelona: Editorial Labor, 1954.

Biographical overview, with a number of questionable facts and observations, such as the remark that "*Goyescas* and *Tonadillas* reveal, without a doubt, the spiritual influence of Albéniz" or that Granados won the 1883 "Concurs Pujol" by *sight-reading* Schumann's Sonata in G Minor. Also an article on Granados's son Eduardo.

B14. "Un aniversari artístic: La primera audició de la *Iberia*." *Mirador: Setmanari de Literatura, Art, i Política* 4, no. 176 (1932): 2.

The author recalls the evening of June 16, 1905, when Albéniz, Roviralta, (Marian) Andreu, the countess of Castellà, and Granados gathered at the home of Malats for a first reading of selections from Albéniz's *Iberia*. (According to the author, Malats sight-read "Triana" from a manuscript copy.) In addition, the Barcelona city council was urged to name streets after Malats, Albéniz, and Granados.

B15. "La Argentina. Sprightly Spanish Dancer Sings as She Snaps Castanets." *New York Herald*, February 11, 1916, p. 12.

A review of the performance by native Spaniard "La Argentina" at the Maxine Elliot Theater, February 10, 1916. "There is no doubt whatever about the charm of the dancer, but there is a certain monotony about her dancing when it fills the greater part of an evening. . . . One of her dances yesterday was *The Tango of the Green Eyes*, written by Enrique Granados especially for her New York debut, and when it was applauded she by a graceful gesture transferred the honors to the composer, who was sitting in a box."

B16. "De Arte." *Diario de Barcelona*, January 28, 1913, p. 1324.

A review of the second performance of *Elisenda*, January 26, 1913, at the Granados Academy. Participants included the composer, Srta. Lluró, Srs. Mares and Perlló, and other instrumentalists. "Dos temperamentos igualmente poéticos como los de los señores Mestres y Granados habian coincidido en esa producción para crear una obra de una gran delicadeza de sentimiento y de una distincion artística". (Two equally poetic temperaments as those of Mestres and Granados have coincided in that production to create a work of great delicacy of sentiment and artistic distinction.)

B17. "Associació de Música 'da Camera'." *Revista Musical Catalana* 11 (1914): 287.

Review of the June 27, 1914, performance by Conchita Badia of the *Tonadillas* at the Palau de la Música Catalana: "per la traça amb que estàn escrites ningú diría què fossin del nostre temps. Ingenues, bellugadices . . . ens transporten a l'època dels *petimetres* i de les *majas*" (from the design of the *Tonadillas*, one could hardly say that they are a product of our own times. Ingenuous, fluttering, they transport us back to the era of dandies, of *majas*."]

B18. "Associació de Música 'da Camera.'" *Revista Musical Catalana* 13 (1915): 23.

Review of the November 14, 1915, concert at the Palau de la Música Catalana at which Granados performed Grieg's Concerto in A Minor, in his new capacity as Artistic Director. "Per a la inauguració del present curs comptà l'Associació de Música 'da Camera', amb el valiós concurs del seu director artístic, el mestre n'Enric Granados". (For the inauguration of the current season, the Association of Chamber Music counts on the welcome cooperation of its Artistic Director, Enrique Granados.)

B19. "Associació Musical de Barcelona." *Revista Musical Catalana* 5 (1908): 47.

Review of a series of Lenten concerts at the Liceu sponsored by the Musical Association of Barcelona, including a performance by Granados and Saint-Saëns of that composer's transcription for two pianos of Chopin's Sonata in B-flat Minor ("la transcripció a dos pianos feta per ell mateix de la Sonata en si bemol menor de Chopin") and Granados's performances of Grieg's Concerto in A minor and Saint-Saëns's Concerto No. 5.

B20. "Associació Wagneriana." *Revista Musical Catalana* 1 (1904): 57.

Review of Granados's Chopin concert sponsored by the Wagner Association February 17, 1904: "La seva tècnica pot dirse que es avuy del tot perfecta." (One can say that by now his technique has been perfected.) Josep Roviralta (author of the poem "Boires baixes") gave an introductory lecture.

B21. "Associació Wagneriana." *Revista Musical Catalana* 1 (1904): 151.

Commentary on Granados's June 19, 1904, Schumann recital sponsored by the Wagner Association. "Lo més notable de la vetllada foren las exquisidas *Escencas d'infants*, a les que'l senyor Granados donà una interpretació molt ajustada y ben sentida". (The high point of the evening was the *Scenes from Childhood*, to which Mr. Granados imparted an engaging and deeply felt interpretation.) Other participants included Frank Marshall, pianist, and Francisca Mercé, soprano.

B22. Aviñoa, José. *La música i el modernisme*. Barcelona: Curial Edicions Catalanes, 1985.

An expansion of the author's 1983 dissertation which traces musical developments in Barcelona from 1880 to 1910, with emphasis on subscription series founded during this period. Granados's founding of the Society of Classical Concerts and his efforts to foster Catalan lyric theater (there are thirty-five references to the composer throughout the book) are of greatest interest.

B23. Bannard, Joshua. "Enrique Granados: 1868 [*sic*]-1916." *Monthly Musical Record* 46, no. 546 (1916): 162.

An evaluation of the composer: "Granados learnt much from a study of past masters . . . he everywhere expressed himself alone and in his own terms. As a result, some of his work is hurried, inconsequent, over-decorated. Yet his unclouded inspiration [may be found] on every page, and it is such that lives forever in the memories of men." Unfortunately, most of Bannard's dates are incorrect.

B24. "Barcelona: Eugeni [*sic*] Isaye." *Revista Musical Catalana* 1 (1904): 125.

Review of the first of Belgian violinist Eugène Ysaye's two Barcelona appearances in May, 1904, under the auspices of the Philharmonic Society. Granados was the pianist and the concert included various works of Bach, a paraphrase of *Siegfried's Idyll*, and Brahms's Sonata in D Minor, this last performance being "especially noteworthy."

B25. "Barcelona: Teatre Principal." *Revista Musical Catalana* 3 (1906): 54.

During this season Granados and von Sauer (on his third tour of Barcelona) each presented two solo recitals at the Principal. Granados presented several of his Scarlatti transcriptions. "Totes elles d'una extraordinaria forsa expressiva y d'una varietat admirable." (All of these [have] an extraordinary expressive force and an admirable rhythmic variety.)

B26. Benko, George. "*Reverie-Improvisation*, by Enrique Granados." *Clavier* 6, no. 7 (1967): 27-36.

Reproduction and history of an improvisation recorded in 1916 by Granados in the Aeolian studios of New York. A technician had surreptitiously left the recording equipment on while Granados improvised a short piece. The original piano roll was donated to International Piano Archives and later transcribed by *Clavier*.

B27. Bertran, Marcos Jesús. "El año musical en Barcelona." *La Vanguardia*, January 1, 1900, pp. 2-3.

A review of musical activities in Barcelona during 1899, including the city's premiere of *María del Carmen* at the Teatre Tívoli in May of that year. "*María del Carmen* . . . es una obra de potente inspiración y de finísima labor de orquesta". (*María del Carmen* . . . is a work of great inspiration, with attentiveness to details of orchestration.)

B28. Boas, Robert. "Lille." *Opera* 37 (1986): 71-73.

A review of a production of *Goyescas* at Lille, November 1, 1986. "It was a good idea of the Opera Royal de Wallonie to revive . . . *Goyescas*. Less happy was the decision to entrust the *mise en scène* to the Spanish emigré playwright Fernando Arrabal, who, abetted by the decor and costume departments, proceeded to impose his own interpretation . . . the result was an evening of depressingly familiar anti-Romantic clichés: cars, derelict permanent sets littered with cranes and wrecked hairless, pseudo-naked supernumeraries . . . [and] humdrum modern costumes."

B29. Bohle, Bruce, ed. "Enrique Granados." In *International Cyclopedia of Music and Musicians*. 11th ed., 327. New York: Dodd, Mead, 1985.

Biographical outline. Lists works by category, with names of individual compositions within a larger set.

B30. Boladeres Ibern, Guillermo. *Enrique Granados: Recuerdos de su vida y estudio crítico de su obra por su antiguo discípulo* (Enrique Granados: Recollections of His Life and Critical Study of His Works by a Former Student). Barcelona: Editorial Arte y Letras, 1921.

A largely anecdotal memoir of the author's piano studies with Granados during the first decade of the twentieth century. Boladeres Ibern provides information on Granados's priorities as a teacher (his interest in the *mecanismo*, i.e., the physical aspects of piano playing, in pedaling, and in the piano's orchestral sonorities). Selected piano works are discussed; contains an (incomplete) catalogue of works. The first full-length study on Granados.

B31. Bonet y Cembrano. "Granados." *Joventut* 7 (1906): 154-55.

A review of Granados's two solo recitals at the Teatre Principal, March 1 and 3, 1906, in preparation for a tour of several Spanish provinces. Gives complete programs as well as encores. Granados performed some of his newly edited Scarlatti sonatas on this occasion (see **Biography**, p. 24 for citation).

B32. Borowski, Felix. "Fourth Program of the Twenty-Fifth Season (1915-16) of the Chicago Symphony Orchestra," published by the Orchestral Association, Orchestral Hall, Chicago.

Program notes for November 5 and 6, 1915, performances by the Chicago Symphony of *Dante*, conducted by Frederick Stock. The author describes relationship between Dante's *Divina Commedia* and Granados's symphonic poem, which was given its American premiere at this performance with mezzo-soprano soloist Sophie Braslau.

B33. "Brillante epílogo de los homenajes de Granados." *La Vanguardia Española*, February 9, 1957, p. 17.

An account of a colloquium sponsored by the Escuela de Periodistas at Barcelona's Athenaeum. After speeches by various musicians and city officials, the following ideas were discussed: the erection of a Granados monument, a concert of his symphonic music, and the need for a completely new edition of his works, "muy particularmente su creación sinfónica, inexplicadamente poco conocida" (especially the symphonic works, inexplicably little known).

B34. Brody, Elaine. "The Spaniards in Paris." In *Paris: The Musical Kaleidoscope, 1870-1925*, 168-89. New York: George Braziller, 1987.

An overview of the musical interaction between French musicians and the "Spanish colony" in Paris at the turn of the century. Emphasis on Albéniz, Granados, Viñes, and Falla. A photograph on page 173 is misidentified as Granados. Most of the factual information on the composer is drawn from Ricardo Viñes's diary.

B35. ---. "Viñes in Paris: New Light on Twentieth-Century Performance Practice." In *A Musical Offering: Essays in Honor of Martin Bernstein*, ed. Edward H. Clinkscale and Claire Brook, 44-62. New York: Pendragon Press, 1977.

Drawn from Viñes's unpublished diary, this article discusses late nineteenth- and early twentieth-century performance practice as perceived by pioneer of new music pianist Ricardo Viñes, with whom Granados briefly shared lodgings in Paris. Also included are Viñes's impressions of Charles de Bériot, who taught Granados, Viñes, and Ravel.

B36. Broekhoven, J. van. "*Goyescas* (*The Rival Lovers*): A Spanish Opera in Three Pictures." *Musical Observer* 13, no. 3 (1916): 134-35.

Broekhoven discusses the apparent absence of Spanish musical genius, commenting that "while the composers of other countries have worked with success this Spanish mine of jewels, the Spaniards themselves--with few exceptions--have failed to take advantage of the opportunity within their grasp. The first attempt to regain this opportunity is the opera *Goyescas*, a most promising achievement." Fourteen musical examples enhance a synopsis of the opera.

B37. Camuto, Alessandro. "Trieste." *Opera* 33 (1982): 619-20.

Review of the Italian-language version of *Goyescas* given at the Teatro Verdi, February 4, 1982. "The opera had been absent from the Italian stage since 1937. . . . Gert Meditz's conducting over-emphasized the orchestration, resulting in a rather crude and summary reading of the piece, a reading that neutralised the excellent work of the chorus. On stage a great deal of energy was wasted with violence more associated with *verismo* than with the elegance prescribed (albeit spasmodically) by Granados's score."

B38. Cardona, Rodolfo. "Granados' Spain." Paper presented at the "Granados and *Goyescas*" Symposium, Harvard University, Cambridge, January 23, 1982.

A discussion of historical events during Granados's lifetime, including the Revolution of 1868, Spain's loss of her colonies in 1898, and the Setmana Trágica (Tragic Week) of 1909 (to which Granados refers in B379), during which violent uprisings by Barcelona's workers resulted in numerous deaths and more than 3,500 arrests.

B39. Carreras i Granados, Antoní. *Granados*. Series title: *Gent Nostra*. Barcelona: Litoclub, 1988.

A fifty-page treatment by the composer's grandson of Granados's life and works. Especially valuable are the more than seventy photographs (many taken from the family archives and not reproduced elsewhere). Primarily, Carreras recounts personal anecdotes and describes Granados's friendships.

B40. Casals, Pablo. *Joys and Sorrows* (As told to Albert E. Kahn). New York: Simon and Schuster, 1970.

Autobiography offers a brief synopsis of the great cellist's friendship with Granados, tracing their association from Granados's performances with the Crickboom Quartet (a reproduction of an 1897 recital program by Casals, Crickboom, and Granados is included) to the composer's death. For the general reader.

B41. Castilla, Alfonso de. "España aquí." *Las Novedades*, January 27, 1916, p. 6.

Commentary on the January 28, 1916, Metropolitan Opera premiere of *Goyescas*, concluding with a roster of prominent Spaniards then working in the United States, including María Barrientos, Lucrezia Bori, Conchita Supervía, Pablo Casals, and Miquel Llobet.

B42. Chase, Gilbert. "Albéniz and Granados." In *The Music of Spain*, 150-65. 2d rev. ed. New York: Dover Publications, 1959.

The now classic English-language survey of Spanish music places Granados in a historical perspective vis-à-vis Spanish music. In so doing, Chase draws several parallels between Granados and Albéniz. An excellent introduction.

B43. Chase, William B. "Opera Founded on Paintings: The *Goyescas* of Enrique Granados Received with Favor by Metropolitan Audiences." *Opera Magazine* 3, no. 3 (1916): 10-13.

A summary of the spirit and creation of the January 28, 1916, Metropolitan Opera premiere of *Goyescas*. Information on the career of Anna Fitziu, the first Rosario, who had earlier sung on Broadway. Also contains information on Spanish and Spanish-language operas performed in the United States prior to *Goyescas*. Background on Granados as an opera composer contains some errors in dating.

B44. Chavarri, Eduard L. "Records de N'Enric Granados." *Revista Musical Catalana* 13 (1916): 188-90.

Homage to Granados, with details on Chavarri's orchestration of Granados's *L'Himne dels morts*.

B45. Collet, Henri. *Albéniz et Granados*. Paris: Editions Le Bon Plaisir, 1948.

Approximately twenty pages on Granados's life, thirty-five on his works. The most complete source of dates, locations, and repertory of Granados's public appearances. Reference to his friendship with Joaquín Nin. The "Works" section includes an overview of Granados's *oeuvre*, with references to several missing and unfinished compositions.

B46. ---. *L'Essor de la Musique Espagnole au XX siècle* (The Development of Spanish Music in the Twentieth Century). Paris: Editions Max Eschig, 1929.

Survey of early twentieth-century developments in Spanish music, with several references to Granados's role in the "Spanish musical renaissance." Written from the standpoint of musical criticism rather than musicology.

B47. Comellas, Jaume. "Memòria d'Enric Granados." *Revista Musical Catalana*, 2d ser., 4, nos. 33-34 (1987): 10-12.

An interview with Granados's son-in-law, Antoní Carreras i Verdaguer, on the occasion of his loan of numerous Granados manuscripts and documents to Barcelona's Centre de Documentació Musical. Carreras explains his motivation in making the donation, and also mentions Granados's friendship with Spanish composer Oscar Esplá.

B48. "Concert for Benefit of War Sufferers from the Paris Conservatory to be Held at Carnegie Hall on Wednesday, March 15, 1916." *New York Herald*, March 12, 1916, NYPL.

Ignaz Paderewski, the Flonzaley Quartet, Ernest Schelling, and Granados were scheduled to appear in an all-French program (Saint-Saëns, Massenet, Daquin, Couperin) as a benefit for the French war effort. Although it turned out that Granados did not participate in the concert (he left the United States March 11), several biographers have made the error of including him as a participant.

B49. "Concert Granados." *Revista Musical Catalana* 8 (1911): 89-90.

Review of Granados's March 11, 1911, recital at the Palau de Música Catalana which featured his own works, including premieres of *Cant de les estrelles* and *Goyescas*. On *Goyescas*: "L'impressió que causen la premiera vegada que s'escolten no es pas d'aquelles dominadores; però això es degut al caracter general de les obres d'en Granados, el qual es enemic de tota violencia: en mig del sentiment fondo que les inspira, hi plana sempres una dolça placidesa, que constitueix potser el llur major encìs." (The impression caused by a first hearing of *Goyescas* is not a startling one; this is due to the character of Granados's works in general, which are completely lacking in violence: buried within the deep sentiment which motivates every work, however, lies a sweet placidness which in fact constitutes each work's principal charm.)

B50. "Concert Granados-Malats." *Revista Musical Catalana* 4 (1907): 224.

Review of the September 30, 1907, two-piano concert by Granados and Malats at the Teatre de Novetats. (This concert was a repeat of a performance given on June 9, 1899, also at the Novetats.) "Rares vegades se donarà'l cas de sentir plegats a dos pianistes de tant renom com en Granados y en Malats". (Rarely does one have occasion to hear two pianists of such renown as Granados and Malats on the same concert.)

B51. "Concert Malats." *Revista Musical Catalana* 1 (1904): 239.

A review of the October 29, 1904, concert by Joaquím Malats at the Teatre de Novetats, which included Granados's *Allegro de concierto*. "No menys felís estigué-en la interpretació del *Allegro de concert* de Granados, obra distinguida, de marcat caràcter espanyol y d'execució difícil, que en mans d'en Malats resultà brillantíssima". (He was no less fortunate in the *Allegro de concierto* of Granados, a distinguished work of marked Spanish character and technical challenges, which, in Malats's hands, was brilliantly rendered.)

B52. "Concerts Crickboom." *Revista Musical Catalana* 3 (1906): 122.

Review of May 26 and 28, 1906, concerts by Granados and Crickboom at the Teatre Principal. "[La Sonata de Beethoven] hi alcansa, secundat admirablement per en Granados, la ovació més grossa de la nit". (Their admirable joint interpretation of Beethoven's 'Kreutzer' Sonata received the biggest ovation of the evening.)

B53. "Concerts Risler-Granados." *Revista Musical Catalana* 3 (1906): 102.

Review of joint recital on April 28 and 30, 1906, at Barcelona's Teatre Principal. In addition to Mozart's Concerto in E-flat for Two Pianos, K. 365, works of Schumann and Saint-Saëns, Granados and Risler performed *Three Romantic Waltzes* of Chabrier: "Apreciables per la seva originalitat, però d'un sentiment tant baladí, que solament la colorida y brillanta execució de dos artistes com en Risler y en Granados pot realsar". (Arresting in their originality, although perhaps a trifle shallow in sentiment, which only the colorful and brilliant execution of two artists like Granados and Risler can bring to life.) The orchestra was conducted by Crickboom.

B54. "Concerts de Tardor." *Revista Musical Catalana* 7 (1910): 347-49.

Review of Granados's November 12, 1910, appearance with violinist Jacques Thibaud at the Palau de Música Catalana. "No menys dignes de recordança foren els dos últims concerts, que, malgrat l'aparent aridesa de llurs programes, comprenent cada un d'ells tres sonates no més, atragueren un públic prou nombrós". (No less worthy of mention are the two last concerts [of this series], which, despite the apparent aridity of programming, each consisting of three sonatas, no more, attracted a large public.)

B55. "Concerts varis." *Revista Musical Catalana* 3 (1906): 84-85.

Review of Ricart Vives's performance of four Granados-Scarlatti sonatas at the Círcol Barcelonès. "Encara qué l'auditori . . . no era'l més indicat pera ferse just cabal de les obres y qualitats esmentades, tampoch escassejà als joves artistes els aplaudiments que's mereixen". (Although the audience . . . may not have been the best prepared to appreciate the above-mentioned qualities, neither did it stint on the applause the artist merited.)

B56. Cooke, James E. *Great Pianists on Piano Playing*. Philadelphia: Theodore Presser, 1913.

Brief descriptions of pianists prominent early in this century, including Ernest Schelling, Granados's friend and associate in the United States.

B57. "Mr. Copeland's Recital: A List of Unfamiliar Pieces for the Pianoforte Played." *New York Times*, December 7, 1915, p. 13.

A review of George Copeland's December 6, 1915, Aeolian Hall recital, in which he played one of Granados's *Twelve Spanish Dances*, "which had the most of the Spanish characteristic [*sic*]."

B58. Corredor, J. *Conversations with Casals*. Translated from the French by André Mangeot. New York: Dutton, 1956.

Descriptions of Granados's piano playing, with emphasis on his skill as an improviser.

B59. "Correspondencies: Madrid." *Revista Musical Catalana* 1 (1904): 62-63.

Notice of Granados's winning of the contest sponsored by the Madrid Conservatory for his *Allegro de concierto*. "Acabaré ab duas noticias referents a dos mestres catalans. L'una d'ellas es l'haver sigut premiat en un concurs obert pel Conservatori d'aquesta capital un *Allegro de concierto* pera piano, que's destinarà al darrer curs de carrera, original del distingit compositor l'Enrich Granados". (I will conclude with news of two Catalan musicians. One of these was declared winner in a contest sponsored by the Conservatory of this capital for an *Allegro de concierto*, to be used in the last level of the curriculum--an original work by the distinguished Enrique Granados.)

B60. "Cronica." *La Esquella de la Torratxa* 1065 (1899): 362-63.

A laudatory review of the Barcelona premiere of *María del Carmen*, May 31, 1899. Attention, however, is drawn to the weak libretto, although numerous high points are given special mention: "L'element pintoresch prepondera sobre l'element dramatisch. Granados paga tribut á aquest element pintoresch de una manera brillant". (The picturesque predominates over the dramatic. Granados, however, pays tribute to this picturesque element in a brilliant way.)

B61. Crutchfield, Will. "A Treasury of Voices, from Galli-Curci to Lily Pons." *New York Times*, June 23, 1985, sec. 2, p. 20.

Interview with William Seward, collector of opera memorabilia, who acquired from Amelita Galli-Curci "a notebook of drawings and musical sketches by Enrique Granados. . . . It contains preliminary versions --some significantly different from the published ones--of his popular *Tonadillas*."

B62. "Culp and Grenados [*sic*] Furnish White House Program." *Musical Courier*, March 16, 1916, NYPL.

An account of Granados's March 7, 1916, White House performance. "The President, Mrs. Wilson, and Miss Wilson are said to have been particularly gratified at the excellence of the program rendered and to have expressed their gracious appreciation."

B63. Curet, Francesc, ed. "Intents de Teatre Líric Català: Enric Granados." In *Historia del Teatre Català*, 436-39. Barcelona: Editorial Aedos, 1967.

Discusses various figures in Catalan theater with whom Granados collaborated (Mestres, Gual, Feliu i Codina) and outlines the composer's involvement in Catalan modernism.

B64. Cuspinera, C. "Enrique Granados." *Diario de Barcelona*, April 22, 1890, pp. 5075-76.

An enthusiastic review of Granados's official Barcelona debut at the Teatre Líric, April 20, 1890. Includes names of the assisting artists and comments on Granados's abilities as both pianist and composer. The reviewer compares Granados's present style (at this concert he performed his *Arabesca* and the *Serenata española*) with his pre-Paris compositions. To the reviewer, these latter had seemed "modest, [although] we can remember several concert mazurkas that could be compared to those of Chopin" ("algunos trabajos modestos entre los cuales recordamos algunas mazurkas de concierto que podían figurar dignamente entre las de Chopin").

B65. "Date Set for Opera in Spanish." *New York Herald*, January 17, 1916, p. 12.

"At last the date for the American premiere of *Goyescas* has been set. . . . The plot, entirely original with the librettist, was inspired by the life and paintings of his compatriot, the artist Goya, and presents three episodes such as might have occurred in the heyday of his career."

B66. Davis, Peter G. "The Spanish Piano School and Its Star Pupil." *New York Times*, July 31, 1977, sec. 2, pp. 13-16.

Reviews one of Alicia de Larrocha's recording of *Goyescas*. Discusses the importance of Granados both as an indirect influence on Miss de Larrocha's playing and in relation to Spanish music: "Granados was perhaps the most important of this trio [Albéniz, Falla, Granados]--there's no telling what directions he might have explored had it not been for his untimely death. . . . As a technical tour-de-force *Goyescas* presents a formidable challenge--Granados . . . spares the player very little in terms of elaborate passagework, interweaving subsidiary themes and complex rhythmic patterns."

B67. "Dear Musical America." *Musical America*, April 9, 1916, NYPL.

A summary of the reaction of many contemporary artists to the torpedoing of the *Sussex*. "The sinking of many ships since then, and now the Granados tragedy, will, no doubt, result in all of them [foreign artists in the U.S.] . . . staying here for the summer."

B68. Del Arco. "Mano a mano: Natalia Granados [de Carreras]." *La Vanguardia Española*, January 22, 1957, p. 14.

An interview with the composer's youngest daughter, Natalia, during which she describes her father's creation of *Goyescas*: "He had started it but broke off, in one of those crises of modesty to which he was always prone. But my mother asked him to continue, so he took it up again." Before the thwarted Paris premiere of *Goyescas*, Granados's finances were extremely precarious.

B69. De Larrocha, Alicia. "Goya of Music: Alicia de Larrocha Talks about Granados." *Opera News* 32, no. 6 (1967): 6-7.

Interview commemorating the hundredth anniversary of Granados's birth. The author describes Granados's love of improvisation and mentions a memorial concert by Artur Rubinstein in Barcelona given shortly after Granados died.

B70. ---. "Granados." (With the assistance of Edmund Haines.) *High Fidelity Magazine* 17 (1967): 56-58.

A discussion of the interpretation of Granados's piano works by the foremost Granados specialist, with emphasis on rubato and ornamentation.

B71. ---. "Granados, the Composer." Translated from the Spanish by Joan Kerlow. *Clavier* 6, no. 7 (1967): 21-23.

The Spanish pianist outlines Granados's three creative periods (nationalistic, romantic and "goyesca"), describes the characteristics of each, and cites representative works from each area.

B72. Del Campo, Angel. *Granados*. Madrid: Publicaciones Españoles no. 473, 1966.

Written by the music critic of the Madrid daily, *Pueblo*, this series of five essays contains commentary on current topics, including quotes by Granados's musical contemporaries and headlines from various Madrid newspapers in the days preceding Granados's death. Discusses cultural scene in Madrid and Barcelona during Granados's time.

B73. Delclós, Tomás. "El músico Douglas Riva rescata obras inéditas de Granados escritas en 1888." *El País*, March 29, 1984. Douglas Riva Collection, New York.

A description of the contents of *Album: Paris, 1888*, which contains sketches and finished piano works. Many of the works have humorous or mysterious titles and many are dedicated to young women or to Granados's mentors.

B74. "Demands That Spain Act: Madrid Authority Wants German Merchantmen Seized." *New York Times*, April 15, 1916, p. 3.

Commentary of prominent Spaniards on the torpedoing of the *Sussex*, including Amadeo Hurtado on neutrality policies. Spanish Premier Romanones is quoted as suggesting reprisals against Germans. Mentions telegram sent to Madrid from Spanish artists living in Paris, urging Madrid to take action against Germans.

B75. Demarquez, Suzanne. *Manuel de Falla*. Translated from the French by Salvator Attanasio. Philadelphia: Chilton Book Co., 1968.

A biography of the Andalusian composer that contains several references to Granados and to Frank Marshall.

B76. "Des de Nova York." *Revista Musical Catalana* 13 (1916): 88-89.

A brief report on the New York operatic season of 1916, including the premiere of *Goyescas*. "Les *Goyescas* pianistiques . . . han sofert una magnífica ampliació a l'ésser traslladades a l'escena. . . . Llàstima que, no havent estat secundat degudament pel llibretista . . . el mestre Granados no ha pogut fer propiament una òpera, sinó . . . un gran poema musical realçat plàsticament per l'espectacle escènic". (The *Goyescas* for piano . . . have undergone a magnificent expansion in being moved to the stage. . . . It is a pity that, not having properly secured the right librettist, . . . Granados has not created an opera, but rather a great musical poem for the stage.)

B77. "Des de Nova York." *Revista Musical Catalana* 13 (1916): 242-43.

A brief obituary. "El gran mestre Enric Granados també ha estat víctima de la lluita implacable." (The great master Enrique Granados is also a victim of this voracious war.)

B78. "*Dos marchas militares*." *Revista Musical Catalana* 7 (1910): 109.

Announcement of the publication by Casa Dotesio (Barcelona) of the four-hand work: "Inspirades y elegantíssimes, com les mateixes de Schubert, són les dues marxes militars d'en Granados, dignes de figurar en el programa més serios". (Inspired and supremely elegant, like Schubert's, these two military marches are worthy of appearing on the most dignified concert program.)

B79. Eames, Emma. Interview. "Echoes of Music Abroad: Most Typical of Spanish Composers Lionized in Paris." *Musical America*, August 1, 1914, p. 11, NYPL.

An interview with American opera singer Eames (wife of singer Emilio de Gorgoza), who recalls the beginning of her friendship with Granados during his 1914 Paris tour. Recounts a performance at the home of Robert Bliss, the first secretary of the American Embassy in Paris, in which Granados performed *Goyescas* and some of the *Spanish Dances* and de Gorgoza performed several of the *Tonadillas*. (He converted some of the *maja*'s songs by changing the masculine and feminine pronouns in the text.)

B80. "Eleven Thousand Dollars for Granados: Six Guest Artists at Benefit for Late Composer's Children." *New York Times*, May 8, 1916, p. 9.

Account of the May 7, 1916, memorial concert which featured Barrientos, Culp, Paderewski, Kreisler, Casals, and McCormack and "attracted a crowd that could not be accommodated in the great auditorium." Paderewski, Kreisler, and Casals (who had never performed together before) played Beethoven's "Archduke" Trio. Autographed programs were sold at five dollars apiece and Mme. Paderewski sold "Polish refugee dolls" in the foyer.

B81. "L'Enric Granados a París." *Revista Musical Catalana* 11 (1914): 140-42.

Collection of translated press clippings reviewing Granados's April 4, 1914, recital at the Salle Pleyel, the Paris premiere of *Goyescas*. "Ens féu conèixer tot el primer llibre de les *Goyescas* i dues obres de segón llibre. Confesso que no sé judicar les darreres . . . però les primeres, que m'eren un xic familiars, m'han acabat de convèncer que'ns trobem al davant de lo millor que la música de piano ha produit a Espanya". (He acquainted us with the whole first book of *Goyescas* and also two pieces from the second book. I confess that I do not know how to judge these last . . . but the first, which are somewhat familiar to me, have just convinced me that they belong in the front rank of all the piano music Spain has produced.) G. Jean-Aubry, *La Tribune Musicale*.

B82. "Enrique Granados." *Musica* 2 (1916): 53-54.

This obituary mentions Granados's negotiations with the Teatro Colón in Buenos Aires for a premiere of *Goyescas* to be held on June 2, 1916. The writer suggests that Granados planned to travel to Buenos Aires for the Latin American premiere, and that these negotiations were finalized during his stay in New York.

B83. "Enrique Granados." *Musical Emporium* 9, no. 77 (1916): 1-2.

A lengthy obituary with generally accurate biographical information. The same number also contains a description of a memorial concert organized by Italian pianist Stefaniani, which took place in Madrid at the Palace Hotel, April 15, 1916. The *Infanta* Isabel attended the performance, which included the *Tonadillas* (sung by Srta. Cecilia Sánchez), three movements of *Goyescas* (Sr. Aroca), orchestral renderings of several *Spanish Dances* (directed by Stefaniani), and concluded with one of Liszt's symphonic poems and the Prelude from *Die Meistersinger*.

B84. "Enrique Granados y Campiña." *Ilustración Musical Hispano-Americana* 3 (1890): 282-83.

The reviewer introduces Granados to Barcelona's musical community after his official debut April 20, 1890. In a biographical sketch, the date of Granados's studies with Pedrell is given as 1884 (only vaguely established by many biographers); since Pedrell founded and edited the *Ilustración Musical* we can assume this date to be accurate. On Granados's style: "El género *brillante* ha cesado de ser. . . . Granados será de los buenos artístas que buscarán siempre el aplauso en el arte puro". (The flashy genres have ceased to be. . . .

Granados will be among those fine artists who will seek applause only as a reward for pure art.)

B85. "Enrique Granados and His Opera *Goyescas*: Interesting Facts about the Spanish Composer Whose Novelty Is Soon To Be Brought Out by the Metropolitan Opera Company." *Musical Courier*, December 23, 1915, NYPL.

Introduces Granados and his wife, Amparo, to the American public. General biographical information.

B86. "Enrique Granados Plays: Composer of *Goyescas* Makes Debut as Pianist--Anna Fitziu Aids." *New York Times*, February 23, 1916, p. 13.

A review of Granados's February 22, 1916, Aeolian Hall appearance, which featured his *Danza lenta*, *Danza valenciana*, *Allegro de concierto*, selections from *Goyescas*, and selected Scarlatti-Granados sonatas. Granados also accompanied Fitziu in *Tonadillas*. The reviewer mentions the confusion as to which came first, the piano score or the opera, *Goyescas*. "Unusual and interesting recital program . . . a delight to those on whom conventional piano recitals may have begun to pall."

B87. Ericson, Raymond A. "Granados Given a Lovely Tribute: Alicia de Larrocha Devotes an Evening to His Music." *New York Times*, December 8, 1967, p. 60.

Review of de Larrocha's December 7, 1967, all-Granados recital at New York's Carnegie Hall, which consisted of the *Escenas románticas*, three of the "Popular Spanish Songs," and the entire *Goyescas* suite, including "El Pelele." "The musical world of the Spanish composer Enrique Granados is very special, highly perfumed and poetic. . . . Ordinarily a pianist would not devote an entire evening to his music."

"The *Goyescas* suite was played without interruption--Miss de Larrocha paused only once in its performance--the music created a hypnotic atmosphere . . . [of] somber, playful, or dreamlike moods."

B88. ---. "Little Orchestra Revives *Goyescas*." *Musical America* 76 (1956): 26-27.

A review of the October 15, 1956, performance of *Goyescas* in concert version by the Little Orchestra Society of New York at Town Hall. "Time has neither dimmed nor brightened the opera's merits. Considering that the score is a development of a series of piano pieces, it is less patchy than might be supposed, but the instrumentation, for all its color, is sometimes clumsy. . . . Its net effect is less striking than the piano *Goyescas*, which are excellent pieces of their genre."

B89. "Ernest Chausson." *Pel & Ploma* 3 (1899): 1.

This obituary of the French composer mentions Granados's rendering of a piano reduction of *María del Carmen* (whose Barcelona premiere had recently taken place) in early June, 1899, at the Cau Ferrat in Sitges. "El malhaurat Chausson era dels pocs que sostenien desinteressadament el moviment artístic català . . . i encara no fa tres semmanes ens recordava la nit passada al Cau Ferrat escoltant *La Fada* den Morera i la *María del Carmen* den Granados". (The unfortunate

Chausson was among the few [foreigners] who sustained a disinterested involvement in Catalan artistic movements . . . and it was not three weeks ago that we all spent an evening at the Cau Ferrat listening to *La Fada* by Morera and *María del Carmen* by Granados.)

B90. "Mr Ernest Schelling." *London Times*, December 10, 1913, p. 13.

A review of Schelling's December 9, 1913, Queen's Hall recital, the London premiere of *Goyescas*. A generally positive assessment of Schelling's playing, on *Goyescas*; however the reviewer comments that "[Schelling] played the Spaniard's music without making us aware that there was much in it."

B91. "Ernest Schelling Exploits a Spaniard." *New York World*, March 27, 1913, NYPL.

Review of Ernest Schelling's March 26, 1913, Carnegie Hall recital, at which he gave the American premiere of *Goyescas*, a work which, according to the reviewer, is "supposed to illustrate a little slumming expedition to Madrid by the Duchess of Alba and her lover the painter Gorja [*sic*]. . . . The audience was large and appreciative."

B92. "España y la America Latina en Nueva York." *Las Novedades*, November 18, 1915, p. 5.

Comments on Spanish and Latin American artists performing in New York during the 1915-1916 season, with remarks on first performances of Granados's works in New York.

B93. "Espectacles-Audicions Graner." *Revista Musical Catalana* 3 (1906): 54.

Commentary on the Graner repertory, including productions at the Teatre Principal of Rossiñols's *L'Alegria que passa* and Granados's *Picarol*, described as "verament notables per l'acert y bon gust que hi presideix" (truly notable for the expertise and good taste which presided).

B94. Esteban, Julio. "Master Lesson on a Granados Dance." *Clavier* 6, no. 7 (1967): 39-40.

The Madrid-trained pianist claims that Granados was "more knowledgeable and, in intimate feeling, more inspired" than Albéniz. Reflects on interpretive details and technical challenges in *Spanish Dance*, No. 6, "Rondalla Aragonesa."

B95. Ester-Sala, María. "Un manuscrit scarlattià retrobat." *Revista Musical Catalana* 5 (1988): 221.

Short history of Vidal Llimona y Boceta's 1904 edition of *Domenico Scarlatti (1685-1757). Veintiséis Sonatas Inéditas.* (*Transcripción para piano de Enrique Granados, precedidas de un estudio biográfico-bibliográfico-crítico de Felipe Pedrell*) and the 1988 discovery in Barcelona of the previously lost manuscript.

B96. "El estreno de *Goyescas* en Nueva York." *Musical Emporium* 19, no. 76 (1916): 4-5.

Along with a synopsis of the plot, the author explains how the opera *Goyescas* came to be given in New York rather than Paris. Also quotes reviews (positive only) from the New York press; these amplify the author's markedly chauvinistic views on Spanish art: "Granados, como lo hizo antes Albéniz, ha llevado al extranjero, para popularizarlos y glorificarlos, los aires característicos de España, fuente de inagotable inspiración. . . . Del éxito grande de *Goyescas*, todos los españoles pueden ciertamente vanagloriarse". (Granados, like Albéniz before him, has taken abroad for the purpose of popularization and glorification, the essential qualities of Spain, the inexhaustible source of inspiration. . . . All Spaniards can congratulate themselves on the enormous success of *Goyescas*.")

B97. "El estreno de la ópera *Goyescas*." *Musica* 2 (1916): 36.

An account of Granados's 1916 New York tour, in both its social and artistic aspects, with emphasis on his induction into the Hispanic Society of North America and subsequent presentation of an original piano-vocal score of *Goyescas* to the Society. "[Granados] fué inscrito en el cuadro de españoles ilustres al lado de Zuloaga y Sorolla, regaló al Museo el original de *Goyescas*. Allí quedará expuesto en una vitrina especial". (Granados, admitted into the company of illustrious Spaniards like Zuloaga and Sorolla, presented the Museum with the original of *Goyescas*. There, it was displayed in a special glass case.)

B98. Fasolt, Rémy. "Le Jury du Concours Diémer de 1909." *Musica* 81 (1909): 93.

The author gives a history of the Diémer prize, sponsored triennially by the Paris Conservatory. Granados was a member of the jury in 1909, when the contest took place May 3 and 4. The article identifies the other jurors and describes the requirements for entrants.

B99. Feminal. "El mestre Enrich Granados y la seva esposa." *Ilustració Catalana* 14, no. 109 (1916): 240-42.

An account of Granados's stay in New York, with background on his wife, Amparo, and on his family life.

B100. Fernández-Almagro, M. "Ecos de la vida literaria: Evocación de Granados." *La Vanguardia Española*, May 2, 1958, p. 14.

A review of Antonio Fernández-Cid's biography of the composer. "El hombre que fué Enrique Granados--generoso, reservado, aprensivo, grave--vive en el libro de Antonio Fernández-Cid . . . con la información y el sentido crítico a que el autor nos tiene acostumbrados". (The man Granados--generous, reserved, apprehensive, serious --lives in Fernández-Cid's book . . . with the abundance of information and critical sense we expect of this author.)

B101. Fernández-Cid, Antonio. *Granados*. Madrid: Samarán, 1956.

Possibly the most ambitious treatment of Granados to date. One-hundred page biography contains collected personal recollections of the composer by individuals like daughter Natalia and student Frank Marshall; thus a highly subjective, conversational tone is mixed with factual information. Contains the best summary of Granados's negotiations with the Paris opera, for example. The second half of the book contains subjective impressions on Granados's works.

B102. "Festa de la Música Catalana (Veredicte)." *Revista Musical Catalana* 4 (1907): 144-45.

Granados's name appears with Antoní Nicolau, Domingo Mas y Serracant, Lluís Millet, and Francesc Pujol as jury member for awarding prizes sponsored by the Festival of Catalan Music.

B103. Finck, H.T. "New York Hears Spanish Opera." *Opera News*, January 29, 1916, pp. 3-5. Reprint in *New York Post*.

"It is only by the production of novelties that operatic art can continue. Spain, like Russia, ought to be a fertile field, and in *Goyescas* we have found much music of haunting national charm."

B104. Fiol Gonzalez, E. "Las prácticas de la guerra y el derecho de los neutrales." *La Esfera* 3, no. 119 (1916): n. p.

A polemic against Germany and its violation of neutrality. Calls for a public statement on the part of the Spanish government.

B105. "Friends of Music Applaud Mr. Granados." *New York Herald*, January 24, 1916, p. 13.

A brief and not particularly insightful review of Granados's Ritz-Carlton appearance January 23, 1916: "The novelty of hearing him in a whole programme of his own works drew one of the largest audiences that has attended concerts of the Friends of Music. . . . He first played several *valses poéticos*, charmingly Spanish in rhythm." (This last description of a thoroughly non-Spanish work gives an idea of the critic's understanding of Spanish music.)

B106. Fuenmayor, Domingo de. "Presencia de Enrique Granados: A los treinta y nueve años de ser torpeado el 'Sussex'." *Diario de Barcelona*, June 15, 1955, p. 4.

The author, who is from Lleida and knew Granados personally, interviews Enrique Roig of the Liceu Conservatory, singer María José Antonín, and Julio Pons, a student of Granados's, all of whom describe some personal recollection of the composer.

B107. "La Gala del Orfeò." *La Veu de Catalunya*, March 14, 1911, p. 1.

In this review of Granados's March 11, 1911, appearance at the Palau de la Música Catalana (at which *Azulejos*, *Cant de les estrelles*, and the first book of *Goyescas* were premiered), the reviewer also mentions the March 12 Lenten concert by the Orfeó Català at which Joan Lamote de Grignon's orchestration of *Andaluza* and *Rondalla* were performed. "[Lamote de Grignon] ha cuidat el menor detall escullint a propòsit les diferentes cordes que més poguessin enrobustar l'original". (Lamote de Grignon has cared for every detail, choosing exactly the right instruments for enhancing the original.)

On *Goyescas* the reviewer comments that "Coloquio en la reja" seems "more inspired" than the more pianistic "Quejas" and the "Fandango." Of the *Cant de les estrelles*: "Les veus blanques repetint com un eco les darreres frases, encara que'l procediment no siga nou, sab en Granados emocionar fondament. En canvi la presencia del piano y orga influía el desequilibri, però lo cert es que hi mancava homogenitat". (The [use of] vibrato-less voices, echoing the last phrases, is not a new idea; Granados, however, knows how to draw forth great emotion here. On the other hand . . . we found both piano and organ to be too much . . . and certainly the work lacked homogeneity.) See B225, 299.

B108. Gandara, Francisco. "Noted Spanish Composer Here to See His Opera." *New York Times*, December 19, 1915, p. 7. Reprint in *Chicago Tribune*, June 4, 1916, and in *Musical Observer* 13, no. 2 (1916): 78 under title "Enrique Granados."

This memoir (which unfortunately contains much incorrect information on Granados's youth) recalls meetings with and impressions of Granados dating from 1911. "Critics said he was less original but more of a genius than Debussy, better balanced than Richard Strauss, as full of vigor as Giordano and Leoni, and as replete with sentiment as the Russians Mussorgsky and Borodine." Gandara also evaluates an impromptu performance of *Dante*: "I can still see him [Granados] seated at the piano, waiting for silence, then striking the first notes of what he called a 'sketch'--in reality, his symphonic poem, *Dante*, a masterpiece of contrapuntal vigor."

B109. Gelatt, Roland. "Music Makers." *High Fidelity* 5 (1955): 49-50.

Discusses Granados's plans for a symphony (a work that remained unfinished at the time of his death) and the possibility of its completion by Rafael Ferrer (see B190).

B110. "Gent notable de Catalunya." *Catalunya Artística* 2 (1901): 522-23.

A brief synopsis of Granados's achievements with a fragment of *Follet* in piano reduction. The author also compares *María del Carmen* with *Picarol*: "En la *María del Carmen*, del plorat Feliu y Codina, y el *Picarol*, de l'Apel.les Mestres, plenas abdues de filigranas, que fan sentir ab tensió el jayent simpátich de la música popular de l'horta de Murcia, la primera, y de la musa catalana la segona". (In *María del Carmen*, by the unfortunate Feliu y Codina, and *Picarol*, by Apel.les Mestres, both adorned with filigree, [Granados] aptly recalls the popular music of the orchards of Murcia in the first work, and the Catalan muse in the second.)

B111. Goodfriend, James. "De Larrocha: *Goyescas*." *Stereo Review* 39, no. 4 (1979): 138.

A review of de Larrocha's (third) recording of *Goyescas* on London, CS 7009, 1977. "Granados, following the nationalistic precepts of his teacher Felipe [*sic*] Pedrell, based much of the suite on traditional Spanish styles (northern, not Gypsy) and fragments of popular eighteenth-century song. These elements, without at all dissociating themselves from the whole, come through strongly and idiomatically in de Larrocha's performance."

B112. "*Goyescas.*" *Las Novedades*, January 27, 1916, pp. 9-10.

Scene-by-scene synopsis of the opera, including stage directions, song texts, and details of scenery.

B113. "*Goyescas*, by Enrique Granados." Program notes for The Little Orchestra Society, Inc., New York, October 15, 1956. Thomas Scherman, conductor, with Pilar Lorengar (North American debut), Mignon Dunn, Davis Cunningham, Martial Singher, and the American Concert Choir.

"What distinguishes the music of *Goyescas* in both versions from much other Spanish music . . . is its comparative lack of gypsy, Andalusian, flamenco or *cante jondo* melodic and rhythmic and harmonic usages. The folk background that Granados cultivated was rather that of northern Spain. . . . Granados is a much more narrowly Spanish composer than Albéniz."

B114. "Las *Goyescas* de Granados en Berlin." *Destino*, October 26, 1940, p. 12.

An announcement of the Berlin premiere of *Goyescas*, directed by Prof. Dr. Niedecken-Gebhardt, of the Berliner Teater, "the capital of the Reich." "Sin duda el público germano espera este estreno con profundo interés, teniendo en cuenta la simpatía con que son recibidas nuestras manifestaciones artísticas. . . . La música de Granados infundirá a los mismos el fuego de nuestro espíritu racial latente en cada nota de la partitura". (Without a doubt the German public is awaiting this premiere with great interest, considering the sympathy with which our artistic endeavors are received. . . . The music of Granados will communicate the fire of our indigenous spirit, latent in every note of the score.)

B115. "Les *Goyescas* a Nova York." *Revista Musical Catalana* 13 (1916): 78-83.

A compilation of (translated) press clippings from reviews of the New York production of *Goyescas*. All clippings are identified, Granados is upheld as emblem of Spanish musical nationalism, and only positive reviews are cited.

B116. "*Goyescas* Premiere January 28: Granados's Opera To Be Sung in Spanish at the Metropolitan." *New York Times*, January 19, 1916, p. 12.

Announces date and cast, comments on this first opera to be performed in Spanish at the Metropolitan. Mentions that the composer and librettist had been assisting conductor Gaetano Bavagnoli and that the Spanish dance numbers "(of great importance in this work) will be done by Rosina Galli and Guiseppe Bonfiglio."

B117. "The *Goyescas* Production." *Musical America*, February 1916, NYPL.

Commentary on the premiere of *Goyescas*: "It must be confessed that the production reflects much credit on the Metropolitan. Such deficiencies as may be remarked in the interpretation of the little Spanish opera are more than offset by its features of excellence and by the sumptuous beauty of the settings in which the three brief stage pictures are framed. . . . So, if not that artistically important, the production of *Goyescas* has a certain significance in the fast-growing annals of American music appreciation."

B118. "*Goyescas*, Spanish Opera: Brilliant Music, Not Dramatic." *New York Herald*, January 29, 1916, p. 12.

A review of the January 28, 1916, New York premiere of *Goyescas*. "Musically, this work is interesting chiefly in that it is said to be real Spanish music . . . there is precious little that is reminiscent or familiar. But dramatically the work is out of joint . . . interest lags and the work suffers from anti-climax. For all that, *Goyescas* is an interesting work for two acts, and its melodies and rhythms are very engaging. Its lavish production again illustrated the 'art for art's sake' attitude of the Metropolitan. And last night's applause was the public acknowledgement of its gratitude for this latest novelty."

B119. "Mr. Grainger's Recital: A Program of Pianoforte Pieces with Folk-Song Elements." *New York Times*, December 9, 1915, p. 15.

Review of Australian pianist and composer Percy Grainger's December 8, 1915, Aeolian Hall appearance, which included the New York premiere of "El Pelele," a work "full of Spanish color."

B120. "Gran Teatro del Liceo." *La Vanguardia Española*, December 10, 1939, p. 5.

A review of the Liceu's 1939 revival of *Goyescas*, chosen by the recently victorious Franco regime to inaugurate the reopening of the opera house, "now freed from the stultifying atmosphere in which the Communists, enemies of all that signifies purity and nobility in art, had enveloped it." ("El Liceo, libre ya de aquella atmósfera mefítica en que lo habían envuelto los rojos, reñidos con cuanto significara puro y noble arte".) Gives the cast and other works that filled out the program, including the performance of several of Granados's piano works by Alicia de Larrocha. "The evening began and ended with the National Anthem, to which the audience listened, arms raised in salute, full of patriotic fervor" ("plena de fervor patriótico").

B121. "Granados." *Musical America*, December 25, 1915, NYPL.

Lists awards bestowed upon the composer, including the Cross of Charles III and (upcoming) membership into the Hispanic Society of North America.

B122. "Granados." *Las Novedades*, January 6, 1916, p. 6.

Information on the publication of *Goyescas*: "La Casa Dotesio de Barcelona, editora de las composiciones pianísticas . . . *Goyescas*, impresas en 1912, le concedió el permiso para convertirlas en ópera: permiso que, en opinión del mismo compositor, revela gran generosidad, pues probablemente pocas casas editoriales lo hubieran concedido sin hacer, a cambio, grandes exigencias". (Casa Dotesio of Barcelona, Granados's publishers of *Goyescas* in 1912, gave him permission to convert it into an opera, a permission which, in the opinion of the composer, seems extremely generous, given that probably few publishers would have given it without demanding something in return.)

B123. "Granados." *Vell i Nou* 2 (1916): 12.

A discussion of the organization of a protest against Germany in reaction to the torpedoing of the *Sussex*. "Els centres artístics de Barcelona--per iniciativa del Círcol de Belles Arts--s'han reunit per fer una protesta i per testimoniar un homenatge al nostre gran artísta, víctima ignocent de la gran bogería que s'ha desencadent sobre Europa". (Artistic centers in Barcelona--under the initiative of the Círcol de Belles Arts--have united in protest, and to pay homage to our great artist, an innocent victim of the mania that is sweeping Europe.)

B124. Granados de Carreras, Natalia. "*Goyescas* and Enrique Granados." Translated from the Spanish by Norman P. Tucker. *Granados and "Goyescas,"* 8-10. Boston: Boston Athenaeum, 1982.

The essay by the composer's daughter (which contains several factual errors) serves as a centerpiece for this exhibition catalogue, compiled by Norman P. Tucker, Ann Wadsworth, and Pamela Hoyle to commemorate the 75th anniversary of the composer's death. Also included in the catalogue are a synopsis of *Goyescas*, a chronology of important dates in Granados's life, and a checklist of the exhibition, with designs and photographs relating to the Metropolitan Opera premiere of *Goyescas*.

B125. "Granados, Composer, is Probably Lost." *New York Times*, March 27 1916, p. 3.

Witnesses from the *Sussex* are quoted as saying that Granados and Amparo were last seen clinging to a small raft. Although a boat was sent out to search for the couple, no trace was found. Contains several incorrect biographical details on the composer.

B126. "Granados's *Dante* Heard for First Time in Chicago." *Chicago Monitor*, November 8, 1915, NYPL.

A review of the Chicago Symphony's performance of *Dante*, November 5 and 6, 1915. "Interesting, and somewhat of a relief, to realize that this young Spaniard has almost nothing in common with the modern radicals . . . no trace of the striving after the new and strange merely for the sake of getting off the beaten track."

B127. "Granados Is Here." *New York Evening Post*, December 15, 1915, NYPL.

Introduces Granados to the American public, with particular reference to the Suite on Gallician Themes.

B128. "Granados May Be Safe: Hope That the Composer and His Wife Are on a Hospital Ship." *New York Times*, April 1, 1916, p. 3.

At this time, still no positive confirmation of Granados's death had reached the Spanish Embassy and rumors circulated that an unidentified couple on a hospital ship was in fact the composer and his wife.

B129. "Granados, Pianist, in American Debut." *Toledo Times*, February 6, 1916, NYPL.

A review of Granados's January 23, 1916, appearance at the Ritz-Carlton Hotel, sponsored by the Society of the Friends of Music: "A large gathering that included most of the prominent pianists now in New York applauded Mr. Granados with great warmth." A joint appearance with Casals; singer Maria Gay had also been invited to participate but did not appear. "The composer made it known upon his arrival from Spain that dwellers in this section of the globe had no conception of real Spanish music, and intimated a desire to do some missionary work after *Goyescas* had its baptism at the Metropolitan."

B130. "Granados Plays." *New York Post*, January 24, 1916, NYPL.

A review of Granados's joint appearance with Casals at the Ritz-Carlton Hotel, January 23, 1916. "Mr. Granados played with much feeling for color, rhythm, and nuance . . . if his piano music is a foretaste of joys to come in his opera it promises much."

B131. "Granados Plays His Own Works: Spanish Composer-Pianist Heard by New Yorkers. Anna Fitziu Sings His Songs." *Musical America*, March 1916, NYPL.

A review of Granados's February 22, 1916, Aeolian Hall appearance with Fitziu. "Most of it [the music] is no more distinctly Spanish than the music of MacDowell is distinctly American. . . . It might just as well have been composed in Paris or Vienna. As a pianist he is very pleasing . . . his octave playing was perfect."

B132. "Granados, Schelling, y *Goyescas*." *La Prensa*, November 26, 1950. Schelling Archive, New York.

An account of Schelling's role in the New York premiere of *Goyescas*. The occasion of this article is a performance almost twenty-five years later of a ballet created by the choreographer Ana Ricarda on Schelling's (unpublished) orchestration of "El amor y la muerte" at New York's Century Theater. The performance received seventeen curtain calls. "Y la Ricarda . . . crea un bellísimo balet con el que perpetía el recuerdo de dos genios, Granados y Schelling". (Thus Ricarda creates . . . a beautiful ballet which perpetuates the memory of two geniuses, Granados and Schelling.)

B133. Greely-Smith, Nixola. "Granados in New York: Soul of Spanish Composer is Not for Sale." *Kansas City Times*, n.d., NYPL.

An interview with the composer in New York's Hotel Claridge. Granados is quoted as saying "I am not a rich man . . . but I can say that I have written no cheap music." The writer comments that "far from having the sketchy character of modern music, this [new] opera . . . has the firmness, the solidity . . . of Goya himself."

B134. "Mr. Grenados [*sic*] Plays Piano, Miss Fitziu Sings His Music." *New York Herald*, February 23, 1916, p. 13.

A review of Granados's February 22, 1916, Aeolian Hall recital. "Mr. Granados is an interesting pianist. A fine rhythmic sense . . . is always evident, and he colors his tones skilfully. The *Goyescas* suite, from which the opera took its principal themes, was the most important contribution."

B135. Gual, Adrià. *Mitja Vida de Teatre: Memòries.* Prologue by Maurici Serrahima. Barcelona: Editorial Aedos, 1957.

Background on the production of *Blancaflor* (Barcelona, 1899) and Granados's association with Gual's Teatre Intim. Also contains Gual's personal impressions of the composer.

B136. Guillemot, Jules. Untitled review quoted in *Revista Musical Catalana* 6 (1909): 198-99.

Review of the June 2 and 9, 1909, performances at the Salle des Agricultures in Paris by Granados and violinist Jacques Thibaud. "Han sigut triomfals . . . y'l triumf ha estat ben merescut". (They triumphed . . . and a well-deserved triumph it was.)

B137. Hackett, Karleton. "Spanish Opera at the City Club." *Chicago Post*, n.d., NYPL.

Portion of a review of the May, 1916, "tabloid performance" of *Goyescas* by the Society Hispano-Americano at Chicago's City Club. The performance took place soon after the torpedoing of the *Sussex*; according to the reviewer, all that Granados had earned during his U.S. tour was lost with him in the form of currency.

B138. Halperson, M. von. "Spanien's Musik und Granados' *Goyescas.*" *Sonntagsblatt der New-Yorker Staats-Zeitung*, January 23, 1916, NYPL.

A discussion of the New York premiere of *Goyescas*. Includes an overview for the general reader of developments in Spanish opera, a biographical sketch of the composer, and remarks on Granados's style. "Seine Oper gliedert sich, dem Volkscharacter entsprechend wie natürlich in einzelne Nummern, aber ohne die sklavische Unlage der alten italienisichen Oper." (His opera, in accordance with its character, is articulated naturally, in individual numbers, without the slavishness of the old Italian opera.)

B139. Hammond-Brake, Mavis. "Granados: A Personal Portrait." Transcription and translation of a talk by Conchita Badia. Recorded Sound: *Journal of the British Institute of Recorded Sound* 77 (1980): 57-61.

A personal and anecdotal reminiscence of Badia's friendship with her teacher, Granados.

B140. Hansen, Mark. "The Catalan School of Pedaling in the Teaching of Enrique Granados and Frank Marshall." In *The Pianist's Guide to Pedaling*, ed. Joseph Banowetz, 220-29. Bloomington: Indiana University Press, 1984.

A summary of Granados's *Método teórico práctico para el uso de los pedales del piano*, along with a discussion of Frank Marshall's derivative *Estudio práctico sobre los pedales del piano* and *La sonoridad del piano*. Some treatment of the history of the so-called Catalan school, numerous musical examples, and commentary by Alicia de Larrocha.

B141. Hess, Carol A. "Enric Granados i la vida musical barcelonina entre 1891-1916." *Actes del Sisè Col.loqui d'Estudis Catalans a Nord-Amèrica (Vancouver, 1990)*, 469-81. Ed. Arseni Pacheco and Karl Kobbervig. Montserrat: Publicacions de l'Abadia de Montserrat, 1992. (Translated by Albert Muth.)

An exploration of Granados's activities in Barcelona's musical community from his debut there to his departure for America in 1915. His participation in the founding of several musical organizations and the interaction of these groups in this period of rapid artistic expansion and change are emphasized.

B142. "Homenatge an En Granados." *Revista Musical Catalana* 7 (1910): 369.

Announcement of an upcoming Granados testimonial. "Uns quants admiradors de l'eminent pianista y compositor Enric Granados, volent festejar el nomenament que se li ha fet per a formar part del Jurat encarregat de l'adjudicació del Gran premi del Conservatori de París, han organitzat un homenatge que tindrà lloc pel mes de Janer". (Several admirers of the eminent pianist and composer Enrique Granados wish to celebrate his nomination to the Jury in charge of awarding the Grand Prize of the Paris Conservatory; they have organized a commemorative ceremony to take place in January.)

B143. "Homenatge al Mestre Granados." *Revista Musical Catalana* 8 (1911): 54-55.

Details of the February 12, 1911, ceremony at Barcelona's Sala de Cent honoring Granados. List of presiding officials and description of ceremonies.

B144. "Honors Spanish Composer." *New York Herald*, February 2, 1916, p. 15.

A description of Granados's induction into the Hispanic Society of America, January 19, 1916. The Society's president, Archer M. Huntington, presented Granados with an engraved silver medal.

B145. "Hope Granados Has Been Saved: Unidentified Man and Wife Aboard Rescue Ship Believed to Be Spanish Composer." *Toledo Times*, April 8, 1916, NYPL.

"The Spanish embassy states that although Enrique Granados . . . and his wife are reported missing, no positive confirmation of their deaths was received." A man and a woman whose condition was such that they were unable to speak were picked up by a hospital ship; it was believed that the couple was Granados and his wife.

B146. Hull, A. Eaglefield. "The *Goyescas* of Granados." *Monthly Musical Record* 47, no. 2 (1917): 220-21.

A brief and extremely subjective description of the piano suite.

B147. Iglesias, Antonio. *Enrique Granados: su obra para piano*. 2 vols. Madrid: Editorial Alpuerto, 1985.

A short biography contains several photos and reproductions of documents, among them Granados's birth certificate. The bulk of the book is a catalog of piano works (arranged alphabetically) with rather superficial descriptions of each piece. Iglesias's dating of works is extremely speculative. Useful features include publication information and a table giving Kirkpatrick and Longo numbers for Granados's Scarlatti transcriptions.

B148. "An Interview with Señor Enrique Granados on the Duo-Art Pianola." *New York Times*, March 12, 1916, sec. 2, p. 15.

Essentially an advertisement for the Duo-Art player piano (manufactured by the Aeolian company). Granados comments on the accuracy of the reproduction, exclaiming, "My portrait!" after hearing his own interpretation played back.

B149. Jardí, Enric. "Titelles i Música" and "Wagner, Música i Teatre" (Puppets and Music; Wagner, Music, and Theater). In *Els Quatre Gats*. Barcelona: Editorial Hedes, 1972.

Describes activities of Els Quatre Gats, the important café and artistic center in Barcelona at the turn of the century modelled after Montmartre café society. Jardí discusses clientele, musical programs, and the shadow puppet shows then popular, for which Granados and Malats provided accompaniment on at least one occasion.

B150. Jean-Aubry, G. "Enrique Granados." *Musical Times* 57 (1916): 535-37.

A condensation and translation of the author's more comprehensive treatment of Granados in B151.

B151. ---. "Enrique Granados." In *La Musique et les Nations*, 115-26. London: J & W Chester, 1922.

A perceptive and realistic assessment of Granados's accomplishments, written by a contemporary shortly after the composer's death. Discusses the piano version of *Goyescas* (in addition to the weaknesses of the operatic score), the *Twelve Spanish Dances*, and the *Tonadillas*. Jean-Aubry also compares Granados's accomplishments with those of Albéniz and considers Granados's role in the late nineteenth-century Spanish musical renaissance.

B152. ---. "Enrique Granados et la Musique d'Espagne." *Correspondant* 263/227 (1916): 309-20.

A general discussion of musical developments in late nineteenth-century Spain with classification of major composers from this period, i.e. Pedrell (whose accomplishments as a composer are somewhat exaggerated), Olmeda, Albéniz, Granados, Falla, and Turina. Aubry reflects on French receptivity to prevailing trends in musical nationalism and assesses Granados's output: "Ce sont vraisemblablement, avec quelques unes des *Danses Espagnoles*, les *Goyescas* et les *Tonadillas* qui garderont dans l'avenir la mémoire d'Enrique Granados et qui lui donnent dès à présent une place particulière dans l'histoire de la musique." (Truly it is because of the *Spanish Dances*, the *Goyescas*, and the *Tonadillas* that Granados will be remembered in the future and hold his assigned place in the history of music.)

B153. Jones, J. Barrie. "Enrique Granados: A Few Reflections on a Seventieth Anniversary." *Music Review* 47 (1987): 16-23.

An assessment of Granados's output, with discussion of previous scholarly opinion. Speculation on Granados' exposure to French music, and specific commentary on modality, key-schemes, mordents, and use of thematic reminiscences in *Escenas poéticas*, *Allegro de concierto*, *Goyescas*, and the Scarlatti transcriptions.

B154. Kehler, George. *The Piano in Concert*. Metuchen, N.J.: Scarecrow Press, 1982.

Gives repertory for an otherwise undocumented recital given by Granados in Girona, Spain, 1905. The program included Scarlatti-Granados transcriptions I, III, IV, IX, XV (alla toccata).

B155. Kobbé, Gustave. *The Complete Opera Book*. Edited and revised by the Earl of Harewood. London: Putnam, 1963.

Gives La Scala cast for Milan performance of *Goyescas* and also mentions a 1963 performance in Florence with Perez, Campanez, Oncina, and Cesar.

B156. Konstantin, Rozensil'd. *Enrico Granados*. From *The History of Spanish Music*. Moscow: Muzyka, 1971, 88 pp. In Russian. Below annotation from RILM Abstracts 5 (1971): 175, by Irina Medvedeva.

"Sketches the life and work of Granados in relation to the development of the Spanish art and culture of the late 19th and early 20th century. Analyzes the *Danzas españoles*, *Colección de Tonadillas*, and *Colección de canciones amatorias*."

B157. ---. "The *Goyescas* of Granados." *Sovetskaja muzyka* 32, no. 1 (1968): 87-89. In Russian. Below annotation from RILM Abstracts 2 (1968): 55, by Grigorij Sneerson.

"A comparison of the piano suite with Granados's opera of the same name. An analysis of both compositions, including their connections with the . . . paintings and drawings of Goya. . . . The patriotic and historical themes, the sphere of legend, the grotesque, the accusing irony--all remain unrevealed in the music of the opera and the suite [although] the suite is rich in melodic material, harmony, rhythms, and texture."

B158. Langhi, Ugo Ramellini. "Ricordi di un 'prince charmant' della musica." *La Scala* 23 (1960): 51-54.

Biographical information on the composer and synopsis of *Goyescas*. "La scomparsa di Granados ha lasciato un gran vuoto nella musica, vuoto che sino ad ora non è stato colmato." (The disappearance of Granados has left a great void in music, a void which as yet has not been filled.)

B159. Larrad, Mark. "The Catalan Theater Works of Enric Granados." Ph.D. diss., University of Liverpool, 1991.

On the basis of his discovery of Granados's Catalan lyric dramas in Paris, the author argues that the prevailing view of Granados as a composer of piano music and songs needs re-evaluation. The stage works based on texts by Apel.les Mestres, *Petrarca*, *Picarol*, *Gaziel*, and *Liliana* (*Follet* was not recovered), form the basis of Larrad's discussion of Granados's dramatic style from the viewpoint of structure, harmony, melody, and orchestration. Granados's relation to the Catalan *Renaixança* and the modernist movement is also explored, and an attempt is made to view the Catalan theater works from the perspective of native operatic traditions in Spain.

B160. ---. "The *Goyescas* of Granados." B.A. thesis, University of Liverpool, 1988.

This 170-page essay discusses the musical materials of *Goyescas*, with emphasis on thematic transformation, harmonic language, ornamentation, and sources. Two appendices--a tentative chronology of Granados's piano compositions and a catalogue of Granados's own recordings--are also included.

B161. Livermore, Ann. "Granados and the Nineteenth Century in Spain." *Musical Review* 7 (1946): 80-84.

Summarizes artistic conditions in Spain from the post-Napoleonic era through Granados. Discusses the isolation of the Iberian peninsula, the rise of the middle class, and lack of ecclesiastical patronage.

B162. ---. *A Short History of Spanish Music*. New York: Vienna House, 1972.

Survey of Spanish music with emphasis on Granados as an opera composer, based on author's studies with Granados's student, Conchita Badía. Details on *María del Carmen*.

B163. Llates, Rosendo. "Granados: Señor de la música." *Señor* 11, no. 42 (1966): 56-64.

Anecdotal memoir based on the author's studies at the Granados Academy. Describes Granados's priorities as a teacher and his working habits as a pianist. Also gives details on the torpedoing of the *Sussex* and the conflicting accounts of Granados's death. Some witnesses claimed that Granados threw himself into the water without knowing how to swim. His wife, a good swimmer, followed him, and the two of them sunk and died in an embrace. Others say that the composer saw that his wife was drowning and tried to save her.

B164. Lleget, Mario. "Estampes Barcelonesas. Sobre Enrique Granados." *El Correo Catalan*, February 22, 1957, p.3.

Anecdotal commentary on a performance of *Intermezzo* and the orchestrated version of several of the *Spanish Dances* by the Orquesta Franz Schubert in Barcelona.

B165. Lliurat, F. "Enric Granados." *Revista Musical Catalana* 13 (1916): 139-40.

Brief obituary of the composer.

B166. Llongueras, Joan. "De N'Enric Granados." *Revista Musical Catalana* 13 (1916): 191-92.

An homage to Granados (by the Dalcroze specialist at the Granados Academy) that seeks to place the composer's accomplishments in the wider perspective of Catalan musical history.

B167. Llopis, Arturo. "El recuerdo de Enrique Granados. Un aniversario: 24 de marzo de 1916." *La Vanguardia Española*, March 24, 1963, p. 37.

An interview with Natalia Granados de Carreras at her home, where her husband, Dr. Carreras, maintained "a temple consecrated to the memory of the composer of *Goyescas*." On Granados's lack of business sense, Natalia comments: "Malvendía sus obras. . . A una casa de música de nuestra ciudad, cedió por cien pesetas sus partituras más hermosas". [He sold himself cheap . . . he released some of his most beautiful scores to at least one Barcelona publisher for only a hundred *pesetas*.]

B168. "Londres." *Revista Musical Catalana* 11 (1914): 256-65.

Translations of reviews from the London press on the June 20, 1914, concert in Albert Hall by the Orfeó Català, at which Granados's *Elegía eterna* was performed with María Barrientos as soprano soloist. "La *bocca chiusa* constituí un fons agradós al cant bellament refinat de la Sra. María Barrientos en el solo de l'*Elegía eterna*, d'en Granados". (The use of *boca chiusa* provided a pleasing background for the melody so beautifully shaped by Sra. María Barrientos in the solo of *Elegía eterna*, by Granados.) Quoted (in translation) from *Sunday Times*, June 21, 1914.

B169. Longland, Jean Rogers. "Granados and the Opera *Goyesca*." *Notes Hispanics* 5 (1945): 95-112.

One of the more scholarly treatments of *Goyescas*. After remarks on the genesis of the opera, the author discusses the work's actual title ("The authors said they intended to entitle 'our opera *Goyesca* not *Goyescas*, as through carelessness it has come to be called'") and the work's subtitle, *Literas y Calesas*. Describes finalization of Rouché's offer to produce the work in Paris. Main emphasis, however, is a description of the manuscript of *Goyescas* that Granados presented to the Hispanic Society of America.

B170. Lopez, Rosa Angelica. "Granados's *Escenas Románticas*: Its Romantic Sources and Progressive Features." D.M.A. diss., University of Texas at Austin, 1982.

An analysis of the *Escenas románticas* which attempts to compare Granados's harmonic and formal techniques with those of Chopin, Schumann, and Liszt. The author also discusses Granados's use of modality.

B171. Lowenberg, Alfred. *The Annals of Opera*, vol. 1. Geneva: Società Bibliographica, n.d.

Lists performances of *Goyescas* in Paris (December 17, 1919, performed in French, with translation by Louis Laloy), Buenos Aires (August 8, 1929), and Barcelona (Summer 1940).

B172. Madriguera, Paquita. "Enrique Granados." *Clave: Voz de la Juventud Musical Uruguaya* 43 (1961): 16-20.

Personal data on Granados, including health, marriage, family life, and financial hardships. (The author, a former Granados pupil, later married guitarist Andrés Segovia.) Describes Granados's frustration at sacrificing composing in order to earn a more stable living as a teacher. Refers also to Granados's liaison with a young woman; according to the author this relationship hastened Granados's return to Spain after the United States tour, even though this meant travelling in a non-neutral ship.

B173. Manegat, Julio. "La muerte de Enrique Granados." Barcelona, May 1956, 5 pp. Unidentified source, Douglas Riva Collection, New York.

Biographical information on the composer (includes an eleven-measure sketch of the scherzo of Granados's projected *Sinfonía española*) with numerous references to contemporary press articles that reported on the torpedoing of the *Sussex*.

B174. "*María del Carmen*, de Granados." *Mirador*, December 5, 1935, p. 8.

A discussion of the opera and its restaging at the Liceu in 1935, directed by Joan Lamote de Grignon and featuring Conchita Badia. "La seva bellísima veu i la seva profunda musicalitat brillaren igualment a l'escena, malgrat haver de lluitar amb una orquestra d'una densitat excepcional d'instrumentació. . . . Més que un paper d'acompanyant, l'orquestra té sovint un paper de protagonista". (Badia's lovely voice and profound musicality shone equally on the stage, despite having to combat a heavily-scored orchestral part. . . . More than accompaniment, the orchestra acts as a protagonist.)

B175. Marquez Villanueva, Francisco. "Literary Background of Enrique Granados." Paper presented at the "Granados and *Goyescas* Symposium," Harvard University, Cambridge, January 23, 1982.

Describes Granados's literary interests, including background on his librettists and an assessment of their abilities, with particular emphasis on Gabriel Miró. References to Miguel de Unamuno's *En torno al casticismo* enhance a discussion of the *tonadilla* genre as it relates to *Goyescas*.

B176. Marshall, Frank. *Estudio práctico sobre los pedales del piano*. Madrid: Unión Musical Española, 1919.

A series of pedal studies for piano students, based on Granados's *Método teórico práctico para el uso de los pedales del piano* (see B140).

B177. ---. *La sonoridad del piano*. Barcelona: Boileau, n.d.

A collection of easy to intermediate Romantic piano pieces using Granados's system of pedal notation.

B178. Martinotti, Sergio. "Note critiche su Granados." *Chiagana* 34 (1967): 131-41.

A comparison of the character of Granados's music with that of Albéniz and Falla. Biographical sketch, overview of works, with references to minor works. "Piú che pittoresca, la musica allora parrà pittorica: seppure il musicista ambisca ad una piú coreografica rappresentazione." (More than picturesque, the music will seem pictorial, even though the musician aspires to a more choreographic representation.)

B179. Mas-López, Edita. "Apeles [*sic*] Mestres: Poetic Lyricist." *Opera Journal* 13-14 (1980-81): 24-33.

Biographical summary of Granados's primary librettist, with plot synopsis and English translation of passages from *Petrarca*, which Granados completed in 1900.

B180. "Masnou." *Revista Musical Catalana* 12 (1915): 312-13.

A review of a concert of *Goyescas*, *Tonadillas*, various *Spanish Dances* by Granados and Conchita Badia in Masnou, September 18, 1915.

B181. Mason, A. L. "Enrique Granados." *Music and Letters* 14 (1933): 231-38.

Describes significant aspects of Granados's life, contrasts Spanish and Anglo-Saxon cultures, assesses Granados's output, and offers justification for performance of specific piano and operatic works. Anecdotal biographical information is based on Mason's conversations with Ignacio Tabuyo of the Madrid Conservatory.

B182. McGrigor, Albert. "The Catalan Piano School." Liner notes for *The Catalan Piano Tradition*, Sound Recording no. 109. International Piano Archives. New York: Desmar, 1970.

A discussion of characteristics of the so-called Catalan Piano School as handed down by Granados's teacher, Pujol. A history of recording and commentary on the performances on this disc by Granados, Albéniz, Malats, Marshall, and de Larrocha (nine years old at the time of recording).

B183. Meléndez, Lluís. "Avui fa 22 anys que va morir Enric Granados." *Ultima Hora*, March 24, 1938, p. 2.

A commemorative article which compares German behavior during World War I to that of the late 1930s. Meléndez comments that the U-boat that struck the *Sussex* was the first German vessel to defy a British blockade of the Channel ("el primer que va burlar el bloqueig anglès del Canal"). In conclusion, the writer mentions his puzzlement that Granados's works have been met with "an inexplicable indifference" and that *Goyescas* has yet to be performed at the Liceu, "where [by contrast] representations of the most trivial works take place in any given season."

B184. Mestres, Apel.les. "Enrich Granados." *In Historia viscuda: Volves musicals*, 57-63. Volume 5 of complete works. Barcelona: Salvador Bonavía, 1929.

A personal memoir that emphasizes Granados's improvisatory ability and the extreme nervousness of his character, including the composer's agitation on the day before he was to depart for New York. Mestres refers to one of his own poems, *Atila* (based on testimony of witnesses from the *Sussex*), which "faithfully describes the composer's tragic death and that of his poor wife, Amparo."

B185. Millet, Lluís. "Granados." *Revista Musical Catalana* 13 (1916): 187.

An homage to Granados by a co-founder of the Orfeó Català.

B186. Miró, Gabriel. "Los huerfanos de Granados." *La Esfera* 3, no. 131 (1916): n. p.

An attractive photograph of the six Granados children accompanies this fictionalized account by Spanish author and family friend of how the news of the composer's death reached the Granados home. Miró also describes the contents of Granados's luggage as discovered by the orphans: clothing, books, and, fortunately, the score of *María del Carmen* which, according to the eldest son, Eduardo, was the only copy of the opera.

B187. Montoliu, Manuel de. "A la memoria de Enrique Granados." *Diario de Barcelona*, February 13, 1957, p. 3.

A friend of the composer recalls soirées at Granados's home in the Carrer Fontanella. He also cites the origins of Granados's Romanticism ("the school of Chopin, Mendelssohn, Schubert, Schumann, and Wagner") and comments on Romanticism in general: "El adjetivo 'romántico' se lo da hoy en día un sentido equivocado, y para muchos significa exclusivamente sentimental". (Nowadays the adjective 'Romantic' is used wrongly, for to many it signifies sentimentality.)

B188. Montsalvatge, Xavier. "En silueta: Enrique Granados." *La Vanguardia Española*, November 15, 1961, p. 32.

An objective assessment of Granados's output in which the author incorporates a discussion of the origins of the composer's style: "Granados representó la época y el ambiente, con todas sus gracias y debilidades . . . las obras pianisticas menores representan un documento de la vida artística barcelonesa de un interés incuestionable". (Granados represented the epoch and the atmosphere, with all its delights and frailties . . . the minor piano works are documents of artistic life in Barcelona and are of unquestionable interest.)

Montsalvatge also cites *zarzuela* composers Arieta, Chapí, and Bretón as primary influences on Granados's style.

B189. ---. "Las *Goyescas* líricas de Enrique Granados." *Destino*, December 9, 1939, pp. 8-14.

The Catalan composer announces the first performance in Spain of *Goyescas*, scheduled for the Liceu on December 9, 1939. (Montsalvatge mentions that the same company to perform at the Liceu had unsuccessfully attempted a Spanish premiere in San Sebastian some years earlier.) The entire article is written in the inflated prose typical of the early *franquista* period, with numerous references to Granados's love of *patria* and exaggerated praise for Periquet's abilities. The author gives an incorrect date for the Madrid premiere of *María del Carmen*.

B190. ---. "Una importante obra de Enrique Granados, inedita." *Destino*, April 16, 1955, pp. 33-34.

Montsalvatge discusses conductor Rafael Ferrer's discovery of the first movement of a Symphony in E Minor by Granados, which Ferrer found in piano reduction form with annotations for proposed orchestration. According to Ferrer, "Granados wrote for the piano, but he possessed an unfailing sense for orchestration . . . many of his piano works seem to be derived from orchestral ideas." ("Granados escribía para piano pero tenía el sentimiento exacto de la orquesta . . . se ha dicho que muchas obras pianísticas de Granados parecen extractos de ideas sinfónicas".)

Ferrer believes that the work was composed sometime between 1904 and 1910, after Granados had given up a markedly popular Spanish style and had embraced "a Romantic ideology." Ferrer also mentions his discovery of the manuscript of a nearly completed piano piece, *Tango de los ojos verdes*.

B191. Moragas, Rafael. "En el gran teatro del Liceu: Ante la representación de la ópera *María del Carmen* del compositor Enrique Granados." *El Dia Gráfico*, November 30, 1938, pp. 2-3.

The first of a two-part series on *María del Carmen*, scheduled for the Liceu on December 1, 1938, proposed by the Republican government: "Que ahora el Gobierno de la Republica española . . . como ofrenda a un gran músico española, víctima de una Alemania totalitaria, os ofrece en el escenario del Gran Teatro del Liceu". (The Republican government of Spain . . . as a gesture to a great musician, who was a victim of totalitarian Germany, offers to you, the public, [*María del Carmen*] on the Liceu stage.)

B192. ---. "El monumento a Enrique Granados." *La Noche*, January 31, 1933, p. 8.

Describes a meeting at the home of J. M. Roviralta, a co-author of the poem "Boires baixes." Casals called the meeting to organize activities in honor of Granados, including the construction of a monument and a concert of unpublished works (Moragas does not specify which) by the Orquesta Casals. Casals comments that even in 1933, Granados's works "are still barely known" in Barcelona.

B193. ---. "Música i musiqueta." *Pel & Ploma* 4 (1903): 143-44.

A general article which contains a review of the April 4, 1903, premiere of *Follet* for a private audience at the Liceu. Addresses questions on the sophistication of Barcelona's audiences and the viability of Catalan theater. In addition to discussing poor performance conditions, Moragas remarks on Granados's development since his earlier Catalan opera, *Picarol*: "El mestre català ha pogut demostrar . . . la evolució artística qu'ha fet desde *María del Carmen* i *Picarol*". (The Catalan master has been able to demonstrate . . . his artistic evolution since *María del Carmen* and *Picarol*."]

B194. ---. "Records d'Enric Granados." *Mirador*, December 5, 1935, p. 8.

Moragas's light, conversational recollection of the first hearing of *Goyescas* at an informal recital in the summer of 1910. The author lists half a dozen invited guests, among them Wagner's daughter Isolda and critic Joaquím Pena. In addition to *Goyescas*, Granados performed the Liszt Sonata in B Minor.

B195. Morgades, Lourdes. "Localizados en París cinco manuscritos de obras escénicas de Enrique Granados." *El País*, February 18, 1990, n.p. Douglas Riva Collection, New York.

An account of British musicologist Mark Larrad's discovery of five lyric dramas (*Miel de la Alcarria*, *Petrarca*, *Picarol*, *Gaziel*, *Liliana*) in the archives of the French publishing house, Salabert. The article states that a contract between the composer's oldest son, Eduardo, and Salabert indicates that the French house has held the manuscripts since the late 1920s.

B196. ---. "Una obra inédita de Granados será estrenada en Estados Unidos." *El País*, May 29, 1987, n.p. Douglas Riva Collection, New York.

A discussion of the upcoming performance on June 14, 1987 (Rockport, Massachusetts), of the Serenade for Two Violins and Piano. The American pianist Douglas Riva was given the eight-minute work by Granados's daughter Natalia Granados de Carreras. Riva estimates that the Serenade was composed between 1907 and 1910.

B197. Morrison, Bryce. "Granados: The Complete Piano Music of Granados recorded for CRD by Thomas Rajna." *Musical Opinion* 99 (1976): 203-4.

Favorable review of Thomas Rajna's "gradual assimilation and recording of the complete piano works of Granados . . . a labour of love rather than of duty. . . . Some years ago Granados might have been called a sentimentalist. Today he would be considered an escapist, and the loss inherent in such an attitude is ours." Compares Granados's use of thematic metamorphosis to that of Liszt.

B198. Muñoz, Eduardo. "Teatro de Parish: *María del Carmen*." *El Imparcial*, November 13, 1898, p. 2.

After commenting that Granados ought not to be confused with another Granados (a popular composer of *boleros* and *pasacalles*) Muñoz reviews the Madrid premiere of *María del Carmen*, which featured Marina Gurina, confining his comments largely to the weakness of the libretto, which "lacks harmonious verses . . . and fluidity" ("hacen falta versos armoniosos . . . fluidos"). Muñoz also comments on Granados's departures from standard *zarzuela* formulae and the public's reaction to these innovations: "El público acostumbrado á los 'antiguous moldes' . . . se extraña y como que se disgusta. ¿Dónde están las romanzas con su fermata intercalada en el texto? ¿Dónde los duos á la antigua usanza? Anoche lo oía decir á algunos señores de las butacas, 'Esto es wagneriano y deben llevarlo al Real!'"

(The public, accustomed to conventional models . . . is surprised and taken aback. Where are the romances with the built-in fermatas? Where are the customary duets? Last night two gentlemen in the audience were heard to comment: "This is pure Wagner--and they should take it to the [Teatro] Real!")

B199. Nagin, Carl. "Spanish Night at the Opera: Granados Celebration in Boston." *Cambridge Express*, February 6, 1982, p. 21.

A review of the Boston Concert Opera Company's performance of *Goyescas* during the two-week Granados festival in Boston and Barcelona that commemorated the 75th anniversary of the composer's death. Discussion of main ideas in *Goyescas* (sexual tension and jealousy, clash of social rank) and observations on Spanish music in general. "Spanish music, for its nuance and national character, has an insular quality that, like the plays of Garcia Lorca, translates badly beyond its borders except in its most popular forms. American audiences, long nurtured on Carmen and Ravel's *Bolero*, have missed authentic Spanish compositions by Albéniz and Granados."

B200. Neufert, Kurt. "Die Opernregie des Berufsprovokateurs. Nancy: Ein Abend mit Granados' *Goyescas* and de Fallas *La vida breve* in der Inszenierung Fernando Arraballs." *Opernwelt* 27 (1986): 50.

Review of the April 15, 1986, revival of *Goyescas* (with Falla's *La vida breve*) at Nancy: "Düftig und unergiebig, jedoch nicht so unergiebig, wie sich die Oper nun in der Regie von Arrabal gab." (Uninspired and insufficient, however not as insufficient as the direction of Arrabal might have us imagine.)

B201. "New Grenados [*sic*] Opera." *New York Herald*, January 30, 1916, p. 11.

Discussion of the New York premiere of *Goyescas*. "The work takes only an hour in performance, including two entr'actes, yet it calls for . . . four important singers and three complete sets of scenery. This, in itself, is almost sufficient to defeat its chances of performance in most opera houses. . . Was it worth all that?"

B202. "New Music from Spain: Granados's Tone-Poem Stirs Chicago." [Unidentified source]. November 8, 1915, NYPL.

"Mr. Stock produces [Granados's] *Dante*, the first symphonic music of the acclaimed composer to be heard in America . . . [the performance reflected] the power, passion and individuality of a remarkable piece."

B203. "The New Opera, *Goyescas*." *Vogue*, November 15, 1915, NYPL.

"Granados . . . is doing for Spain what Chopin did for Poland and Grieg for Norway. [He] was discovered by Ernest Schelling, the noted pianist . . . [who] has already popularized excerpts from *Goyescas* in his piano recitals; 'Gallant Compliments,' 'Lovemaking,' and 'Fandango' especially, have been many times appreciatively received by the public."

B204. Newman, Ernest. "The Granados of the *Goyescas*." *Musical Times* 58 (1917): 343-47.

Shows instances of pianistically conceived passages in the opera score. Also cites similar procedures in the symphonic poem, *Dante*. Newman calls attention to Granados's unusual procedure of writing an opera based on a pre-existent work, "hitherto unprecedented in the history of music."

B205. Nin, Joaquím [*sic*]. "Pobre Granados!" *Revista Musical Catalana* 13 (1916): 194-95.

Reflections on the untimely deaths of Spanish composers Granados, Albéniz, and Malats.

B206. ---. *Pro Arte* and *Ideas y comentarios*. Barcelona: Dirosa, 1974. First published in France in 1909, n.p.

A discussion of musical practices in early twentieth-century Spain, with emphasis on concert programming and music education.

B207. "Una nova sala de concerts." *Revista Musical Catalana* 9 (1912): 24.

Description of the new concert hall and its adjoining classrooms built for the Granados Academy by Granados's long-time patron, pharmacist Dr. Salvador Andreu i Grau. The new building was located at the foot of Avenue Tibidabo.

B208. "Noves." *Revista Musical Catalana* 2 (1905): 88.

A review of the March 31, 1905, concert at the Salle Pleyel (Paris), featuring Granados and Crickboom. Granados performed six of his Scarlatti transcriptions: "[Granados] ha obtingut darrerament a París un remarcable triomf". (Granados has recently achieved a remarkable triumph in Paris.)

B209. "Noves." *Revista Musical Catalana* 6 (1909): 120.

Announcement of Granados's appointment to the Diémer Prize Committee, whose auditions would take place in Paris May 3 and 4, 1909, under the auspices of the Paris Conservatory. "Felicitem ab entusiasme a nostre compatriota y distinguit amic Granados, qui portarà per primera vegada . . . a un tan renomenat Concurs, la representació de la nostra Catalunya". (We congratulate with enthusiasm our compatriot and distinguished friend, Granados, who represents Catalonia for the first time in this renowned competition.)

B210. "Noves." *Revista Musical Catalana* 7 (1910): 109.

Announcement that the Granados Academy would initiate a Society of Chamber Music Concerts: "que's regirà en la mateixa forma que la 'Filharmonica' de Madrid" (to be organized in the same fashion as the Philharmonic Society of Madrid). The mainstay of the Barcelona series would be the newly founded "Trio Granados," composed of Granados, Perelló (violin), and Raventós (cello).

B211. "One of Four Principals to Show Notable Artistry." [Unidentified source], NYPL.

"Although a considerable number of over-zealous persons applauded with suspicious enthusiasm, their exertions had only a negative effect. . . . Enrique Granados is a gifted composer and his compositions disclose marked originality; but *Goyescas* will not bring him enduring fame. What the fashionable and large audience will chiefly remember of last night's performance must be the ill-timed applause that did not come from the main portion of the house and the celerity with which Mr. Granados came before the curtain."

B212. "One Thousand Twelve Dollars for Granados Orphans." *New York Times*, May 15, 1916, p. 9.

Since the American pianist Ernest Schelling had been unable to appear at the May 7, 1916, benefit concert in New York, he organized his own benefit in Spokane, Washington, which garnered the amount mentioned in the title.

B213. "Orfeó Català: Concerts de Quaresma." *Revista Musical Catalana* 7 (1910): 55.

Review of public premiere of *Dante* at the Palau de la Música Catalana, which was part of a six-concert Lenten series in 1910 (see B247 on private premiere). "La bona impressió que'ns va causar allavors ha sigut ara molt millorada escoltada en més favorables condicions". (The fine impression made before is now much improved, heard in these more favorable new conditions.)

B214. Orrey, Leslie, ed., with Gilbert Chase, advisory ed. *Encyclopedia of Opera*. New York: Charles Scribner's Sons, 1976.

Cites, in addition to other performances of *Goyescas*, a Royal College of Music (London) performance given on July 11, 1951.

B215. Ors, Eugeni. [Untitled]. *Pel & Ploma* 85 (1902): 260-74.

A discussion of the poem "Boires baixes" by Josep M. Roviralta and Luis Bonnin, the inspiration for one of Granados's symphonic poems. "Es un poema estrany. En ell se fónen lo real i lo ideal, lo intern i lo exterior, la natural i 'ls somnis". (It is a strange poem. In it are contained [allusions to] the real and the ideal, the internal and external world, what is natural and what is dreamlike.) The article also includes a synopsis of the poem, fragments of its various sections, drawings by its co-author, Bonnin, and a fragment of Granados's symphonic poem.

B216. "Pablo Casals Discusses New Music of Spain." *New York Herald*, January 23, 1916, p. 11.

An interview with Casals, in which he states that "the first real Spanish work to make any definite impression on American audiences was Enrique Granados's piano suite, *Goyescas*. . . . A national school has sprung up within the last thirty years in Spain. . . . Now we have at least twenty composers worthy of serious consideration who not only write excellent music but write in a distinctly Spanish idiom. Enrique Granados is the leader and the most important composer in the new movement."

B217. Packard, Dorothy Ream. "Searching Spain for Background Color." *Clavier* 6 no. 7 (1967): 23-27.

For a general audience. Ms. Packard interviews Granados's daughter, Natalia Granados y Carreras, who mentions that Granados wore leather wrist-straps while practicing the piano, presumably to strengthen his technique.

B218. "Palau de Belles Arts." *Revista Musical Catalana* 8 (1911): 220-21.

Information on the 1910-11 symphonic and operatic season at the Palau de Belles Arts, including the premiere of *Liliana*, a "scenic arrangement" ("arranjament escenic") of the poem by Apel.les Mestres. "L'obreta, qual llibre es d'una simplicitat enamoradora, perd en aquests moments, un xic el caracter simple que le es caracteristic, perquè la música li dóna una certa trascendencia que sens dubte no té pas". (The little work, whose libretto expresses a charming simplicity, sometimes loses character; the music, however, lends [the libretto] a certain transcendence it doesn't actually possess.)

B219. Palau, Enric. "La tràgica mort d'Enric Granados." *La Nau*, March 24, 1928, p. 5.

This eulogy piece includes a poem by Apel.les Mestres, "En la mort de l'Enric Granados."

B220. "Palau de la Música Catalana." *Revista Musical Catalana* 5 (1908): 103-4.

Review of April 10, 1908, performance by Granados and violinist Marian Perelló of three sonatas, including one by Belgian contemporary Lekeu: "Es veritat que la sessió mereixia un públic molt més nombrós, però ja sabem que al gros públic l'atrau més que la calitat de la bona música, la quantitat d'ella, y el programa de la sessió que'ns ocupa no comportava més que tres obres". (It is true that the performance deserved a much larger public, but we are aware that the greater public is attracted more by quantity of music rather than by its quality, and this performance consisted of only three works.)

B221. "Palau de la Música Catalana: Concerts de Quaresma" (Lenten Concerts). *Revista Musical Catalana* 9 (1912): 80-81.

A review of the March 3, 1912, concert by Granados and Thibaud at the Palau. "En llurs interpretacions va desplegar el pianista català aquella fantasia plena de nerviositat que dóna tant de color al seu estil i que tantissim plau a son devot auditori". (In his interpretations, the Catalan pianist displayed that incredible imagination, so full of nervous energy that gives such color to his style and which so immensely pleased his devoted listeners.)

B222. "Palau de la Música Catalana." *Revista Musical Catalana* 12 (1915): 115-16.

Review of the March 1, 1915, benefit concert for the French Red Cross, often incorrectly given as the premiere of "El Pelele" (see B326). Granados also performed "Quejas o la maja y el ruiseñor," selected *Tonadillas* with Francisco Viñas, and, with Montoriol-Tarres, four-hand works of Saint-Saëns and Berlioz.

B223. "Palau de la Música Catalana: Concert Schwind, Cassadó i Longàs." *Revista Musical Catalana* 12 (1915): 343.

Brief review of October 10, 1915, concert. Granados's *Madrigal* for cello and piano was performed by Catalan cellist Gaspar Cassadó and Granados's student Frederic Longás. Often given incorrectly as the first public performance of *Madrigal*; the piece was actually premiered May 2, 1915, at the Sala Granados.

B224. "Palma de Mallorca." *Revista Musical Catalana* 2 (1905): 105.

Commentary on the 1905 appearance in Mallorca of Granados and the Orchestra of Barcelona. Among the works performed "under Granados's intelligent baton" was the Prelude to the third act of *Follet*, which, along with the other selections, "received a well-deserved, enthusiastic reception."

B225. Pangloss. Untitled review. *La Publicidad*, March 15, 1911, p. 4.

A review of Granados's March 11 concert at the Palau de la Música Catalana (see B107, 299). On the second number of *Goyescas*, "Coloquio en la reja," the author writes: "Es el que entraña el mayor valor artístico. Es una página de las que figurarán en el mundo musical moderno". (It is [the part] that carries within itself the greatest artistic value. It is a page out of the world of modern music.)

This reviewer is more impressed than other critics with *Cant de les estrelles*: "Granados abandona . . . los derroteros de la música española y nos transporta a una música completamente espiritual". (Granados abandons . . . the usual direction of Spanish music and transports us to a kind of music that is completely spiritual.)

B226. Parsons, Armand. Twenty-Sixth Program of the Sixty-Seventh Season (1957-58) of the Chicago Symphony Orchestra, published by the Orchestral Association, Orchestral Hall, Chicago.

Program notes for the Chicago Symphony's performance of the *Intermezzo* from *Goyescas* on April 10 and 11, 1958, conducted by Fritz Reiner. Gives history of the work. "For this [premiere] performance Granados added an Intermezzo between the first and second acts, or *tableaux*: this Intermezzo, played on this occasion, has come to be one of Granados's most popular compositions."

B227. Pedrell, Felip. "Granados: Danzas Españolas para piano." In *Lirica Nacionalizada*, 29-33. Paris: Librería Paul Ollendorf, n.d.

One in a series of informal writings on Spanish musical nationalism, the above article quotes praises from well-established European composers (Grieg, Cui, Massenet) for Granados's *Twelve Spanish Dances*.

B228. ---. "Nuestros pianistas en Paris." *Musicalerías*. Valencia: F. Sempere y Compañia, n.d.

A discussion of Granados's "free transcription" ("transcripción libre") of Scarlatti keyboard sonatas in which Pedrell compares the Scarlatti-Granados sonatas with earlier transcriptions by Tausig and von Bülow.

B229. ---. "La personalitat artística d'En Granados." *Revista Musical Catalana* 13 (1916): 173-74.

This homage to Granados, written shortly after the composer's death, contains the following curious assessment: "No experimentà jamai cap feblesa d'assimilació exòtica, ni la temptadora, però corruptora, francesa que ha inutilitzat a tants". (He never experienced the slightest weakness towards the assimilation of the exotic, nor the tempting yet corrupting influence of France which has ruined so many.)

B230. Pena, Joaquím. "Concert Granados." *Joventut* 3 (1902): 214.

In a review of a concert by students Jordá, Sostres, Icart, and Via of the Granados Academy March 27, 1902, at the Sala Chaissaigne. Pena assesses the Academy's effectiveness: "L'Academia de piano qu'ha establert el distinguit pianista Granados está donant ja fruyts profitosos". (The Academy for piano, which was established by the distinguished pianist Granados, is already offering its remarkable results.)

B231. ---. "Concerts." *Joventut* 1 (1900): 237.

A generally encouraging yet honest assessment of Granados's efforts to promote symphonic and chamber music in Barcelona through the founding of the Society of Classical Concerts (Societat de Concerts Clàssics). Like others who reviewed the same concert, Pena comments that while a less than perfect ensemble may be acceptable during the organization's early stages, an artist of Granados's stature should do no less than raise the orchestra to a level comparable to that of his own piano playing.

B232. ---. "Concerts." *Joventut* 1 (1900): 638-39.

An extremely negative review of the fourth and fifth Classical Concerts in which Pena comments on the mediocre quality of the orchestra and certain weaknesses in Granados's conducting.

B233. ---. "Concerts, Concert Casals." *Joventut* 1 (1900): 301-2.

A review of the second and third Classical Concerts, directed by Granados. Here, Pena comments on the difficulties of making a career as a musician in "backward" Spain ("en aquesta atrasada terra") and congratulates Casals for overcoming numerous obstacles.

B234. ---. "Crònica musical: varias." *Joventut* 2 (1901): 53.

Commentary on the demise of the Society of Classical Concerts, the subscription series Granados founded. "Es trist que desaparegui una Societat qu'havia comensat ab una sort que no á tothom li es fácil conseguir". (It is sad that the Society had to disappear, especially given that it began with the sort of good fortune that is difficult to come by.)

B235. ---. "Musichs que fugen." *Joventut* 3 (1902): 383-85.

Pena's comments on a short-lived collaboration between Granados, Albéniz, and Morera in an effort to promote Catalan lyric theater. Unfavorably compares the musical climate of Barcelona to that of Madrid.

B236. ---. "Teatres: Líric-Català." *Joventut* 2 (1901): 165-67.

An unenthusiastic review of Morera and Rusiñol's *Cigales y formigues* and (Granados's) *Picarol* in which Pena expresses frustration towards composers who strive for nothing more than a facile imitation of Wagner.

B237. Periquet, Fernando. "*Goyescas*: How the Opera Was Conceived." Translated from the Spanish by S. de la Selva. *Opera News*, January 29, 1916, p. 12.

Description of the difficulties that arise between composer and librettist when a text must be set to pre-existing melodies: "One day we talked of taking those ravishing melodies to the stage--we used to quarrel like schoolboys--he, wanting to keep to his original ideas; I despairing of finding its expression within the counted syllables." Also refers to plot and production considerations.

B238. ---. Letter to the Editor. *New York Times*, February 27, 1916, sec. 2, p. 6.

The librettist's rebuttal of a *New York Times* piece of January 23, 1916, in which it was stated that "The *toreador*, Paquiro, and the young officer Fernando [characters in *Goyescas*] can hardly be claimed as peculiar to Goya or to this opera." Periquet replied that Paquiro is modelled after one of Goya's 620 bullfighters of the "Corridos de Toros" and that a Captain of the Royal Guard (Fernando) is found in the etching "Tal para cual."

B239. Peyser, Herbert F. "Granados Here for Production of *Goyescas*." *Musical America* 23 (1915): 3.

An interview with the composer upon his arrival in New York City in December 1915. Discusses the gestation of *Goyescas* (see **Biography**, p. 26 for Granados's comments).

B240. Pfeifer, Ellen. "Boston Concert Opera: Granados's *Goyescas*." *High Fidelity/Musical America* 32 (1982): 32.

A review of Boston Concert Opera's production of *Goyescas*, under conductor David Stockman, on January 29 and 31, 1982. "The opera bears little resemblance to the piano pieces. It seems almost a different work." Discusses Granados's procedure in reworking the piano suite into an opera.

B241. Phillips, Harvey E. "Reports: New York." *Opera News* 33 (1968-69): 24.

A review of the Opera Theater of the Manhattan School of Music's revival of *Goyescas*, March 14-16, 1969. "The music is lushly beautiful, indulging in a kind of fluid dissonance that is a sophisticated distillation of authentic Spanishness. . . . But what is one to say of the stage action? The story, a model of simplicity in the worst sense, lends itself to many awkwardnesses, a few of which were avoided. All reservations aside, one was thankful for the rare chance to encounter this fascinating work of the short-lived twentieth-century Spanish musical renaissance."

B242. "Pianoforte Recitals." *Musical Times* 55 (1914): 47.

Brief review of the first performance of *Goyescas* (Book One) in London: "Mr. Ernest Schelling's pianoforte playing is always interesting. On December 9 [1913] at Queen's Hall the interest was enhanced by the performance of a descriptive Suite by the Spanish composer, Granados, which proved of fascinating brilliance and colour. The four movements are entitled *Goyescas*."

B243. Pillois, Jacques. "Un Entretien avec Granados." *S.I.M. Revue Musicale* 10, suppl. 1-4 (1914): 7.

French scholar and litterateur Jacques Pillois gives account of an informal conversation with Granados during the composer's 1914 visit to Paris. Pillois mentions a production of *Jardins de Murcie* at Paris's Odéon theater and elicits the composer's comments on Stravinsky's *Rite of Spring*, which Granados had heard in concert version, conducted by Pierre Monteux, during the 1914 visit. Apparently Granados found the rhythmic structures of the work particularly impressive: "C'est prodigiuex de rythme."

B244. Pomés Pont, Antonio. "Enrique Granados: 1867-1916." *Musica* (n.d.): 76-77. Douglas Riva Collection, New York.

A brief survey of the composer's accomplishments and discussion of the goals of the now defunct Camarote Granados, a small museum and archive founded in the early 1960s and housed at the Hotel Manila, Barcelona.

B245. Powell, Linton E. "Granados, Albéniz, and Their Contemporaries." In *A Short History of Spanish Piano Music*, 47-90. Bloomington: Indiana University Press, 1980.

Biographical sketch of the composer, musical examples of an opera fantasia by Granados's teacher, Joan Baptiste Pujol, and quotes by period critics. Introductory material on the piano works of Granados's lesser-known contemporaries, such as Nicolau, Alió, Morera, and Malats.

B246. "La presentación de Granados." *Las Novedades*, January 27, 1916, p. 16.

Discusses Granados's New York recital debut: "La Sociedad de los Amigos de la Música, formulada por dilettanti de los más ricos y cultos de Nueva York, invitó a Enrique Granados para que hiciera su presentación en uno de los conciertos que la agrupación celebra en el elegant Hotel Ritz-Carlton". (The Friends of Music, composed of the wealthiest and most cultivated dilettantes in New York, invited Granados to make his debut at the elegant Ritz-Carlton Hotel.)

B247. "Una producció notable." *Revista Musical Catalana* 5 (1908): 119.

Review of the premiere of *Dante* ("L'Entrada de l'Infern" and "Episodi de Paolo y Francesca") at the Palau de la Música Catalana before a private audience. Sñrta. Serra performed the mezzo-soprano part and Granados conducted, unfortunately, after only two rehearsals. "Està clar que ab una sola audició no es possible ferse càrrec d'una obra concenciosa y sólida . . . com es aqueixa . . . esperem sentirla en sa forma definitiva y completa". (Clearly it is impossible to effectively judge a thought-out, solid work such as this after only a single hearing . . . [therefore] we hope to hear it in a complete and definitive form.)

B248. "El pròximo concierto del Maestro Granados." *Las Novedades*, February 17, 1916, p. 12.

Description of upcoming concert February 22 and interview with Granados, in which the composer states: "Conozco los puntos flacos de mi música: pero en tanto que la generalidad se deleita con ella saboreando las cualidades que pueda encerrar para cautivarle, los críticos muchas veces se complacen en apuntar los trazos débiles". (I am aware of the weak points in my music, but whereas the majority of listeners let themselves take pleasure in the music, many times the critics gratify themselves by taking note of the weaker passages.)

B249. Puaux, René. "Granados: Silhouettes espagnoles." [Unidentified source], Schelling Archive, New York.

Reviews the reports of various witnesses on the *Sussex* and also refers to a 1916 letter from President Wilson to the German government on the torpedoing of the vessel: "La fameuse note du 19 avril, adressée par le president Wilson à l'allemagne, [a protesté] contra la guerre sous-marine et [a déclaré] que l'Amerique ne supporterait pas un attentat plus". (The famous note of April 19, sent by President Wilson to the Germans, protested against submarine warfare and declared that the United States would not tolerate one more attack.)

Field Marshall Hindenburg's response is quoted and "Granados's assassin" (i.e. the commander responsible for the torpedoing, Lieutenant Pustkuchen) is identified.

B250. "La qüestió de la Banda Municipal." *Revista Musical Catalana* 7 (1910): 148-57.

Describes Granados's participation in a meeting of August 17, 1910, to debate the selection of a new director for Barcelona's Municipal

Band. The official jury's choice provoked some controversy, and this article describes the ensuing protest and Granados's role therein.

B251. R.R.M.C. "Obres líriques de Granados sobre textos d'Apel.les Mestres." *Revista Musical Catalana* 6 (1989): 496.

A discussion of British musicologist Mark Larrad's discovery of five previously lost stage works (see B159, 195), with brief commentary on each. Although never performed during Granados's lifetime, *Petrarca* now earns Larrad's strong preference. "Mark Larrad creu, molt convençut, que sería interessant de reposar-les, i remarca especialment els valors musicals de *Picarol* i *Gaziel*". (Mark Larrad is strongly convinced that it would be extremely worthwhile to revive these works; he comments especially on the musical value of *Picarol* and *Gaziel*.)

B252. "Rehearsal of *Goyescas*." *New York Herald*, January 27, 1916, p. 13.

A description of the final dress rehearsal of *Goyescas* at the Metropolitan Opera. "Attended by a larger audience than has been at any Metropolitan Opera House dress rehearsal in several years, the new Spanish opera *Goyescas* was given its final preparation at noon yesterday. On similar occasions only a few persons have attended and there have been no public demonstrations, but yesterday's gathering applauded each act almost in the manner of a first night audience." Among the distinguished guests were Mrs. Vincent Astor and Mrs. Richard Aldrich.

B253. "Revista de espectáculos. *Liliana*." *Diario de Barcelona*, July 10, 1911, pp. 9345-46.

Review of the July 9, 1911, premiere of *Liliana* at the "Greek pavilion," the Palacio de Bellas Artes, conducted by Jaime Pahissa. Compares the scenery by Vilamara, Moragas, and Alarma with the overall design of the various *tableaux*; these latter were designed by librettist Apel.les Mestres. Gives a synopsis of the plot, cast, and describes some performance problems: "El poeta Apel.les Mestres ha desarollado este cuento en versos harmoniosos que no siempre llegaban á los oídos de los assistentes, por las dimensiones y condiciones acústicas del local". (The poet Apel.les Mestres has spun out this tale in harmonious verses, which, however, did not always reach the ears of the audience due to the dimensions and acoustical properties of the hall.)

B254. "Revista de Madrid." *Diario de Barcelona*, November 20, 1898, p. 12,618.

A report on the November 12, 1898, Madrid premiere of *María del Carmen*. "*María del Carmen* tiunfa en toda la línea . . . me alegro de que la obra haya caido en buenos manos y felicito al señor Granados por su triunfo. Los hombres del oficio . . . echan de menos algun duo o alguna romanza de la antigua escuela". (María del Carmen triumphed in every sense of the word . . . and I for one am delighted that the work fell into capable hands, and I congratulate Mr. Granados on his triumph. Some in this business . . . miss some duo or romance of the conventional school.)

B255. *Revista Musical Hispano-Americana* 8, no. 4 (1916).

This entire number is devoted to Granados and includes letters of bereavement, critical commentary, and personal recollections by contemporary musicians and critics. Among the contributors are Debussy, Saint-Saëns, d'Indy, Fauré, Esplá, Bretón, Turina, Vives, and Millet. (Manuel de Falla's reminiscence is also published in that composer's *Escritos sobre música y músicos* [Madrid: Espasa-Calpe, 1950], 25-26.) Juan José Mantecón (pp. 14-15) describes a symposium on the *tonadilla* given by Granados, Periquet, and Linares Rivas at Madrid's Athenaeum in 1913.

B256. Ricarts i Matas, Josep. *Concerts celebrats a Barcelona de música sinfónica i de camera desde l'any 1797 fins el present.* Vols. 1 and 2. At The Josep Ricart i Matas Institute of Musical Documentation and Research (Reial Acadèmia Catalana de Belles Arts de Sant Jordi), Barcelona, n.p., n.d.

Ricart i Matas's personal catalog of all instrumental concerts in Barcelona. Contains dates, locations, programs, and personnel for all of Granados's solo, chamber, and conducting appearances in Barcelona, from a student performance in 1886 to his last appearance in 1915, shortly before he sailed for New York. Vol. 1 (1797-1901) is cross-referenced according to repertory and personnel; successive volumes list concerts in chronological order. Extremely complete, over one hundred concerts in which Granados participated are cited (with an occasional omission).

B257. Riera, Juan. *Enrique Granados: Estudio.* Prologue by Fernando Colás. Lérida: Institutos de Estudios Ilerdenses de la Excma. Diputación Provincial de Lérida, 1967.

A study to commemorate the centennial of Granados's birth, with emphasis on his association with Lérida, his birthplace. In addition to an extremely general discussion of Granados as composer, teacher, and individual, one chapter is dedicated to "El Leridanísmo de Granados," in which dates of his Lérida appearances and subsequent ceremonies and *homenatges* sponsored by the city are cited.

B258. Rinaldi, Antonio. [Untitled article, unidentified source]. January 1, 1916, n.p. NYPL.

"Granados has been largely advertised as having been discovered and imported by Ernest Schelling. This seems a very foolish move on the part of Schelling's manager. It has no value in increasing Schelling's reputation and might well have placed Granados, a composer whose fame has preceded him from Spain, in the misrepresentative light of a protégé."

B259. Risler, Eduard. "Una carta d'en Risler a n'en Granados," *Revista Musical Catalana* 2 (1905): 109.

In an encouraging letter, Alsatian pianist Joseph Eduard Risler praises Granados for his March 31, 1905, concert in Paris: "Feya llarch temps que no havia jo sentit una tal impressió d'un pianista. Los vostres Scarlattis y Chopins restaràn inoblidables pera mi". (It has been a long while since I felt such a strong impression from a pianist. Your Scarlatti and Chopin will remain unforgettable for me.) Risler also offers to arrange Parisian contacts.

B260. Riva, Douglas J. "Enric Granados: Composer, Performer, and Teacher." *Catalan Review: International Journal of Catalan Culture* 1 (1986): 101-14.

A synopsis of Granados's accomplishments, drawn from the author's 1982 doctoral dissertation and his studies at the Marshall Academy, formerly the Granados Academy (see B262).

B261. ---. "Enrique Granados." *New Grove Dictionary of Opera*. Forthcoming.

Riva divides Granados's stage works into three areas: (1) Nationalist (incidental music for *Miel de la Alcarria*, *María del Carmen*, the incomplete *Ovillejos*), (2) Catalan Modernist (all collaborations with Gual, Mestres, and Miró), and (3) *Goyescas*. Dates and synopses of the operas are given. Under separate headings Riva gives more detailed synopses of *Goyescas* and *María del Carmen*.

B262. ---. "The *Goyescas* for Piano by Enrique Granados: A Critical Edition." Ph.D. diss., New York University, 1982. Ann Arbor: University Microfilms.

A study of *Goyescas* based on a comparison of: a facsimile of the manuscript, Frank Marshall's copy, printer's proof copies with Granados's corrections, and sketches of various movements. A lengthy secondary topic is found in a discussion of discrepancies in editions of *Spanish Dance* no. 7, "Valenciana."

B263. ---. "El Llibre d'Apunts d'Enric Granados." Translated from the English by Joan Malaquer i Ferrer. *Revista de Catalunya* 28 (1989): 89-106.

A study of one of Granados's sketchbooks, now housed at the Pierpont Morgan Library, New York (see B328). Riva summarizes Granados's ideas on orchestration as reflected in various sketches and also notes discrepancies between the sketches and published versions of various *Tonadillas*.

B264. ---. "Master Class: A Newly Discovered Mazurka by Granados." *Keyboard Classics: The Magazine You Can Play*. January/February 1985, 20-22, 38-39.

An account of Riva's 1981 discovery of several piano miniatures in a sketchbook entitled "Album: Paris, 1888." The album, long in the possession of Granados's daughter Natalia, contains eleven solo piano pieces and a "fifteen-minute [piano] duet," *En la aldea*. According to Riva, the album represents the "earliest record we have of the young Granados striving to become a mature composer." The mazurka is reproduced in this issue.

B265. Rodriguez, Santiago. "Master Class: Granados's *Spanish Dance* No. 5." *Keyboard Classics: The Magazine You Can Play*. March/April 1982, 19-23.

The Cuban pianist's interpretive ideas on the "simplicity and accessibility" of *Spanish Dance* no. 5 ("Playera").

B266. Rostand, Claude. "Une Grande première: *Goyescas* de Granados." *Disques* 58 (1953): 438-39.

Review of Leopoldo Querol's 1953 recording of *Goyescas* on the Ducretet-Thomson label. "C'est en tout cas un événement . . . Granados n'est présent aux catalogues 78 ou 33 tours qu'avec les enregistrements . . . de quelques oeuvres aimables et mineurs . . . nullement susceptibles de donner au public la moindre idée de la grandeur de ce musicien sous le rapport de l'inspiration, de la beauté d'invention, ni de l'écriture pianistique." (This is in any case an event . . . the only works of Granados available on 33 or 78 RPM recordings are minor, innocuous . . . in no way capable of affording the public the slightest appreciation of the grandeur of this musician, his inspiration, the beauty of his invention or his way of writing for the piano.)

B267. Ruiz-Pipó, Antonio. "Enrique Granados y Campiña." *New Grove Dictionary of Music and Musicians*, ed. Stanley Sadie. 7:628-29. London: Macmillan, 1980.

A "Life and Works" article by the Spanish conductor whose main intent seems to be that of placing Granados in a broader context. List of works and dates of some compositions are inaccurate.

B268. Sagardia, Angel. "Programas del Liceo. Granados y *María del Carmen*." *El Diluvio*, January 4, 1939, n.p.

Commentary on the performance history of *María del Carmen*. In a discussion of the 1896 Madrid premiere of Feliu y Codina's play, Sagardia mentions that the Spanish author Clarín endorsed the work. In his commentary on the November 12, 1898, premiere of the opera, Sagardia identifies the theater incorrectly but quotes the contemporary critic Eduardo Bustillo: "Algunos motivos y situaciones están tratados por el gran maestro demasiado alto y brillantemente para el 'vulgo zarzuelero'". (Some motifs and dramatic situations are treated in too exalted and lofty a fashion by the master for the common *zarzuelist*.)

B269. "Sala Estela." *La Esquella de la Torratxa* 21 (1899): 834.

An enthusiastic review of Granados's and Malats's two-piano recital at the Sala Estela December 22, 1899. The concert was sponsored by the Philharmonic Society and featured vocal selections performed by Sra. Jane Bathori and Emil Engel, in addition to the Sonata for Two Pianos, K. 448 by Mozart and two Saint-Saëns works for two pianos. The reviewer inaccurately states that this is their debut as a two-piano team; in fact, Granados and Malats gave two-piano recitals at the Teatre Novetats on June 9 and 18 of the same year.

B270. "Sala Granados." *Revista Musical Catalana* 9 (1912): 51.

Description of the February 4, 1912, ceremonies that inaugurated the newly constructed Granados Academy, Avenue Tibidabo. Pharmacist Salvador Andreu i Grau was the main donor and Granados presented a short concert.

B271. "Sala Granados." *Revista Musical Catalana* 9 (1912): 195.

A review of the May 19, 1912, concert by violinists Perelló and Frigola and pianist Ricart Vives. Among other works, they performed a composition listed simply as *Dança*, by Granados. (Since no reference to this string work appears in any other source, it is probably a transcription of one of the *Twelve Spanish Dances*.)

The same article reviews the July 7, 1912, chamber music concert at the Sala Granados which included the premiere of *Elisenda*, for piano and chamber orchestra. "L'obra, en el nostre concepte, es de lo més important . . . que ha sortit de l'exquisida ploma d'en Granados". (The work, in our view, is the most important . . . to flow from Granados's exquisite pen.) Gives background on the work.

B272. "Sala Granados." *Revista Musical Catalana* 9 (1912): 374-75.

Review of the November 3, 1912, concert by Granados and Crickboom at the Sala Granados. This article also reviews another concert in the same location, given in early December, in which Granados and Perelló performed Lekeu's Sonata. "L'interpretaren amb un profund sentit". (They interpreted the work with profound sensitivity.)

B273. "Sala Granados." *Revista Musical Catalana* 10 (1913): 56.

Notice of a second performance of *Elisenda* on January 26, 1913, along with other works by Vivaldi and Franck. Performers included A. Brossa, E. Casals, and M. Perelló (violins), P. Marés (cello), Granados, Frank Marshall, and Federico Longàs (piano), and Sñrta. Lluró (soprano) (see B271, 315).

B274. "Sala Granados." *Revista Musical Catalana* 12 (1915): 184.

Review of the May 30, 1915, solo recital by Granados at the Granados Academy. The reviewer noted Granados's extended improvisation on various Chopin works: "Amb el més gran romanticisme traduí el pensament chopinià compendiat en pàgines com el *Nocturn*, òp. 1, el *Vals*, òp. 64, núm. 2, la *Berceuse* i la *Polonesa-fantasie*, òp. 22". (With a grand, Romantic gesture he translated the Chopin into a compendium of the following pages: the Nocturne, op. 1, the Waltz, op. 64 no. 2, the *Berceuse*, and the *Polonaise-Fantasy* [op. 61, given incorrectly as op. 22].)

B275. Salazar, Adolfo. "Enrique Granados." In *La música contemporanea en España*, 189-204. Madrid: Ediciones la Nave, 1930.

Outlines Granados's career and discusses his role in Spanish Romanticism.

B276. Salvador, Miguel. "The Piano Suite *Goyescas* by Enrique Granados: An Analytical Study." D.M.A. diss., University of Miami, Coral Gables, 1988.

A stylistic and structural analysis of *Goyescas*. Emphasis on Granados's harmonic vocabulary, including the composer's use of ninth and augmented sixth chords, of pedal points, and his approach to modulation. An extended discussion of Goya's Madrid precedes this objective description of the composer's mature style.

B277. Salvat, Joan. "Enric Granados: Notes biogràfiques." *Revista Musical Catalana* 13 (1916): 197-207.

Homage to Granados and comprehensive biographical treatment of the composer. Details on his performing career in Barcelona.

B278. Samulski-Parekh, Mary M. V. "A Comprehensive Study of the Piano Suite *Goyescas* by Enrique Granados." D.M.A. diss., University of Missouri-Kansas City, 1988.

Biographical treatment of the composer and attempt to relate Granados's stylistic tendencies to Goya and to late-nineteenth-century artistic developments in Spain.

B279. "Schelling Charms in Unheard Spanish Work: Pianist in Recital at Carnegie Hall Plays *Goyescas* by E. Granados, a Known Writer in His Country." *New York American*, March 27, 1913, NYPL.

A review of Schelling's March 26, 1913, recital at Carnegie Hall. "Señor Granados has been hailed as 'The Chopin of the South'. . . his *Goyescas*, . . . really distinct tone-poems, [have] much of the fluency and charm of the Polish composer's works: exquisite color and artistic proportion."

B280. "Mr. Schelling's Recital: Spanish Pieces by a Spanish Composer, Granados, Heard for First Time." *New York Times*, March 27, 1913, p. 11.

"It is true, however, that Mr. Albéniz saw Spain through the veil of the modern Frenchman. Mr. Granados is submitted to no such foreign influence. The Spain that is embodied in his music is authentic . . . [yet] what he has written is a personal, individual expression."

B281. Schoenberg, Harold. "Colorful World of Old Spain." *New York Times*, March 15, 1959, sec. 2, p. 74.

A review of a performance by the Manhattan Opera Orchestra and Concert Chorale directed by Anton Coppola at the Manhattan School of Music, March 14, 1959. Schoenberg comments: "Nothing much really happens and the ending does not work at all. . . . But those who know the piano version know how beautiful the music is, and it is just as beautiful in its orchestral dress. . . . Despite the harmonic sophistication of the music it is basically sweet and simple, with one gorgeous tune following another."

B282. ---. "Goya Captured in Music." *New York Times*, November 26, 1967, sec. 2, p. 17.

Written a week prior to Alicia de Larrocha's December 7, 1967, Carnegie Hall all-Granados program (for the centennial of the composer's birth), this article assesses the opera *Goyescas*: "It is too bad that *Goyescas* as an opera is not done; it is such a pretty piece. Here is a double bill for somebody: *Goyescas* and Manuel de Falla's *La vida breve*. Anybody listening?"

B283. "Sempronio." "Granados, recordado por su hija." *Diario de Barcelona*, January 19, 1957, p. 4.

An interview with Granados's youngest daughter, Natalia, with emphasis on her discovery of the composer's diary, from which she quotes: "They are his memoirs; one of his former female students just presented them to me. I confess that I never knew they existed." This appears to be the diary the organization Amigos de Granados published in 1966 (see B365).

B284. "Sinfónica de Madrid." *Revista Musical Catalana* 12 (1915): 179.

A review of a performance by the Madrid Symphony of *Dante*, Parts I ("Dante e Virgilio") and II ("Paolo e Francesca"). "Es aquesta una obra que pel tema que l'inspirà s'aparta, naturalment, del caràcter nacional que predomina en quasi totes les produccions d'en Granados. . . . Amagada d'aquesta manera, en part, la personalitat del nostre músic, l'auditori queda un xic confós". (A work whose very theme stands apart from the nationalistic character that predominates in almost all Granados's other works. . . . Given that the composer's personality was thus hidden, in part, the audience experienced some confusion.)

B285. Slonimsky, Nicholas, ed. "Enrique Granados." In *Baker's Biographical Dictionary of Music and Musicians*, 879. 7th ed. New York: G. Schirmer, 1984.

A survey of Granados's accomplishments and list of works, including dates of all the stage works. Some inaccurate biographical information on the "outstanding Spanish composer." "Granados's music is essentially Romantic, with an admixture of specific Spanish rhythms and rather elaborate ornamentation."

B286. ---. *Music Since 1900*. 4th ed. New York: Charles Scribner's Sons, 1971.

In addition to quoting from the New York press after the premiere of *Goyescas*, Slonimsky cites an article in the London *Morning Telegraph* published immediately after Granados's death March 24, 1916.

B287. "Societat Filharmònica." *Revista Musical Catalana* 1 (1904): 82.

Announces a performance of the *Prelude* to the third act of *Follet* by the Philharmonic Society "as part of a recent series of four concerts," conducted by Crickboom.

B288. "Songs and Violin Playing: De Gorgoza and Hemus, Baritones, Miss Bach, Violinist in Recitals." *New York Times*, November 9, 1915, p. 13.

A review of baritone Emilio de Gorgoza's November 8, 1915, Aeolian Hall recital, in which "nothing [on the program was] more interesting than three songs by Enrique Granados . . . marked now by poignancy and intensity of feeling, now by irony. . . . His singing of the Spanish songs contributed to the modern literature, practically unknown to this public . . . [and] made a deep impression on the listeners."

B289. "[Spain's] Greatest Composer." [Unidentified source], NYPL.

A review of Granados's February 22, 1916, Aeolian Hall appearance: "Enrique Granados . . . is beyond question the greatest composer Spain has produced so far, as well as the best pianist."

B290. "Spanish Composer Makes Fortune in U.S." *Detroit News Tribune*, February 20, 1916, NYPL.

Commentary on Granados's financial gains during his United States tour. "During his short stay Granados is said to have drawn about $4,000 from the Metropolitan Opera house . . . at a rate of $800 a performance. In addition, although declining a concert tour, he gave two recitals in New York which must have netted him another thousand." Discusses other sources of income, such as the publication in the United States of his music and his contract with the Aeolian Piano Roll Company.

B291. "Spanish Composer May Have Been Saved: Hope that Enrique Granados and Wife Did not Perish on 'Sussex.'" *Louisville Post*, March 3, 1916, NYPL.

A report from Paris shortly after the torpedoing of the *Sussex*, speculating as to Granados's presence on a hospital ship.

B292. "Spanish Opera to Have Premiere This Week: *Goyescas* by Enrique Granados, Will Be First Opera To Be Sung Here in Spanish--Libretto is Based on Paintings by Famous Artist Goya." *New York Times*, January 23, 1916, sec. 2, p. 56.

This article incorrectly states that *Goyescas* was originally written as "a drama in verse" which Granados set to music. (In fact it was composed before Periquet fashioned his libretto to fit the music.) The characters Rosario and Pepa are likened to the Duchess of Alba and the *maja* of the painting *La Maja y los Biozados*, while Fernando is said to recall "something of Goya himself."

B293. Starkie, Walter. *Spain: A Musician's Journey through Space and Time*. 2 vols. Geneva: Editions Rene Kister, 1958.

A survey of Spanish music which discusses Granados in the context of the history of the *tonadilla*.

B294. Stevens, Denis. "New York City." *Musical Times* 109 (1968): 162.

On Alicia de Larrocha's December 7, 1967, Carnegie Hall all-Granados program: "But it is doubtful whether an entire evening of Granados does him credit: by placing his best works . . . beside compositions of other nationalists, a clearer picture of his personality might have emerged. Much of the music (the *Escenas románticas* and even some of the *Goyescas*) relies on a harmonic and figural language that is too derivative to be genuinely convincing."

B295. Suarez Bravo, F. "Orquesta Sinfónica de Madrid." *Diario de Barcelona*, May 27, 1915, pp. 6667-69.

A review of the May 25, 1915, performance of *Dante*, Parts I and II ("Dante e Virgilio" and "Paolo e Francesca") at the Palau de la Música

Catalana. (The work had been revised after a private hearing in 1908. See B284.) "Aun el primer cuadro solo es demasiado grande . . . el carácter dominante es sombrío y abstruso. Como composición sinfónica, está tratada hábilmente, trabajada en todos sus detalles. Para el efecto en el público acaso debiera haber reservado en el plan general un contrast mayor". (The first movement is still too big . . . the dominant mood is somber and abstruse. As a symphonic composition, it is treated aptly in all details; as for its effect on the public, however, it would have been better to maintain greater contrast in the general scheme.)

B296. ---. "Teatro Lírico: Primer concierto clásico." *Diario de Barcelona*, May 16, 1900, pp. 5896-97.

A review of the first concert presented by the Society of Classical Concerts, the subscription series Granados founded. After questioning the use of the word "classical" in the organization's name (the first concert included works by Grieg, Chopin, and Cramer) Suarez Bravo describes the group's objectives: "crear y organizar la agrupación de una verdadera y compacta masa de instrumentistas de cuerda" (to create and organize a truly cohesive string ensemble).

B297. ---. "Teatro Principal: Primer concierto Granados." *Diario de Barcelona*, March 2, 1906, pp. 2668-69.

A review of Granados's March 1, 1906, solo recital. Surprisingly, the reviewer downplays Granados's activity as a professional concert artist: "Sin ser un concertista profesional, pues la composicion le ha apartado de esta forma de actividad artística". (Without being a professional concert artist, since composition has taken him away from this form of activity.) The review is extremely flattering, however, and Suarez Bravo especially praises Granados's transcription of two Scarlatti sonatas, performed according to the composer's recent edition.

B298. ---. "El violoncellista Pablo Casals." *Diario de Barcelona*, June 22, 1900, pp. 7425-26.

A review of Casal's June 16, 1900, performance of the Saint-Saëns Cello Concerto, op. 33 in the second concert of the Society of Classical Concerts, at the Teatre Líric. The reviewer comments on Granados's conducting in the Mozart Serenade: "Bajo la batuta del maestro Granados, [la orquesta tocó] con la galanura y soltura que requiere una composicion tan ligera y transparente". (Under the baton of maestro Granados [the orchestra played] with an elegance and suppleness required by such a light, transparent composition.)

B299. ---. [Untitled]. *Diario de Barcelona*, March 13, 1911, pp. 3398-99.

A review of Granados's March 11, 1911, concert at the Palau de Música Catalana (see B107, 225). Suarez Bravo comments at length on Albéniz's style, which "revealed a Spanish music clothed in modernity" which Granados successfully carried through in his completion of Albéniz's *Azulejos*, "one number more of *Iberia*."

On *Cant de les estrelles*: "No creemos . . . que en realidad el éxito fuera tan sincero y espontáneo como en las Goyescas . . . tal vez sobre el piano, y bastarían el órgano y los coros". (We do not believe . . . that in reality its success was as sincere and spontaneous as that of *Goyescas* . . . probably the piano was unnecessary, and the organ and choirs alone would have been enough.)

B300. Subirá, José. "El compositor Enrique Granados en Madrid." *Diario de Barcelona*, February 15, 1957, p. 3.

Outlines Granados's associations with Madrid, from his first visits in the mid-1890s to the premiere of *María del Carmen*, to two later performances. A propos of *María del Carmen*, Subirá lists popular *zarzuelas* from the 1898-99 season with which *María del Carmen* had to compete: at the Parish, Chapí's *Curro Vargas*; at the Teatro Zarzuela, *Gigantes y cabezudas*; and at the Apolo ("the cathedral of the genero chico"), *El santo de la Isidro*.

B301. ---. *Enrique Granados: su producción musical, su madrileñismo, su personalidad artística*. Madrid: Z. Ascasíbar, 1926.

An expanded version of a lecture given in Madrid's Sala Aeolian, March 24, 1926, in commemoration of the tenth anniversary of Granados's death. Subirá, who knew the composer, gives a biographical overview and commentary on selected works, with emphasis on *Danza gitana* for orchestra and the *Cant de les estrelles*. Highly descriptive.

B302. ---. *La opera en los teatros de Barcelona*. 2 vols. Barcelona: Ediciones Librería Millá, 1946.

Discusses the January-February 1901 Catalan Theater Festival at the Tívoli theater, including the February premiere of *Picarol*.

B303. "El 'Sussex'." *Diario de Barcelona*, March 27, 1916, p. 4062.

Details on the torpedoing of the *Sussex*, with a description of the ship's proportions and capability. A telegraph sent from the *Sussex* during the attack was answered by a French rescue ship, the *Marie-Thérèse*.

B304. Tarazona, Andres Ruiz. *Enrique Granados: el último romántico*. (Enrique Granados: The Last Romantic). Madrid: Real Musical, 1975.

Generally undocumented biography includes excerpts from Granados's letters to Amparo Gal during their courtship and marriage, and information on Granados's association with Catalan writers, artists, and musicians. Includes a time line linking significant dates in Granados's biography with developments in Spanish literature.

B305. "Tasques d'hivern." *Revista Musical Catalana* 5 (1908): 169-70.

Critic Marcos Jesús Bertran interviews prominent Barcelonese musicians on their plans for the upcoming winter. In addition to discussing his future engagements with Fauré and Thibaud, Granados comments on *Dante*: "La meva idea a l'escriure *Dante* no ha sigut seguir pas a pas la *Divina Comedia*, sinó donar la meva impressió . . . pera això m'inspiro en el cèlebre quadro d'en G. Rosetti sobre'l mateix motiu". (My idea in composing *Dante* was not to follow, detail by detail, the *Divina Commedia*, but rather to give my impression . . . for this, I have found inspiration in the well-known sketchbook on the same theme by G. Rosetti.)

B306. Taylor, Robin Elizabeth. "Enrique Granados: *Goyescas*." M.A. diss., San Jose State University, 1976.

Biographical overview of Granados and analytical commentary on *Goyescas*.

B307. "Teatre del Bosch." *Revista Musical Catalana* 3 (1906): 170.

Background on the difficulties Granados encountered in securing a performance of *Follet*: "La empresa d'aquest teatre, que durant . . . dies seguits vingué anunciant els ensajos y la pròxima estrena del drama lirich d'en Granados *Follet*, ha terminat la temporada sense que dita estrena s'efectués. En cambi, de cop y volta, ha anunciat la estrena de dues altres òperes, que's posaren en escena la mateixa nit". (The management of the [Bosch] theater, which . . . has continued to announce rehearsals and the premiere of Granados's *Follet*, ended the season without the premiere having taken place. Rather, the management has abruptly announced the premiere of two other works, to be staged the very same night.)

B308. "Teatre Principal." *Revista Musical Catalana* 3 (1906): 192.

Review of the October 27, 1906, premiere of *Gaziel*, with Viola, Paricio, Moragas, and set designs by Alarma. "Deixant apart el llibret . . . perquè no volem exercir aquí de moralistes, direm lo molt que'ens ha plagut . . . els inspirats motius de la partitura, realsats per una orquestació finament cisellada. Pera la instrumentació Granados ha aprofitat ab molt de tacte'l seu instrument favorit, el piano". (Leaving aside the libretto [by Appel.les Mestres] . . . since we prefer not to act as moralists here, we will say how pleasing are the inspired motives of the score, realized through a finely honed orchestration. For the instrumentation, Granados exploited his favorite instrument, the piano.)

B309. "Teatro Lírico." *La Vanguardia*, January 31, 1899, p. 9.

A review of the disastrous premiere of *Blancaflor*, held the previous evening at the Líric. The reviewer comments on the numerous production flaws and inappropriateness of the performance space. "Una gran parte del público no vió ni sintió por completo." (Much of the audience could neither see nor hear completely.)

B310. "Teatro del Tívoli: *María del Carmen*." *La Vanguardia*, June 1, 1899, p. 5.

A review of the May 31, 1899, Barcelona premiere of *María del Carmen*, in which the author comments favorably on Granados's orchestration and keen dramatic sense, as demonstrated, for example, by María's second-act entrance. The author also describes the claques in the audience, and expresses the hope that the work will be objectively judged. "Así no hubiese permitido que se colaran dentro los intrusos, y el maestro Granados no habría tenido la faena enojosa de distinguir cuáles fueron los aplausos profesionales y cuáles los sinceros". ([It is to be hoped] that intruders will no longer be permitted to gather in the theater, and that Granados will not find himself confronted with the odious chore of having to distinguish the claques from those who applaud sincerely.)

B311. "Teatres." *Catalunya Artística* 2 (1901): 109-10.

This review of the February 28, 1901, premiere of *Picarol* briefly summarizes the plot and congratulates composer and librettist: "Ab *Picarol* han obtingut l'Apel.les Mestres y el mestre Granados un triomf hermosíssim y la empresa del Teatre Líric Català [ha efectuat] una obra que será segurament la mimada del públich de la temporada vinent, sobre tot si procuran donarli més bona interpretació". (With *Picarol*, Mestres and Granados have secured a great triumph, and the Teatre Líric Català [has produced] a work that will be a favorite with the public in the coming season, especially if the best possible performance can be obtained.)

B312. "Teatros y conciertos: Barcelona. Homenaje al maestro Granados." *Musical Emporium* 4, no. 32 (1911): 4-5.

On February 12, 1911, Granados was honored at the Salón de Ciento de las Casas Consistoriales, presumably for having been selected by Fauré for the Diémer jury. (The Diémer competition had taken place in May 1909. See B98.) The article gives names of political and artistic personalities present at the reception and mentions that in his "delicately worded" acceptance speech Granados urged the municipal representatives present to erect a monument to the recently deceased Albéniz.

B313. "Teatros y conciertos: Barcelona." *Musical Emporium* 4, no. 33 (1911): 3-4.

A review of Granados's premiere of *Goyescas* and other works at the Palau de la Música Catalana, March 11, 1911. On *Goyescas* the reviewer notes "[una] gran riqueza de ideas y de ritmos" (a vast richness of ideas and rhythms); on *Cant de les estrelles* (one of the more enthusiastic reviews) the critic applauds "la idea feliz de disponer en lo alto el coro que simboliza las estrellas . . . coro que, con el de los hombres, situado en el estrado, sostiene un bello diálogo de una delicada poesia" (the apt idea of representing the stars with the higher voices in the choir . . . voices which, with the male chorus placed on the risers, sustain a lovely dialogue of delicate poetry).

B314. "Teatros y conciertos: Barcelona." *Musical Emporium* 5, no. 42 (1912): 4.

A report on the celebration of Dr. Salvador Andreu i Grau's gift of new school facilities to the Granados Academy, where an official inauguration was held at the new building (corner of Tibidabo and Girona) on February 4, 1912, the highlight of which was a concert by Granados. The complete program is given: Prelude in E-flat Minor from the *Well-Tempered Clavier*, Book One, Bach; Sonata in F K. 332, Mozart; Sonata in C Minor ("Pathétique"), Beethoven; "Los requiebros" from *Goyescas* and works of Chopin, Schumann, Schubert, and a Wagner-Liszt transcription.

B315. "Teatros y conciertos: Barcelona." *Musical Emporium* 6, no. 51 (1913): 5.

A review of the second performance of *Elisenda*, held at the Granados Academy January 26, 1913; among the participants were Granados, Perelló, Marés, Mas y Serracant, Longás, Vives, and others. "*Elisenda* . . . obtuvo, lo mismo que cuando se estrenó, un exito unánime que indica que esta obra ha quedado en el repertorio de nuestros conciertos. En verdad lo merece por su exquisita composición y hondo sentimento". (*Elisenda* . . . obtained, as it did on the occasion of its first performance, a unanimous success, which indicates that the work has remained in our concert repertory. Truly this is deserved, due to its exquisite composition and deep sentiment.)

B316. "Teatros y conciertos: Barcelona." *Musical Emporium* 7, no. 66 (1914): 4-5.

A review of the last two season concerts by the Musical Association of Barcelona. The first of these final concerts (June 27, 1914) was Conchita Badia's performance of the *Tonadillas*. "Badia. . . logró en la ejecución de los hermosos *bijoux* del autor de *Goyescas* un notable y merecido éxito por la gracia y viveza con que supo traducir la intención de cada *Tonadilla*". (Badia . . . in these beautiful jewels by the composer of *Goyescas*, attained a notable and deserved success for the elegance and vivaciousness with which she communicated the essence of each *Tonadilla*.)

B317. "Teatros y conciertos: extranjero." *Musical Emporium* 2, no. 18 (1909): 6.

A review of Granados's Paris appearance with Thibaud the previous spring in which they performed Beethoven's "Kreutzer" sonata, Franck's "Sonata in A Major," and other works. The reviewer translated a quote from the French newspaper *Comoedia*: "Según me han dicho, M. Granados es reconocido en España como muy distinguido compositor. Sus obras pianisticas son numerosas, de una pluma original y experta, habiendo producido también obras dramaticas". (From what I have been told, Mr. Granados is recognized in Spain as a distinguished composer. His numerous piano works are from an expert and original pen, having produced dramatic works as well.)

B318. "Teatros y conciertos: extranjero." *Musical Emporium* 9, no. 79 (1916): 8-9.

An account of a June 24, 1916, benefit performance of Mozart's *Abduction from the Seraglio* at London's Aldwich Theater on behalf of the Granados orphans. The benefit was organized by Sir Thomas Beecham, then director of the theater's opera company. The performance took in over four thousand duros and was attended by Prince Henry of Battenberg, the Lord Mayor of London, and ambassadors of Italy, Japan, and Spain. Beecham and his fellow organizers circulated a strongly worded anti-German pamphlet prior to the performance.

B319. "Teatros y conciertos: Madrid." *Musical Emporium* 6, nos. 55 and 56 (1913): 3.

A report on what appears to be the Madrid premiere of the *Tonadillas*, on May 27, 1913, at the Círculo de Bellas Artes. The concert was preceded by a lecture by Periquet on the origin and development of the *tonadilla*; Sra. Membrives then performed the work, which appears to have been favorably received: "Granados ha escrito con su maestría é inspiración diversas composiciones de aquel exquisito género tan popular en el siglo XVIII . . . verdaderos joyas del arte musical español". (Granados has written, with his customary mastery and inspiration, various compositions in this exquisite genre so popular in the eighteenth century . . . truly jewels of Spanish musical art.)

B320. "Teatros y conciertos: Madrid." *Musical Emporium* 6, no. 58 (1913): 3.

An account of Granados's appearance on October 8, 1913 (incorrectly given as October 9), at Madrid's Teatro Real, in honor of the President of the French Republic, Poincaré. Alfonso XIII and his family were present. Granados performed Saint-Saëns's Fifth Piano Concerto on this program of French works. "No obstante cierta frialdad de etiqueta, fueron ovacionadas el eminente pianista catalán Enrique Granados y el no menos notable artista de violín Sr. F. Bordas . . . hicieron verdaderas maravillas de dicción y mecanismo". (Notwithstanding a certain coolness of manner, the eminent Catalan pianist Enrique Granados and the no less notable violinist Sr. F. Bordas . . . were given an ovation for the marvels of expression and technique effected by both.)

B321. "Teatros y conciertos: Madrid." *Musical Emporium* 9, no. 79 (1916): 6.

Announcement that the Granados Academy is temporarily under the directorship of Felip Pedrell, who, in keeping with the founder's desires, has initiated the publication of a journal, *Musiciana*. The first number will be dedicated to the study of musical form as found in piano literature. "El fin de la Academia Granados es hacer obra de cultura entre los músicos en general y en particular entre sus numerosos discípulos". (The goal of the Granados Academy is to promote culture among musicians in general and between its many students.)

B322. "Teatros y conciertos: Madrid." *Musical Emporium* 9, no. 80 (1916): 3.

Review of what appears to be the first performance in Spain of the "Intermezzo" from *Goyescas*, performed by the Madrid Philharmonic under the direction of Pérez Casas at the Sala de Price sometime in late November or early December 1916. "El bellísimo intermedio, primor de gracia y de color español, provocó un entusiasmo delirante". (The lovely Intermezzo, a treasure of elegance and Spanish color, provoked delirious enthusiasm.)

B323. "Teatros y conciertos: Madrid." *Musical Emporium* 10, no.78 (1916): 3.

An account of the May 31, 1916, memorial concert for Granados given by the Sociedad Nacional de Música in Madrid, whose program combined both known and unknown works of the composer, including *Elisenda*, *Navidad* (with members of the Madrid Philharmonic, directed by Pérez Casas), "El Pelele" (Federico Longás), assorted songs, and the *Tonadillas*, performed by Conchita Badia, who had to repeat two "delightful numbers," "Los ojuelos verdes" and "Serranas de Cuenca."

B324. "Terassa." *Revista Musical Catalana* 6 (1909): 64.

Announcement of Granados's upcoming March 7, 1909, appearance in Terassa, at which he was scheduled to perform, among other works, one of his Scarlatti transcriptions.

B325. "Terassa." *Revista Musical Catalana* 8 (1911): 149.

A review of Granados's performance in Terassa on May 12, 1911, a repeat of his March 11 appearance at the Palau de la Música Catalana, with the exception of *Cant de les estrelles*, which was omitted.

B326. "Terassa." *Revista Musical Catalana* 11 (1914): 160-61.

Review of Granados's recital on March 29, 1914, sponsored by the Escola Choral of Terrassa. Performed one of the Scarlatti transcriptions, two *Spanish Dances*, "El Pelele" (premiere), the *Tonadillas* (with Judit Tarragó, soprano), and the first book of *Goyescas*. "Ens [*El Pelele*], creiem, el fragment de les *Goyescas* més valent i més ple de moviment. . . . En Granados, com a pianista, estigué a l'alçada de les seves obres". (We believe that *El Pelele* is the most animated of all the *Goyescas*, the most exciting. . . . Granados, as a pianist, is at his peak.)

B327. Tintorer, Emili. "Teatres: Vetllades artístiques." *Joventut* 5 (1904): 445.

Tintorer discusses the founding of the "Vetllades artístiques," a series of theatrical productions organized by the members of the "Circol de Propietaris de Gracia." Adrià Gual's *Ultima primavera* (*Letzer Frühling*), which Granados conducted, was one of the works presented in this four-evening series.

B328. Turner, J. Rigbie. "Nineteenth-Century Autograph Music Manuscripts in The Pierpont Morgan Library: A Check List." *19th-Century Music* 4 (1980-81): 49-76.

A history of the Pierpont Morgan's acquisition of the Mary Flagler Cary Music Collection, which includes three leaves of *Follet*, two of which are dated October and November 1901, Ripollet and Barcelona. The Pierpont Morgan houses Granados's sketchbook, *Apuntes y temas para mis obras* (see B263), an eight-bar fragment, *Valses: Cartas de amor*, and a letter to an anonymous Frenchman describing *Liliana* (see B382).

B329. "Unió Musical." *Revista Musical Catalana* 1, no. 12 (1904): 265.

Review of the November 20, 1904, concert by the Musical Union, which included Granados's performance of selected *Escenas románticas*, the *Allegro de concierto*, Beethoven's "Spring" Sonata, op. 24 with violinist Sánchez Deyà, and several encores. Appears to have been the premiere of the seldom-performed *Escenas románticas*; the reviewer does not comment specifically on this work, however. "Abdós artistas foren aplaudits ab gran entusiasme per l'auditori". (Both artists were applauded with great enthusiasm by the audience.)

B330. [Untitled]. *Diario de Barcelona*, April 10, 1886, p. 4202.

A review of the April 9, 1886, performance at the Barcelona Athenaeum presented by students in Pujol's class. The reviewer lists participants and works and mentions that two good pianos, a Bernareggi and a New York Steinway, were used.

B331. [Untitled]. *Diario de Barcelona*, January 18, 1897, pp. 737-38.

A review of the January 17, 1897, concert by Catalunya Nova (the choral group founded by Morera), at which Granados performed several of his *Spanish Dances* and the Impromptu. Although the main interest seems to have been the premiere of Morera's *Plany*, the reviewer comments on the reception of Granados's works: "Es ocioso consignar que dicho artísta, cuyos méritos han sido repetidamente sancionados por el público, fue aplaudido calurosamente". (It is idle to point out that this artist, whose merits have been repeatedly approved by the public, was warmly applauded.)

B332. [Untitled]. *Diario de Barcelona*, December 6, 1899, p. 13498.

A review of the December 4 chamber music concert for Philharmonic Society patrons at the Sala Estela, apparently the premiere of the *Valses poéticos* (See **Biography**, p. 11 for press commentary.) Included on the program were a Suite for Violin and Keyboard, the Quartet, op. 47 by Schumann, *Adagio appassionato* by Bruch, and Saint-Saëns's *Rondo capriccioso*.

B333. [Untitled]. *Diario de Barcelona*, November 12, 1900, pp. 12890-91.

A review of the fifth concert presented by the Society of Classical Concerts on November 11, 1900. Of Granados's re-orchestration of Chopin's Concerto in F Minor, op. 21 (performed by Carles Vidiella) the reviewer comments that "A decir verdad, el original de Chopin es muy pobre. Y Granados ha compuesto, á nuestro entender, una obra orquestal notabilísima, especialmente por su claridad y por su delicadeza". (To tell the truth, the Chopin original is really quite deficient. Granados has, to our way of thinking, composed a notable orchestral work, especially so for its clarity and delicacy.)

B334. [Untitled]. *Diario de Barcelona*, February 14, 1902, p. 2042.

A review of the February 13, 1902, concert of all-Catalan vocal music presented by the Musical Association of Barcelona at the Sala Chaissagne, where Srta. Marina Cañizares premiered a song of Granados's, "La boira." "Figuraba en la primera parte, obteniendo mucho menos éxito que el que merecía, 'La boyra [*sic*]' de Granados, composición en la que el canto recitado . . . y el acompañamiento de piano constituyen una obra de gran carácter". (In the first part, and receiving far less recognition than it deserved, figured Granados's "La boyra [*sic*]," a composition in which the recitation of the voice, combined with the piano accompaniment . . . create a work of great character.)

B335. [Untitled]. *Diario de Barcelona*, June 22, 1903, p. 7628.

A review of the June 21, 1903, concert of instrumental music at the Teatre Eldorado, where Granados's Impromptu for piano solo and *Melodía* for piano and violin were premiered by pianist Ferran Via and violinist Lluis Pichot. On *Melodía*: ["Pichot] dió a conocer . . . una *Melodía* para violin y piano del maestro Granados, en la que el interés melódico corrió parejas con el arte que ha presidido á su desarrollo". (Pichot introduced . . . a *Melodía* for violin and piano by maestro Granados, in which the melodic interest unfolded alongside the artfulness of the work's overall development.)

B336. [Untitled]. *Diario de Barcelona*, March 1, 1904, pp. 2730-31.

A review of the February 29, 1904, performance at the Teatre Principal of the Prelude to the Third Act of *Follet*, conducted by Crickboom. "La orquesta ejecutó . . . el preludio del tercer acto del poema dramático del maestro Granados *Follet*, que por la sentida melodía y el brillo de la orquestacion es digno de su autor". (The orchestra performed . . . the Prelude to the Third Act of maestro Granados's dramatic poem *Follet*, which, given its deeply felt melodies and the luster of its orchestration, is worthy of its author.)

B337. [Untitled]. *Revista Musical Catalana* 1, no. 6 (1904): 124.

Memorial concert for Mallorquin composer Antoní Nogueras given by Granados and the Orfeó Català on May 3, 1904, at the Teatre de Novetats. Here, Granados performed that composer's *Melodias populars mallorquinas*. "Las delicadas y características melodias populars mallorquinas . . . trobaren en l'esmentat pianista un interpretador fidel". (The delicate, characteristic Mallorcan melodies found a faithful interpreter in the above-named pianist.)

B338. [Untitled]. *Diario de Barcelona*, January 8, 1906, p. 284.

A review of a concert at the Teatre Principal on January 7, 1906, at which Granados conducted fourteen-year-old Mieczyslaw Horszowski in the Concerto in D Minor, K. 466 (Mozart), the Concerto in G Major, op. 58 (Beethoven), and the *Andante spianato and Grande Polonaise brilliante*, op. 22 (Chopin). The 2reviewer comments favorably on all selections, with the exception of the *Polonaise*: "La orquesta . . . mas bien estorba que contribuye á su realce". (The orchestra . . . obstructed rather than facilitated the realization of the work.)

B339. [Untitled]. *Diario de Barcelona*, October 29, 1906, p. 12341.

Review of the premiere of *Gaziel*, October 27, 1906, including the cast, a plot synopsis, and commentary on the libretto and on the primary musical factors. "*Gaziel* es un poema escrito correctamente . . . pero que no alcanza á ser una obra eminentemente teatral. . . . La música del maestro Granados, como suya, se distingue por una factura sóbria y correcta . . . muy bien cuidada la instrumentacion". (*Gaziel* is a poem that is correctly written . . . but which does not attain the status of an eminently theatrical work. . . . Granados's music distinguishes itself through its altogether appropriate conception . . . [and] thoughtfully conceived orchestration.)

B340. [Untitled, unidentified source]. March 27, 1913, NYPL.

Review of Ernest Schelling's Carnegie Hall recital, March 26, 1913: "All the Granados music had a languor about it that made it on first acquaintance a trifle long."

B341. [Untitled]. *Diario de Barcelona*, March 2, 1915, p. 2716.

A review of a benefit concert for the French Red Cross at the Palau de la Música Catalana, which occasioned an early performance of several of Granados's songs. "La señorita Helena Girlina . . . que dió a conocer por primera vez canciones de Granados muy interesantes: 'No lloréis, ojuelos,' and 'Serranas de Cuenca' . . . de gran originalidad, revela un aspecto muy nuevo en la fisonomía de compositor del maestro Granados". (Miss Helena Girlina . . . introduced the public to some very interesting songs by Granados: "No lloréis, ojuelos" and "Serranas de Cuenca" . . . of great originality, revealing a new aspect of the composer, Granados.)

B342. [Untitled, unidentified source]. N.d., NYPL.

Review of November 5, 1915, premiere of *Dante* in Chicago: "Granados has his individual style . . . risks what few risk these days--slender, two-part writing, and lean-limbed three-part writing in the midst of this fluorescence of tonal abundance . . . something of the assurance of Sir Edward Elgar, whose first symphony will come to mind."

B343. [Untitled, unidentified source]. November [?] 1915, NYPL.

Review of November 5, 1915, premiere of *Dante* in Chicago: "[*Dante*] is a work whose logic is not of mechanisms, but of vital moods. [Granados] is not the type that provides the theorists with material from which to deduce laws: he is not of the persuasion subservient to formulas . . . *Dante* came as a revelation to the audience of the Chicago Symphony this last week."

B344. [Untitled, unidentified source]. N.d., NYPL.

Review of *Dante* premiere in Chicago, November 5, 1915. "The 'free recitative' form which Granados chose was well-adapted to his purpose, only he did not handle the matter gracefully. He gave to the voice little opportunity for declamation or sustained singing, but hurried it along in an awkward sort of way. . . . The music one could admire, but grew weary of the turmoil which ceaselessly boiled up without the inspirational value which should give it vitality."

B345. [Untitled, unidentified source]. December 13, 1915, NYPL.

Commentary on upcoming January 28, 1916, premiere of *Goyescas*. "Throughout the opera he obtains magnificent and original effects by the use of the chorus. . . . The orchestration is brilliant and modern in treatment. . . . The work teems with spontaneous melody and rhythmical vigor."

B346. [Untitled, unidentified source]. N.d., NYPL.

Review of *Goyescas* premiere January 28, 1916. The reviewer comments on the absence of an overtly Spanish quality in Granados's music. "None of the singers who took part in this production, singing in Spanish, is a Spaniard: wherefore the perfection of the Spanish accent and diction cannot be guaranteed. It is said that some of it, notably Miss Fitziu's, was not bad. . . . The management has done more for the stage setting of this opera than it has for some other of the recent productions."

B347. [Untitled, unidentified source]. N.d., NYPL.

Review of *Goyescas* premiere. "Periquet, the librettist, was commissioned to adapt a text to the score, a proceeding against all traditions, yet not inconsistent in this era of progressive musical writing."

B348. [Untitled, unidentified source]. N.d., NYPL.

Review of *Goyescas* premiere January 28, 1916. "The musical action throughout this [first] scene is truly an exemplification of the text, glowing with Spanish color and intense in rhythm. . . . Granados has constructed this part of his opera with a definite intent--that of coordinating orchestra and chorus to simulate the concerted voices of the multitude."

B349. [Untitled, unidentified source]. N.d., NYPL.

Review of *Goyescas* premiere January 28, 1916. "As he scorns diversity of character, so too does Señor Granados scorn external dramatic effect. How much, for example, might have been made of the first entrance of Rosario, or of the quarrel in the dance hall."

B350. [Untitled, unidentified source]. N.d., NYPL.

Review of Granados's January 23, 1916, Ritz-Carlton Hotel appearance. "There is in these *Goyescas* much sincerity, geniality and great ability, but we found less of these qualities in the other pieces played. Nearly all of the other music seemed to be more salon than concert music, and that is always pleasing and interesting. But sometimes it was too long."

B351. [Untitled]. *New York Post*, February 23, 1916, NYPL.

Review of Granados's February 22, 1916, Aeolian Hall recital with Anna Fitziu. "It is considered risky for a pianist to devote a programme entirely to one composer. But when the pianist is also the composer and his name is Enrique Granados, the risk is not great . . . beautiful in melody . . . deeply expressive [Granados's songs] will doubtless be heard around the country . . . as Granados is the latest fashion."

B352. [Untitled]. *New York World*, February 23, 1916, NYPL.

A review of Granados's February 22, 1916, Aeolian Hall appearance: "In reviewing . . . [the opera] *Goyescas*, I said of the music that it smacked of the piano. Last night's exhibition justified the remark. Mr. Granados was on natural ground."

B353. [Untitled]. *Musical America*, May 13, 1916, NYPL.

Discusses the Spanish writer Mariano de Cavia's demands that Germany pay an indemnity to the Granados children after the torpedoing of the *Sussex*. "As long as the German Government denies to the children of Maestro Granados the indemnity which is theirs by right . . .

absolutely no German music, including naturally the modern frivolities of Viennese opera, should be either played or sung in our theaters, concert rooms, salons or schools."

B354. [Untitled, unidentified source]. May 27, 1916, NYPL.

Review of *Goyescas* premiere (concert version) in Chicago, May 1916. "As far as is known, this fragment of last evening was the first performance in Chicago of an opera sung in the Spanish language. The artists of the [Grove] Company were Mrs. Mabel van Grove, soprano; Miss Mabel Corlew, contralto; Stuart Dykema, tenor; and Eusebio Concialdi, barytone [*sic*]. The production was under the direction of Isaac van Grove . . . it was he who played the piano . . . the impression given was altogether delightful."

B355. [Untitled]. *Toledo Blade*, August 5, 1916, NYPL.

Outlines the circumstances leading to Granados's *Reverie-Impromptu*, the improvisation surreptitiously recorded by a technician during the composer's recording session at the Aeolian studios in 1916.

B356. [Untitled, unidentified source]. January 10, Madrid, 1917 [?]. Schelling Archive, New York.

"Notice that the German government will pay an indemnity of 666,000 pesetas to Granados's family. Herr von Jagow, the then German foreign minister, [had] expressed regret for the death of the composer in April, 1916."

B357. Ureña, Pedro Henriquez. "*Goyescas*: precedentes, la interpretación, la concurrencia, la crítica." *Las Novedades*, February 3, 1916, pp. 6-7.

A general discussion of the January 28, 1916, premiere of *Goyescas* and of earlier performances of Spanish operas in New York.

B358. Valls i Gorina, Manuel. "Els compositors. Albéniz i Granados." In *La Música Catalana Contemporània*, 54-59. Barcelona: Editorial Selecta, 1960.

In this introduction to modern music in Catalonia, observations on Granados are brief and general. Refers to the influence of Chopin.

B359. ---. "Enric Granados." In *Història de la Música Catalana*, 151-56. Barcelona: Editorial Tàber, 1969.

An assessment of Granados's *oeuvre* in the more general context of Catalan music. Emphasizes Granados's avoidance of folkloristic elements and lack of susceptibility to Wagnerian influences.

B360. ---. "Granados, inédito." *El País*, April 5, 1984. Douglas Riva Collection, New York.

Valls comments on the concert given at the Municipal Conservatory of Barcelona April 3, 1984, at which some of the pieces from *Album: Paris, 1888* (see B73, 264) were performed. "De las mazurcas, valses, melodías, romanzas sin palabras y piezas similares que integraban la primera parte del programa, asoman las tímidas intuiciones de un joven músico . . . con una estructura formal débil, pero que anuncia el temperamento del post-romanticismo que presidió parte de su creación". (Of the mazurkas, waltzes, melodies, songs without words, and similar pieces that comprised the first part of the program, timid intuitions of the young musician surface . . . with a weak formal structure, but which announce the post-romantic temperament that took precedence in the composer's output.)

B361. Van Vechten, Carl. *The Music of Spain*. London: Kegan Paul, Trench, Trubner, 1920.

For a general audience. The author, a British gentleman-scholar, discusses Spanish operas performed in the United States prior to *Goyescas*.

B362. Vernon, Grenville. "*Goyescas* Sung at Metropolitan: First Performance on Any Stage of Opera by Enrique Granados." *Opera News* 7 (1916): 2-5.

An assessment of *Goyescas*. "A Spanish opera sung in Spanish made its bid for our public's suffrage. . . . Like Charpentier and Moussorgsky and Borodin, Señor Granados is a democrat. He sings not of two or three characters or one love affair, but of the cumulative feelings of the masses . . . little definite characterization in either the story or the music reduced the music allotted to the individuals to a strange similarity of melodic expression."

B363. "Vetllades artísticas." *Revista Musical Catalana* 1 (1904): 178.

Brief, positive review of the July 28, 1904, repeat performance of the Gual-Granados collaboration, *La nuit d'octobre*. Also performed were the "dramatic ballade" ("balada dramàtica"), *Picarol* (Granados/Mestres) and *L'Alegria que passa* (Morera/Russiñol).

B364. Vila San-Juan, Pablo. "En el cincuenta aniversario de la muerte de un gran artísta: los cuatro pianos de Enrique Granados." *La Vanguardia Española*, March 24, 1966, p. 48.

An extremely fanciful account of Granados's life, represented by four pianos he used at various stages of his career. Vila San-Juan describes the cafés in which Granados played before going to Paris, and the horseback-riding accident which killed the composer's father at approximately the same time. The author also refers to the "cultural entity" Amigos de Granados and that organization's commemoration of the fiftieth anniversary of Granados's death.

B365. ---. *Papeles intimos de Enrique Granados*. Barcelona: Amigos de Granados, 1966.

A collection of essays by Vila San-Juan, letters to and by the composer, photographs, sketches, and excerpts from Granados's diary. Unfortunately the diary entries are haphazard, suggesting that Granados did not consistently keep a diary or that various sections were at some point removed.

B366. Villalba, P. Luis. *Enrique Granados: semblanza y biografía.* Madrid: Imprenta Helénica, n.d.

One of the earliest biographical treatments of the composer; some unreliability of dates, however. Includes brief commentary on selected works and information on Granados's patron, Dr. Salvador Andreu i Grau.

B367. Villar, Rogelio. "Enrique Granados." In *Músicos españoles*, 81-96. Madrid: Mateu, n.d.

An essay on the composer and his output. Refers to concerts in Berlin, Brussels, and Leipzig; there is no evidence, however, that Granados performed in these cities. The author reports meeting the composer in Madrid in 1894, and describes the composer's attempts to have his music published in France. Also mentions Granados's election into the Claustro del Doctorado de Músicos Franceses.

B368. ---. "Granados." *Revista de Música* 4, no. 3 (1929): 221-31.

This overview of Granados's life and works is largely culled from the author's *Músicos españoles* (see B367), with the addition of a lengthy quote by Periquet. Refers to Granados's difficulties in securing performances in Madrid. "En Madrid se le había oído muy poco. Tocó con Manén las diez sonatas de Beethoven . . . pensábamos oirle en la Sociedad Nacional un concierto de obras suyas, deseo que no llegó a realizarse, manifestado por él de una manera vehemente en una carta escrita a . . . Periquet". (In Madrid he was heard very little. He played the ten [violin and piano] sonatas of Beethoven with Manén . . . we also thought we might hear him in a concert of his own works at the National Society, a desire that was never realized, but which was vehemently apparent in a letter to . . . Periquet.)

B369. ---. "Granados en Nueva York: El estreno de *Goyescas*." *La Esfera* 3, no. 108 (1916): n.p.

Villar lists Granados's last compositions, including *Madrigal* for cello and piano, *La natividad de los niños* for small string orchestra, and *El tango de la cacerola* for piano. He also mentions a series of Spanish dances Granados was working on for Vaclav Nizhinsky of the Ballets Russes, evidently commissioned by choreographer Mikhail Fokine (no other source mentions this association or the tango).

B370. Viñes, Ricart [*sic*]. "Breu epístola a N'Enric Granados i Campiña." *Revista Musical Catalana* 13 (1916): 192-93.

A short memoir by the Catalan pianist describing his student days in Paris with Granados.

B371. Vives, Amadeu. "N'Enric Granados i l'edat d'or." *Revista Musical Catalana* 13 (1916): 175-83.

A fictionalized memoir of Vives's friendship with Granados. Comments on Granados's tastes in literature, describes Granados's initial encounter with poet Apel.les Mestres, and quotes the composer on the state of musical education in Spain in the late-nineteenth century.

B372. Walthew, Richard H. "Enrique Granados: 1867-1916." *Musical Observer* 19, no. 3 (1920): 14-15.

A brief discussion of *Goyescas*, selected *Spanish Dances*, and the limited extent to which Grandos's music was known in England at the time of his death, despite English fondness for other national schools. "[Granados's music] is fluent, elastic, unforced. It has little constructive interest or sense of climax but flows in whatever direction the mood of the moment may lead."

B373. Weinstock, Herbert. "America." *Opera* 20 (1969): 497-98.

A review of a revival of *Goyescas* by the Opera Theater of the Manhattan School of Music on March 14-16, 1969. "*Goyescas* remains a protracted Spanish bore, manifesting at every two steps forwards and one step back that it was derived from piano pieces. It is a series of Spanish 'effects' but has no dramatic integument and is irritatingly busy."

B374. "When Granados Played for the Emperor of Brazil." *Musical America*, February 12, 1913 [?], NYPL.

Relates the circumstances of Granados's 1878 performance for Peter II (incorrectly identified as Peter I, who had abdicated in 1831) in the Faubourg Saint Germain salon of Mme. Thierry. Granados performed a full recital and ended with a gavotte of his own. (No other source mentions that Granados was in Paris at this time; the article appears to be apocryphal. See B304: 10-11.)

B375. Wilson, Charles. "The Two Versions of 'Goyescas'." *Monthly Musical Record* 81 (1951): 203-7.

Presents a scene-by-scene comparison of the opera and the piano suite, comparing phrase lengths, transitional passages, and abridgements. Also gives examples of other composers who have used their own instrumental works as bases for vocal works.

B376. "Wilsons Give Musicale: Distinguished Assembly Includes about 300 Guests." *Washington Post*, March 8, 1916, p. 4.

An account of Granados's March 7, 1916, White House performance: "Mme. Julia Culp, soprano, and Mr. Enrique Granados, pianist, were the artists of the evening, giving a program which was selected and arranged by Miss Margaret Wilson. The gathering . . . was a very distinguished one, including several Ambassadors and Ministers, representatives of the cabinet and others from official and resident society."

B377. Wirth, Helmut. "Granados." In *Die Musik in Geschichte und Gegenwart*, ed. Friedrich Blume, 5:678-82. Kassel u. Basel: Bärenreiter Verlag, 1956.

A biographical overview, list of works, and commentary on Granados's style and possible influences.

B378. "World's Premiere of Opera *Goyescas*: Enrique Granados's Little Spanish Work Successfully Sung in Native Tongue." *New York Times*, January 29, 1916, p. 7.

Review of the January 28, 1916, premiere of *Goyescas*. "The first opera ever to be sung in [Spanish] in the Metropolitan Opera House. It did not appear that the audience was profoundly moved by that fact. What did appear was that the music apparently greatly pleased the first-night audience, in which the Spanish colony of New York was largely represented. . . . Opening scene brilliant . . . chief roles competently sung."

LETTERS TO, FROM, OR ABOUT GRANADOS

B379. Granados to Malats, Barcelona, August 26, 1909. Douglas Riva Collection, New York.

The composer discusses preparations for a memorial concert for Albéniz, and requests that Malats perform *Iberia* on this occasion. Granados also comments on the summer of 1909 (during which workers' uprisings and numerous acts of violence culminated in the Setmana Trágica): "Nosotros hemos pasado muchas tribulaciones por aquí. Tenía muchos proyectos para este verano . . . pero los acontecimientos me han privado de muchas cosas." (We have been through many tribulations around here. I had lots of plans for this summer . . . but events have deprived me of many things.)

B380. Granados to Malats, Barcelona, August 31, 1910. Douglas Riva Collection, New York.

Granados announces his intention to present a concert the following March at the Palau de la Música Catalana and asks Malats to form part of the committee that will approve his proposal. This letter is often quoted for its closing, in which Granados describes the first book of *Goyescas*, recently completed.

B381. Granados to Malats, Barcelona, December 11, 1910. Douglas Riva Collection, New York.

Granados comments on his progress with *Azulejos*: "Rosina me ha regalado el original de Isaac y lo guardo como oro en paño. . . ¿Quieres que lo tengamos entre los dos? Yo te mandará el original de lo que he escrito." (Rosina [Albéniz's widow] gave me Isaac's original, which I am guarding with my life. . . . Would you like to share it between the two of us? I'll mail you the original of what I have written.)

B382. Granados to a "dear friend," Barcelona, October 22, 1911. MFC G748.J43, Mary Flagler Cary Music Collection, Pierpont Morgan Library, New York.

In this thirteen-page letter (possibly to French critic Georges Jean-Aubry) Granados discusses the "scenic poem" *Liliana*, which had premiered that summer in Barcelona. A synopsis of the plot, highlighted with over eighty measures of musical examples, is followed by the composer's assessment of the premiere, with references to individual portions: "C'est très penible pour ma modestie de vous dire que la scène des grenouilles est d'une efet suprenant." (It doesn't come easily for a modest person to tell you that the Frog Scene makes a striking effect.)

B383. Granados to Schelling, Barcelona, February 3, 1913. Schelling Archive, New York.

Granados is sending Schelling a copy of his recently completed *Tonadillas*: "les *Lieders* de Espagne: inspirés des anciens chants classiques . . . mais tout a fait a moi comme idée. . . .C'est de la musique de *race*" (the *lieder* of Spain, inspired by ancient songs . . . but entirely of my own creation . . . the music of [the Spanish] *people*).

B384. Granados to Schelling, Barcelona, May 9, (1913). Schelling Archive, New York.

Granados expresses gratitude at Schelling's efforts to premiere *Goyescas* in New York. Also expresses his eagerness to meet Schirmer, possibly on the way to visit Schelling at Céligny later in the month. "Je suis en principe decidé à m'y rendre a votre premier appel; mais, il m'est impossible de reculer la seance que la grande corporation de l'Ateneo de Madrid a déjà organisée sur la base de la *Tonadilla* est moi meme. Cette séance doit avoir lieu du 20 au 21 mai. . . . Je puis donc en partant le 24 ou 25 mai arriver a Céligny vers le 27. M. Schirmer y serait t'il?" (In principle I would come at your slightest suggestion; I am, however, committed to appear at a gathering the Ateneo of Madrid has organized, which has to do with my *Tonadillas*. The event will take place on the 20 and 21 of May. . . . I could therefore appear at Céligny around the 27th. Will Mr. Schirmer be there?)

B385. Granados to Schelling, Barcelona, June 10, 1913. Schelling Archive, New York.

Describes his *sainete*, to be performed in Barcelona at the end of June or the beginning of July 1913: "L'oeuvre est un *sainete*, Espagnol, XVIII siècle . . . rempli de *seguidillas*, *calescas*, danses diverses." ["The work is a *sainete*, in eighteenth-century style . . . filled with *seguidillas*, *calescas*, other dances."]

Refers to his beginning work on the opera version of *Goyescas*, and expresses gratitude to Schelling for having arranged a contract with the New York publisher, G. Schirmer.

B386. Granados to Schelling, Barcelona, July 18, 1913. Schelling Archive, New York.

Granados says that he is ill, suffering from an inflammation. He also makes brief mention of the contract with Schirmer.

B387. C. G. Röder (Leipzig publisher) to Schelling, Leipzig, August 25, 1913 (postcard). Schelling Archive, New York.

Röder thanks Schelling for sending *Dante* on the 18th of the month, and assures him that it will be held in Leipzig "for the disposal of Mr. G. Schirmer, New York . . . whose word will be awaited."

B388. Granados to Schelling, Barcelona, August 26, 1913. Schelling Archive, New York.

Granados is still sick and has lost ten kilos. He gives Schelling a list of piano pieces which he will send to Schirmer, including (1) Impromptu, (2) *Sérénade goyesca*, (3) Prelude in D, (4) *Marche militaire*, (5) *Danse à la cubaine*, (6) two *Spanish Dances*, and (7) *Valse de concert*.

Granados mentions his progress on preparing other works for publication: "J'ai en preparation pour d'ici quelques semaines *Valses poetiques* [*sic*] et *Chant des etoiles* [*sic*], pour piano, orgue et choeurs, très important." (I also have in preparation two other works, the *Valses poéticos* and the *Cant de les estrelles*, for piano, organ, and choirs--and very important.)

B389. Rudolph Schirmer to Schelling, New York, September 6, 1913. Schelling Archive, New York.

Schirmer acknowledges receipt of Schelling's cable announcing Granados's acceptance of Schirmer's proposed two-year contract for six thousand French francs yearly as advanced royalty in exchange for turning over all his compositions to Schirmer for publication during that period. Schirmer also supposes that Granados would prefer to be paid in monthly installments.

B390. Schirmer to Schelling, New York, September 9, 1913. Schelling Archive, New York.

In response to Schelling's letter of August 28, 1913, Schirmer indicates that a contract will be sent directly to Granados with a translation and a check for three thousand francs, "being the semi-annual royalties in advance for the first six months of the contract." Schirmer also expresses interest in seeing any of Granados's "operettas," and says that he will do whatever is necessary "to have them receive a fitting performance, either in Paris or some other capital of Europe."

B391. Amparo Gal de Granados to Mrs. Schelling, Barcelona, September 20, 1913. Schelling Archive, New York.

The letter refers to a performance Granados will give in Madrid on October 8, 1913, in honor of the president of the French Republic. Will Mr. Schelling take part, and could he advise Granados as quickly as possible?

B392. Granados to Schelling, Barcelona, September 24, 1913. Schelling Archive, New York.

Granados informs Schelling that the Schirmer contract has been signed and that, with the contract, Granados also sent the publisher (1) two *Spanish Dances*, (2) *Danse a la cubana*, (3) *Marche militaire*, and (4) *Valse de concert*. The composer also mentions his ongoing work on "El Pelele" and discusses the possibility of a concert for two or three pianos by Schelling, Granados, and a Sñr. Tagores when Schelling next comes to Barcelona.

B393. Granados to Schelling, Madrid, October 7, 1913. Schelling Archive, New York.

Discusses the possibility of two joint appearances with Schelling and the Orfeó Català later that year in Barcelona. On the sophistication of Barcelona's audiences Granados remarks: "Je vous dirais très franchement qu'a Barcelone tres concerts . . . c'est toujours comme ça: un pour advertir le monde, un autre pour avoir du monde et le troisième, dangereux." (I would say to you very frankly that in Barcelona giving three concerts . . . is always like this: one is to warn the public, the second to invite them, and the third, a danger!]

Granados accepts Schelling's offer to give a recital in Marseilles later that year.

B394. Granados to Schelling, [Barcelona?], November 11, 1913. Schelling Archive, New York.

Discusses a difference of opinion with Schirmer over the publisher's interest in Granados's theater works. "Mais il demande pour lui les droits d'auteur comme pour les morceaux de piano, et ça ne me combient pas." (He demands the same rights [for the theater works] as for the piano pieces, and this does not suit me at all.)

B395. Schelling to Granados. [Appears to have been written on a train, is dated only "1913."] Douglas Riva Collection, New York.

Schelling tells Granados that he will play *Goyescas* in London on the 10th. (According to other sources, he actually played December 9, 1913, at Queen's Hall. See B90, 242.) He gives a London address and questions Granados about several accidentals in "Quejas, o La maja y el ruiseñor."

B396. Granados to Schelling, Barcelona, February 4, 1914. Schelling Archive, New York.

After Schelling's London appearances, in which he played some of Granados's works, the composer expresses his gratitude: "J'ai lu les journaux anglais et je suis ravis de penser que mon oeuvre promène deja gràce a mon grand ami et artiste, parmi les premiers publiques du monde!! C'est trop pour moi! Merci, mille fois, merci!" (I read the English newspapers and I am delighted to think that my work has made its way--thanks to my great friend and artist--among the world's more important audiences! It's too much! A thousand thanks!)

B397. Sir Henry J. Wood to Schelling, London, May 7, 1914. Schelling Archive, New York.

The British conductor thanks Schelling for sending him the score of *Dante* the previous December and expresses the hope of performing the work in August or September; however, he will need the string parts prior to August 1.

B398. Granados to Schelling, Barcelona, May 29, 1914. Schelling Archive, New York.

Granados describes his plans to go to Paris in June of 1914: "Je part pour Paris le 11. Je dois donner audition privée de mon opera 'Los majos enamorados,' extrait de *Goyescas* (ça c'est pour Schirmer) a ces Mssrs. de l'Opera." (I leave for Paris on the 11th. I must give a private audition of my opera *The Enamored Majos* extracted from the *Goyescas* (that's for Schirmer) to the gentlemen of the Opera.)

B399. Assistant to the General Director, Chicago Grand Opera Company, to Schelling, Chicago, June 22, 1914. Schelling Archive, New York.

The letter reports that the General Director of the Chicago Grand Opera Company, Maestro Campanini, is interested in seeing the score of *Goyescas*, as Schelling had proposed in previous correspondence. Although at present Campanini does not have time to hear the work, he would consider it in the future.

B400. Rudolph Schirmer to Schelling, Bad Reichenhall, July 5, 1914, Schelling Archive, New York.

Schirmer expresses his interest in *Goyescas* and states his willingness to travel to Barcelona to meet Granados "and establish personal relations with him" (this despite Schirmer's unstable health, presumably the motivation for his stay in Europe). Schirmer also promises to discuss with Gatti-Casazza of the Metropolitan Opera the possibility of a New York premiere.

B401. Granados to Schelling, Barcelona, September 30, 1914. Schelling Archive, New York.

Granados informs Schelling that he and his daughter arrived safely in Barcelona after leaving Céligny. "Nous sommes encore arivés a Barcelona avec quelques francs a la poche. J'avais pensé de jouer dans un cinema en cas de ne pas pouvoir sortir de Geneve." (We arrived in Barcelona with a few francs left in our pockets. I had been thinking of playing in a cinema, however, had we been unable to get out of Geneva.)

B402. Memo [undated]. Schelling Archive, New York.

Lists the donors for the "loving cup" presented to Granados in New York before his sailing on March 11, 1916. The contents of the cup totalled $4,100 and were presented in a note for 20,986.35 pesetas. Contributors included the Spanish ambassador Riaño y Gayangos, Mrs. W. H. Bliss, Mr. and Mrs. Robert W. Bliss, Mr. W. T. Carrington, Mr. S. J. de Coppet, Mr. Otto Kahn, Mr. Fritz Kreisler, Mr. Philip Lydig, Mrs. J. Lanier, Mr. W. Leeds, Mr. Clarence Mc Kay, Mr. Ignaz Paderewski, and Mr. and Mrs. Ernest Schelling. Schelling solicited the funds.

B403. Mrs. W. K. Vanderbilt's personal secretary to Philip Lydig [one of the "loving cup" donors], New York, January 27, 1916. Schelling Archive, New York.

Mrs. Vanderbilt regrets being unable to make a donation to the "loving cup," primarily because she feels "there are other more important things which need her help."

B404. Schelling to Spanish Ambassador Riaño, Santa Barbara, California, April 10, 1916. Schelling Archive, New York.

Schelling urges Riaño to speak to the King of Spain on behalf of the Granados orphans. He also describes various problems associated with the memorial concert, scheduled for May 7, 1916, at the Metropolitan Opera House.

B405. Eduardo Granados to Schelling, Barcelona, April 24, 1916. Schelling Archive, New York.

Eduardo inquires into the particulars of his father's business dealings in the United States, including the rights to *Goyescas*. He alludes to contractual problems with Periquet and inquires as to the rights for *María del Carmen*: "Pourrais-je aussi savoir si mon père a convenu l'édition ou representation de son opera en trois actes, que vous devez connaître, *María del Carmen* ou si cette oeuvre est completement libre et de même pour ses autres oeuvres *Follet* et *Petrarca* qui on eté sauveés avec presque tout le reste des bagages." (Could I also learn from you whether my father has secured the edition or representation of his three-act opera, which you must surely know, *María del Carmen*? Or is this work completely available, and the same for his other works, *Follet* and *Petrarca*, that were saved with practically all the rest of his baggage?)

B406. Schirmer to Schelling, New York City May 9, 1916. Schelling Archive, New York.

In a response to Schelling's inquiries regarding the delay of one of Granados's quarterly payments, Schirmer claims that in fact at the time of his death Granados owed the publisher "in the neighborhood of $2,800 for sums advanced." Schirmer remarks that there is no "reason to complain about our treatment of him."

B407. Eduardo Granados to Schelling, Barcelona, July 25, 1916. Schelling Archive, New York.

Eduardo describes his efforts to continue the work of the Granados Academy: "L'Academie pouvait disparaître sans un grand efort de ma part. . . J'ai reuni les professeurs. Ils m'ont declaré être dispossés a continuer avec moi comme avec mon père." (The Academy could have disappeared without great effort on my part. . . . I met with the faculty, they declared themselves willing to continue under my direction, as with my father.)

Eduardo also includes an authorization for Schelling to "withdraw from Schirmer all of [Granados's] manuscripts and musical works" (see **Biography**, p. 33).

B408. Eduardo Granados to Schelling, Barcelona, February 24, 1917. Schelling Archive, New York.

Eduardo continues the discussion of Granados's estate and refers to a growing conflict with Periquet: "a ossé même insulter la mèmoire de notre père" ([Periquet] has even dared to insult our father's memory). Eduardo suggests that Periquet is even trying to hold up further performances of *Goyescas*, possibly because of a notarized contract signed November 16, 1915, which allowed the librettist only thirty percent of the royalties.

3

Works and Performances

CDM= Centre de Documentació Musical, Barcelona
BOC= Biblioteca de l'Orfeó Català, Barcelona
UME= Unión Musical Española, Madrid
MA= Marshall Academy, Barcelona

W1. **A la antigua (Bourée)**

For piano solo. Unpublished. Cited by Iglesias, who believes title refers to a fifteen-measure sketch, *Aire de danza á la antigua*. Probable date of composition 1885.

W2. **A la cubana. I. Allegretto II. Un poco vivo**

For piano solo. New York: G. Schirmer, 1914, catalogued as op. 36. Dedicated to Mme. Silvia de Sa Valle, an acquaintance from Paris. Probable date of composition 1894.

See: B388

W3. **A la pradera**

For piano solo. Madrid: UME, 1966, catalogued as op. 35. Probable date of composition 1908-9.

W4. **Album: Paris, 1888**

For piano solo. Unpublished collection of nearly forty pieces, presumably written during Granados's stay in Paris. In private collection, Douglas Riva, New York. Includes mazurkas dedicated to Pujol and Pedrell, also piano duet, *En la aldea*. See W52.

See: B73, 264, 360

W5. **Allegro appassionato**

For piano solo. Unpublished, although recorded. Iglesias refers to a near-complete manuscript in family archive.

See: D5

W6. **Allegro de concierto**

For piano solo. Madrid: UME, 19-?, catalogued either as op. 46 or op. 15. Dedicated to Malats. First performance Madrid, April 1904; also, Barcelona, March 11, 1911.

See: B51, 59, 153, 329

W7. **Allegro vivace**

For piano solo. Part of *Album: Paris, 1888*. Currently in unpublished manuscript only (see W4). Was published by Catalana d'Edicions Musicals, 1982, later withdrawn. Dedicated to Malats.

W8. **El amor de la Virgen (melodía)**

For piano solo. Unpublished. Iglesias cites a sketch in pencil, with soprano voice filled in.

W9. **Andante**

For violin and piano. Unpublished. Cited by Iglesias.

W10. **Aparición**

For piano solo. Madrid: UME, 1966. Dedicated to Miss Jennie Rutherford Granshaw.

W11. **Arabesca**

For piano solo. Barcelona: *La Ilustración Moderna*, Espasa, n.d. Douglas Riva Collection, New York. Dedicated to Srta. Fernanda de Bejar. First performance April 20, 1890, Barcelona.

See: B64

W12. **Azulejos. Albéniz-Granados**

For piano solo. Paris: Rouart, Lerolle; New York: Breitkopf and Härtel, ca. 1911. Posthumous piano work of Isaac Albéniz, completed by Granados. At CDM: Ms copy with annotations by Albéniz, 15 pp, 34 cm, dated 1910, Barcelona; incomplete autograph of the Granados revision, 6 leaves, 31 cm, signed and dated May 25, 1910.

First performance March 11, 1911, Barcelona.

See: B49, 107, 299, 381

W13. **Balada**

For piano solo. Score lost. First performance February 15, 1895, Madrid.

W14. **Barcarola**

For piano solo. Madrid: UME, 1966, catalogued as op. 45. Reprint by Associated Music Publishers, New York, 1971. Dedicated to Massenet.

W15. **Blancaflor. Libretto, Adriá Gual**

Stage work based on regional folk material. Unpublished. Ms at CDM, 22 x 31 cm, first, second violin and viola parts only. First performance January 30, 1899, Barcelona.

See: B63, 135, 309

W16. **Bocetos: Colección de obras fáciles. I. Despertar del cazador II. El hada y el niño III. Vals muy lento IV. La campana de la tarde** Also includes **Países soñados. I. Palacio encantado en el mar**

For piano solo. Madrid: UME, 1918. Iglesias assigns *Bocetos* op. 25 and *Paises soñados* op. 20, viewing "Palacio encantado en el mar (Leyenda)" as a fifth *Boceto* (B144, 1:76). "Leyenda" however is designated with a Roman numeral I; it appears that Granados intended to compose additional works in this set. In the bound sketchbook *Apuntes y temas para mis obras* (Pierpont Morgan Library, New York), Granados wrote "Bocetos (2 cuaderno)" with the main title "Rayo de luna" and one subtitle, "Contemplación," evidently as plans for another set. Probable date of composition 1900-1905.

First performance March 23, 1913, Barcelona.

W17. **La boira**

For voice and piano. Unpublished. Ms dated 1900, cited by Iglesias. First performance February 13, 1902, Barcelona.

See: B334

W18. **Boires baixes. Prologue, Canso d'amor, Epilogue**

For orchestra. Unpublished. Iglesias cites a manuscript copy. Song *Canso d'amor* (W25) extracted from this work.

See: B215

W19. **Breves consideraciones sobre el ligado**

A pedagogical booklet on producing legato on the piano. Unpublished.

W20. **Canción árabe**

For piano solo. Madrid: UME, 197-? Ms at BOC, 2 leaves with title "Chanson Arabe."

W21. **Canción y danza**

For piano solo. Unpublished.

W22. **Canción morisca**

For piano solo. Barcelona: Espasa, n.d. In *La Ilustración Moderna*. Douglas Riva Collection, New York. Dedicated to "the subscribers of *La Ilustración Moderna*."

W23. **Canción del postillón**

For voice and piano. New York: G. Schirmer (1916). Dedicated to Andreas de Segurola. English translation of original Castilian text by Harold Flammer.

W24. **Canciones amatorias. I. Descúbrase el pensamiento II. Mañanica era III. Llorad, corazón IV. Mira que soy niña V. No lloréis ojuelos VI. Iban al pinar VII. Gracia mía**

For voice and piano. Madrid: UME, 1962. Ms at CDM, 4 leaves, 38 x 31 cm, complete. First performance (selections) April 5, 1915, Barcelona. Complete ms of "Mira que soy niña" in family archive, dated October 11, 1914, and marked "romancero general anónimo."

See: B1

W25. **Canso d'amor. Text by J. M. Roviralta**

For voice and piano. Barcelona: Casa Dotesio (1902). Ms, 4 leaves, 37 cm, of orchestration by the composer's son Eduardo, at CDM. Extracted from orchestral work, *Boires baixes*.

W26. **Canso de Janer**

For voice and piano. Unpublished, cited by Iglesias.

W27. **Cansonetta: El rey y el juglar**

For voice and piano. Unpublished, catalogued by Iglesias as op. 51.

W28. **Cant de les estrelles**

For piano, organ, and chorus. Unpublished. Based on Catalan translation of poem by Heine. Composed 1910. Ms of organ part (10 leaves) and chorus part (15 leaves) at BOC; piano part in Nathaniel Schillkret Collection, New York. First performance March 11, 1911, Barcelona.

See: B49, 107, 225, 299, 301, 313

W29. **Canto gitano**

For voice and piano. Madrid: UME, n.d..

W30. **Capricho español**

For piano solo. Madrid: UME (191-?); Barcelona: Juan Baptiste Pujol, n.d., catalogued as both op. 39 and op. 2. Dedicated to Don Eduard Condé. Probable date of composition 1886-87.

W31. **Carezza (Vals)**

For piano solo. Madrid: UME, 1917, catalogued as op. 38. Dedicated to Pepita Condé (daughter-in-law of Eduard Condé). Probable date of composition 1886-87. Ms at BOC, 8 leaves.

W32. **Cartas de amor (Valses íntimos). I. Cadencioso II. Suspirante III. Dolente IV. Appassionato**

For piano solo. Madrid: UME, n.d.. Iglesias dates the work from 1887; according to Riva the fairly sophisticated writing indicates 1889 or 1890. An undated eight-measure fragment, also entitled *Valses: Cartas de amor* (possibly intended as a second set) at the Pierpont Morgan Library, New York, Koch Collection no. 442, 1 p, 17.5 x 27 cm.

W33. **Chorale of Johann Sebastian Bach**

Transcription for string orchestra. Unpublished. Autograph ms at CDM, 1 leaf, 36 cm.

W34. **La cieguecita de Belén. Based on a poem by Gabriel Miró**

Unpublished stage work for voices, two clarinets, and bassoon. Also known under the title *El portalico de Belén*. Written when two of Granados's children recovered from typhoid during a 1914 epidemic. At CDM: autograph ms of full score and parts of two intermezzi; ms of orchestral parts with piano, 15 leaves, 36 cm; ms of reduced score signed and dated January 3, 1915 (uses material from *Navidad*); ms of Introduction, 9 pp, 35 cm, incomplete orchestration. See W96.

W35. **Clothilde (mazurka)**

Unpublished. For piano solo. Catalogued by Iglesias as op. 1. At MA: complete ms. Probable date of composition 1884-85.

W36. **Concerto for cello and orchestra**

Unpublished, incomplete. Iglesias cites notes for a first movement, "Allegro serio."

W37. **Concerto for piano and orchestra**

Unpublished, incomplete. At CDM: two signed ms sketches of first movement, (1) a piano reduction, 25 leaves, 36 cm; (2) a second (orchestrated) sketch 25 pp (slow introduction for piano solo), both bear dedication "A mon cher maître M. Camille Saint-Saëns."

W38. **Concerto no. 2 in F Minor, by Fryderyk Chopin (orchestration by Granados)**

For piano and orchestra, first movement only. Unpublished. First performance November 11, 1900, Barcelona, with Carles Vidiella, soloist. Score lost.

See: B333

W39. **Cuentos de la juventud. I. Dedicatoria II. La mendiga III. Canción de mayo IV. Cuento viejo V. Viniendo de la fuente VI. * * * VII. Recuerdos de la infancia VIII. El fantasma IX. La huérfana X. Marcha**

For piano solo. Barcelona: Musical Emporium, 1910; Madrid: UME, 1977 and 1983; London: Associated Board of the Royal Schools of Music, 1985. Catalogued as op. 1. Dedicated to the composer's oldest son, Eduardo. Probable date of composition 1900-1906.

W40. **Dante, or La Divina Commedia. I. L'entrada a l'infern II. Paolo e Francesa**

For orchestra and mezzo-soprano. New York: G. Schirmer, 1915, catalogued as op. 21. Second movement vocal solo text from fifth canto, *La Divina Commedia*. Ms at CDM, orchestra parts, 23 x 31 cm. First (private) performance June 1908, Barcelona. Revised and performed publicly May 25, 1915, Barcelona. American premiere by the Chicago Symphony, November 5, 1915.

See: B32, 126, 204, 213, 247, 284, 295, 305, 342-44, 397

W41. **Danza característica**

For piano solo. Madrid: UME, 1973.

W42. **Danza gallega**

Number two of orchestral *Suite on Gallician Themes* (see W131) arranged for cello and piano by the composer. Madrid: UME, 1971. Dedicated to Pablo Casals.

W43. **Danza gitana**

Versions for large and small orchestra. Unpublished. Both mss at CDM, 31 x 35 cm and 22 x 32 cm, respectively.

W44. **Danza lenta**

For piano solo. Madrid: UME, 1966; New York, G. Schirmer 1914, catalogued as op. 37. Dedicated to the memory of Vincent Esteve, a friend and student of Granados. First performance May 8, 1915, Barcelona.

W45. **Deux danses caractéristiques. I. Danza gitana II. Danza aragonesa**

For piano solo. Paris: Salabert, 1931. Number two adapted from Granados's incidental music for Feliu i Codina's stage work, *Miel de la Alcarria* (W91). Probable date of composition 1894. First performance of latter October 28, 1898, Barcelona.

W46. **Dificultades especiales del piano**

Incomplete pedagogical work for solo piano, ms at MA. Three sections: "Dificultades del cuarto y cinco dedo," "Escalas y arpeggios con cambio del primero y cinco dedo," "Elasticidad del cuarto y cinco dedo," Theme and Variations (three complete variations and an incompleted fourth) on previous exercises, 4 leaves, cover.

W47. **La diosa en el jardín**

For voice and piano. New York: G. Schirmer (1915) as *The Goddess in the Garden*. First performance May 7, 1916, New York.

W48. **Dolora en La menor**

For piano solo. Barcelona: Catalana d'Edicions Musicals, 1982. Subtitled "apunte goyesca" ("preliminary *Goyesca*"). First performance November 27, 1984, Madrid.

W49. **Elegía eterna (text, Apel.les Mestres)**

For voice and piano. Madrid: UME, 1962. Dedicated to María Barrientos. Ms at BOC, 6 leaves. First performance June 10, 1914, Barcelona. First performance of (unpublished) orchestral version January 31, 1915, Barcelona.

See: B168

W50. **Elisenda. I. El jardí d'Elisenda II. Trova III. Elisenda IV. La tornada o Final**

For piano, voice, harp, string quintet, flute, oboe, and clarinet. Unpublished. Based on a poem by Apel.les Mestres. Composed 1910. At CDM: ms of orchestral score of movements one and two, 46 pp, 32 cm, another ms of first three movements; 49 pp, 21 x 31 cm; pencilled autograph of the composer at end of second movement, dated June 8, 1912; a third ms copy of first three movements, 32 cm, copied in two different hands. At BOC: ms, 12 leaves. At MA: incomplete piano sketch, no date.

First performance July 7, 1912, Barcelona.

See: B16, 271, 273, 315, 323

W51. **Elvira (mazurka)**

For piano solo. Unpublished. Iglesias quotes the composer's daughter Natalia Carreras as suggesting that the title refers to Granados's mother, Enriqueta Elvira Campiña. Probable date of composition 1884-85.

W52. **En la aldea. Part One: I. Salida del sol. Maitines II. El cortejo (marcha nupcial) III. La oración IV. Regreso (marcha nupcial), Canto (recitado). Part Two: I. La siesta II. Danza pastoril III. Final**

For piano duet. Part of unpublished *Album: Paris, 1888*. See W4.

W53. **Escena religiosa**

Unpublished. For violin, organ, piano and timbales. Ms at CDM, 4 leaves, 37 cm, with the dedication "A la memoria de mi queridísima Doña Cecilia."

W54. **Escenas infantiles. I. Sueños de oro II. Niño que llora III. Otra melodía IV. Hablando formal V. Recitado VI. Pidiendo perdón VII. El niño duerme**

For piano solo. Unpublished. Iglesias suggests that sections of the work were published as part of other series of piano miniatures.

W55. **Escenas poéticas (first series). I. Berceuse II. Eva y Walter [*sic*: Walther] III. Danza de la Rosa**

For piano solo. Madrid: UME, 1912; New York: Dover, 1973. Dedicated to Granados's daughter Solita. Iglesias catalogues the *Escenas poéticas* op. 27, no. 1 and *Libro de horas* op. 27, no. 2 (see W77). Date of composition probably around 1905, especially given that *Die Meistersinger von Nürnberg*, to which "Eva and Walther" is an obvious reference, was first produced in Barcelona that year.

W56. **Escenas poéticas (second series) I. Recuerdo de países lejanos II. El angel de los claustros III. Canción de Margarita IV. Sueños del poeta**

For piano solo. Madrid: UME, 1923.

W57. **Escenas románticas. I. Mazurka II. Berceuse III. * * * Lento con éxtasis IV. Allegretto (Mazurka) V. Allegro appassionato V. Epílogo**

For piano solo. Madrid: UME, 1930. New York: Dover, 1987. Presumably inspired by a romantic liaison with a young student, María Oliveró, to whom the work is dedicated. According to the Dover edition *"Lento, con éxtasis"* was published separately during Granados's lifetime; it eventually acquired the subtitle *El poeta y el ruiseñor*.

First performance November 20, 1904.

See: B170, 329

W58. **Estudio op. posthumous (Andantino espressivo)**

For piano solo. Madrid: UME, 1973.

W59. **Exquise (Vals tzigane)**

For piano solo. Unpublished, cited by Iglesias.

W60. **Follet. Libretto, Apel.les Mestres**

Lyric drama in three acts. At CDM: incomplete ms of piano-vocal score, 22 x 32 cm, includes parts of all soloists but Guille's; an autograph ms of 80 leaves, 36 cm (complete work separated into three acts), Act One and Prelude to Act Three bear the seal of the Granados Academy; choral parts, 24 x 33 cm, six voices; a complete ms of Prelude to Act Three, 32 cm. At the Pierpont Morgan Library, New York: ms fragment three leaves, 27 x 35 cm, dated 1910 "Ripollet and Barcelona," Albrecht 859D, Cary Catalogue no. 117. At MA: ms portion of piano-vocal score, 24 leaves, pencil and ink, portions of Acts One and Two. Marked "empezado el 1er de octubre" (no year).

First performance April 4, 1903, Barcelona. First performance of Prelude to Act Three February 29, 1904.

See: B110, 193, 224, 287, 307, 336

W61. **Fugue in C-sharp Minor, by J.S. Bach**

For strings, flute, oboe, clarinet, bassoon, trumpet, and trombone, arranged by Granados. Unpublished. Ms at CDM, 31 cm. First performance May 15, 1900.

See: B296

W62. **Gaziel. Libretto, Apel.les Mestres**

Lyric drama in three tableaux. Unpublished. First performance October 27, 1906, Barcelona under auspices of the Espectacles Graner. Ms at Salabert Archives, Paris.

See: B159, 195, 251, 261, 308, 339

W63. **Goyescas (Crepúsculo) [Sérénade Goyesca?]**

For piano solo. Unpublished, cited by Iglesias.

See: B388.

W64. **Goyescas, or Los majos enamorados. Book One: I. Los requiebros II. Coloquio en la reja III. El fandango de candil IV. Quejas, o La maja y el ruiseñor. Book Two: V. El amor y la muerte (Balada) VI. Epílogo (Serenata del espectro)**

For piano solo. Madrid: UME, 1912-14. New York: International, (1943), Dover, 1987. Dedications to Emil Sauer; Eduard Risler; Ricardo Viñes; the composer's wife, Amparo; Harold Bauer; and Alfred Cortot. First extant sketches from 1909. At BOC: 1911 facsimile edition (exemplar no. 23), Book One only. At MA: "Los requiebros," ms, 1 leaf; printers' proofs of nos. 1-3, some corrections, verbal indications. Also of "Los requiebros," ms. of pp. 5-6, signed by Frank Marshall, presented to Igor Markevitch, in personal collection, Carlotta Garriga.

First public performance (Book One only) March 11, 1911, Barcelona. New York premiere January 23, 1916.

See: B6, 10, 49, 83, 87, 90, 107, 146-47, 150-53, 225, 242, 262, 276, 278-80, 294, 299, 313, 350, 352, 375, 380

W65. **Goyescas: An Opera in Three Tableaux. Libretto, Fernando Periquet**

New York: G. Schirmer, 1915. (English translation by James Weldon Johnson.) Piano vocal score. Dedicated to Mrs. Ernest Schelling. At CDM: ms of 123 pp with 2 unattached pages, 54 cm, complete opera with corrections (the two loose pages, 144 and 150, are cadenzas from Act Three); ms of Act Three, orchestral score, French text, 40 cm, note on page 109 reads: "D'ici à la fin l'orchestration est de Gabriel Grovlez"; ms of Act Three, finale, 14 leaves, 41 cm, French text, seal of the Archives of the Orquestra Pau Casals. Ms of piano-vocal score with annotations by the composer in Schelling Archive, New York. Presentation ms of piano-vocal score, 82 unnumbered leaves, 7 blank pp, 34.7 x 24.8 cm at Library of the Hispanic Society of America, New York.

First performance January 28, 1916, New York. Other performances include French version (Paris, December 17, 1917), and Italian (Milan, December 28, 1937).

See: B4, 10, 28, 36-37, 41, 43, 65, 76, 82, 88, 97, 103, 112-18, 120, 137-38, 155, 157-58, 169, 171, 189, 199-201, 203-4, 211, 214, 237-41, 252, 292, 354, 357, 362, 369, 372-73, 375, 378

W66. **L'Herba de amor (Pregaria en estil gregoriá)**

Madrid: UME, 1971. For three-part chorus and organ. Catalan text, dedicated to the Virgin of Montserrat. Ms dated February 27, 1914, at the Abbey of Montserrat.

W67. **L'Himne dels morts**

Piano version composed 1897, arranged for string orchestra by Valencian composer Lopez-Chavarri. Madrid: UME, n.d.; Barcelona: Editorial de Música Española Contemporanea, 1983. Dedicated to flood victims of Turia. Facsimile of piano reduction at BOC.

W68. **Impresiones de viaje (Hacia París, ante la tumba de Napoleón)**

For piano solo. Sketch exists in ms, cited by Iglesias. Probable date of composition 1888.

W69. **Impromptu (Allegro assai)**

For piano solo. New York: G. Schirmer, 1914, catalogued as op. 39. Dedicated to Frank Marshall. Complete ms, 6-8 pp, at MA. On February 15, 1895, in Madrid Granados performed an Impromptu; likewise on January 17, 1897 (Barcelona), and on June 21, 1903, his student Ferrán Vía performed a Granados Impromptu; it is not clear which of four possible Impromptus (see W70 and W144) these might be.

See: B388

W70. **Impromptu (Prestissimo)**

For piano solo. Completed ms catalogued by Iglesias as op. 47. See W69.

W71. **Intermezzo (Goyescas)**

For orchestra. Composed as scene-change music for the opera, 1916. Madrid: UME; New York: Schirmer. Composed 1916. Ms at CDM, 14 leaves, 40 cm, bear the seal of the Archives of the Orquestra Pau Casals and of the Sociedad de Autores Españoles.

See: B226, 322

W72. **Intermezzo (Goyescas)**

Arranged from orchestral version for piano solo by the composer. New York: G. Schirmer, 1916. Composed 1916.

W73. **Intermezzos for the Wedding Mass of Dionisio Condé**

For string quartet, harp, and organ. Unpublished. Dedicated to the son of Granados's benefactor, Eduard Condé. At CDM: photocopy of autograph ms for *Introit Prelude*, 5 leaves, 36 cm; autograph ms, 3 leaves, 36 cm. Probable date of composition 1890-92.

W74. **Jácara (Danza para cantar y bailar)**

For piano solo. Madrid: UME, 1973, catalogued as op. 14.

W75. **El jardí d'Elisenda**

A solo piano arrangement of the first movement of the earlier suite by the same name. See W50. Madrid: UME, n.d.; Barcelona: Casa Dotesio, 1913. Dedicated to Pablo Casals.

W76. **Jota aragonesa by A. Noguéra i Balaguer. Arranged by Granados for piano solo and for orchestra**

Unpublished. At CDM: orchestral parts for five movements in ms, 22 leaves, 36 cm; partial piano version in ms, 2 pp, 28 cm. First performance May 3, 1904, Barcelona.

W77. **Libro de horas. I. En el jardín II. El invierno (La muerte del ruiseñor) III. Al suplicio**

For piano solo. A subseries of *Escenas poéticas*, first series (W55) published in same volume. First performance (*En el jardín*) March 23, 1913, Barcelona.

W78. **Liliana. Libretto, Apel.les Mestres**

Lyric drama in one act. Unpublished. First performance July 9, 1911, Barcelona. At CDM: ms of prompter's part, 32 cm; ms of orchestral score, 108 pp, 37 cm, in different hands; ms of vocal parts, 28 leaves, 22 x 32 cm.

See: B1, 159, 195, 218, 251, 253, 261, 382

W79. **Llegenda de la fada**

For orchestra and vocal soloists. Unpublished, incomplete. Ms at CDM, 20 leaves, 23 x 32 cm.

W80. **Madrigal**

For cello and piano. Madrid: UME n.d.; Miami Lakes: Master Music Publications (1980). Dedicated to Pablo Casals. First performance May 2, 1915, Barcelona; New York premiere January 23, 1916. Complete ms in family archive (2 pp), marked "Danza XIII de las escenas gallegas."

See: B10, 223

W81. **Marcha de los vencidos**

For orchestra. Unpublished. At CDM: autograph ms of orchestral score, 29 pp, 37 cm; autograph sketch, signed, of first 10 measures, orchestral score, 37 cm. First performance October 31, 1899, Barcelona.

W82. **Marche militaire**

For piano solo. New York: G. Schirmer, 1914, catalogued as op. 38. Dedicated to Josep Camps, the composer's nephew. According to Iglesias, the second of an incomplete group of six military marches, two of which were arranged for piano duet. See W145. Autograph ms at CDM with annotations, including indication "Op. 37," 2 leaves, 35 cm. First performance October 31, 1915, Barcelona. The autograph ms of the fourth March of the same incomplete set is also at CDM, 3 leaves, 35 cm. (See A10.) Probable date of composition 1913.

See: B388

W83. **María del Carmen. Librettist Feliu i Codina**

Zarzuela in three acts. Unpublished, except for three separate numbers in piano-vocal reduction: "Canción de la zagalica" (Act One, Scene Six); "Canción cartagenera" (Act Two, Scene Two); "Murcianas, baile. Tiempo algo movido de movimiento de malagueña murciana" (Act Two, Scene Ten); Madrid: Pablo Martín (n.d. but probably contemporaneous with early performances). At CDM: incomplete ochestral score of Act One (flute, oboe, clarinet, trumpet, percussion), 32 cm; also a published score under the title *María del Carmen: Murcianas* (Madrid: Pablo Martín, [191-?]), piano/vocal reduction, 7 pp. At the Sociedad General de Autors de España, Madrid: complete score in three volumes (one per act), in several copyists' hands, many annotations in ink and pencil; several pages have been cut out and new material reinserted.[1] First four pages of a copyist's piano reduction at Library of Congress, Washington D.C. Piano-vocal sketch for "Escena final" (2 pp) in family archive; orchestral sketch of same also in family collection.

First performance November 12, 1898, Madrid; first Barcelona performance May 31, 1899; also performed January 28, 1967, Barcelona.

See: B27, 60, 110, 174, 191, 198, 254, 261, 268

W84. **María del Carmen. Prelude**

For piano solo. Unpublished, but recorded, possibly as an improvisation.

See: D152

---

[1] Walter Clark of the University of California at Los Angeles suggests these insertions are not Granados's but originated with the Barcelona productions during the 1930s.

W85. **Mazurka (alla polacca)**

For piano solo. Madrid: UME, 1973, catalogued as op. 2. Probable date of composition 1888-90.

W86. **Mazurka (alla polacca)**

For piano solo. In *La Ilustración Moderna*. Barcelona: Espasa, n.d. Douglas Riva Collection, New York.

W87. **Mazurka in E-flat Major**

For piano solo. Katonah, N.Y.: Keyboard Classics, 1985. Probable date of composition 1888 (from *Album: Paris, 1888*, see W4).

See: B264

W88. **Melodía**

For violin and piano. Score lost, first performance June 21, 1903, Barcelona.

See: B335

W89. **Melopea**

Lyric drama, incomplete. At MA: ms of Act Two, 1 p, scored for orchestra and harmonium, marked "para copiar"; ms of "Scene" from Act Two, Catalan text, orchestrated, 1 p.

W90. **Método teórico práctico para el uso de los pedales del piano**

Pedagogical manual on pedaling, introduction to Granados's system of pedal notation. Madrid: UME, 1954.

W91. **Miel de la Alcarria**

For orchestra. Incidental music for Feliu i Codina's drama of the same title. At CDM: ms of orchestra and choral parts, 31 cm; ms of much of Act Two (pages 9-26), 36 cm.

See: B197, 261

W92. **Minuetto**

For pedal piano. Barcelona: Llobet y Mas, n.d. Probable date of composition 1886-87.

W93. **Minuetto de la felicidad**

For piano solo. Unpublished. Cited by Iglesias and Tarazona, probably in family archive.

W94. **Moment musical, Schubert-Granados**

For piano solo. Transcription of Schubert original. Cited by Iglesias and Tarazona, probably in family archive.

W95. **Moresque y canción árabe**

For piano solo. Madrid: UME, (191-?). Probably two independent works published together; *Moresque* contains detailed expressions markings while *Canción árabe* (incomplete?) has none. *Moresque* is dedicated to the composer's mother.

W96. **Navidad. Finale**

For double quintet, wind and strings, with piano (from *La cieguecita de Belén*, see W34). At CDM: ms of full score, 31 cm; autograph score, 12 leaves, 36 cm, incomplete parts; ms copy with corrections by different hands, 14 leaves, 37 cm, flute part bears dedication of Eduardo Granados, Madrid, 1922. First (public) performance May 31, 1916, Madrid.

See: B323

W97. **Ni así la distingue**

For piano solo. Unpublished, cited by Tarazona.

W98. **La nit del mort. Poema de desolació**

For orchestra. Unpublished, unfinished. At CDM: autograph ms with corrections of orchestral score, 18 leaves, 37 cm, first 26 measures missing; ms of string parts 22 x 31 cm.

W99. **Obras fáciles para la educación del sentimiento (Andantino espresivo)**

For piano solo. Unpublished. A ms of nos. IV through VII is cited by Iglesias.

W100. **L'ocell profeta (lied)**

Voice and piano. Madrid: UME, 1972. Text by the Contessa del Castellà. Autograph ms at CDM, 2 leaves, 31 cm, with annotation "Cansons del Poeta: Lieders" (*sic*). First performance June 22, 1911, Barcelona.

W101. **Oriental (Canción variada, Intermedio y Final)**

Madrid: UME, 1973. For piano solo. Dedicated to Juan Marqués, a student.

W102. **Ornamentos**

Unpublished, incomplete pedagogical essay. Examples of mordents extracted from piano literature.

W103. **Ovillejos o La gallina ciega (Sainete lírico)**

Lyric drama. Unpublished, incomplete. Based on a drama by Feliu i Codina. At CDM: incomplete ms 69 leaves, 31 cm; libretto, 66 leaves, 23 cm.

See: B261, 263, 385

W104. **Paisaje**

For piano solo. Madrid: UME, 1913, catalogued as op. 35. Dedicated to Ernest Schelling. Ms at BOC, 8 leaves. Probable date of final revision 1912-13.

W105. **El pedal**

Unpublished. A pedagogical booklet on pedaling technique.

W106. **El pelele (Goyesca)**

New York: G. Schirmer, 1915. For piano solo. Completed 1913. Dedicated to pianist Montoriol-Tarrés. First performance, March 29, 1914, Terassa (Spain).

See: B119, 222, 326, 392

W107. **Pequeña romanza**

For string quartet. Madrid: UME, 1975.

W108. **Petrarca. Libretto, Apel.les Mestres**

Lyric drama on the poem by Mestres. Never performed, unpublished. Ms in Salabert archives, Paris. Granados may have begun sketches for the work as early as 1899.

See: B159, 179, 195, 251, 261

W109. **Picarol. Libretto, Apel.les Mestres**

Lyric drama in one act. First performance February 28, 1901, Barcelona. Ms in Salabert archives, Paris.

See: B93, 110, 159, 195, 236, 251, 261, 311

W110. **Prelude in D**

For piano solo. Score missing; however, in a letter of August 26, 1913, Granados comments on the revisions he is making in this work and his plans to send it to Schirmer.

See: B388

W111. **Preludio**

For piano solo, in F Major. Part of *Album: Paris, 1888*. See W4.

W112. **Quintet in G Minor. I. Allegro II. Allegro casi andantino III. Presto molto**

For piano and string quartet. Madrid: UME, 1973. At CDM: autograph ms of string parts with designation op. 49, annotations and corrections, and date of premiere; autograph ms of second movement, 8 leaves, 27 x 36 cm.

First performance February 15, 1895, Madrid.

W113. **Rapsodia aragonesa**

For piano solo. Madrid: UME, 1901. Ms dates from 1901.

W114. **Reverie-Improvisation**

For piano solo. Evanston, Ill.: 1967. An improvisation recorded at the Aeolian Company during Granados's 1916 visit to New York. The composer contracted to record ten of his own works on piano rolls; the technician left the recording equipment on, however, while Granados improvised. This work, *Reverie-Improvisation*, was later transcribed by International Piano Archives and *Clavier* magazine.

See: B26

W115. **Romanza**

For violin and piano. Madrid: UME (1971). Dedicated to Don Lázaro Clariana.

W116. **Romeo y Julieta**

For piano solo. Unpublished. Ms in Nathaniel Schillkret Collection, New York. At MA: arrangement for two pianos (subtitled "Poema"), 1 p, beginning only.

W117. **Rosamor**

Lyric drama, incomplete. At MA: incomplete pencil sketch (Act Three, Scene Two), piano reduction with instrumentation indications, ca. 1900; Act Three, Finale, complete orchestration, marked "para copiar," 1 p only; Act Two, Finale, incomplete, marked "para copiar"; Act Two in copyist's hand, complete score, only partially orchestrated.

W118. **Sardana**

For piano solo. New York: G. Schirmer, 1914, catalogued as op. 37. Dedicated to Ernest Schelling. Probable date of final revision 1912-13.

W119. **Serenade**

For two violins and piano. Unpublished; incomplete manuscript was completed by Glen Kirchoff, 1988. First performance April 4, 1914, Paris. Photocopy of ms in Douglas Riva Collection, New York.

See: B196

W120. **Sérénade goyesca [Goyescas (Crepúsculo)?]**

For piano solo. Score missing; however, in a letter of August 26, 1913, Granados comments on the revisions he is making in this work and his plans to send it to Schirmer.

See: B388

W121. **Serenata española**

For piano solo. Unpublished, lost. Often confused with an Albéniz work of the same name, whose title, however, is usually given in French. First performance April 20, 1890, Barcelona.

See: B64

W122. **Si al Retiro me llevas (Tonadilla)**

Madrid: UME (1971). Voice and piano. Text by "an unknown eighteenth-century author."

W123. **La sirena (Vals Mignone)**

For piano solo. Published in *La Ilustración Moderna*, Espasa, Barcelona, n.d. Douglas Riva Collection, New York. Also published in Keyboard Classics, Katonah, N.Y.: November 12, 1989, pp. 38-39.

W124. **Six Expressive Studies in the Form of Easy Pieces (Seis estudios expresivos en forma de piezas fáciles). I. Theme, variations, and finale II. Allegro moderato III. El caminante IV. Pastoral V. La última pavana VI. María**

For piano solo. Madrid: UME, (191-?). The fifth piece, *La última pavana*, is based on the poem *La condesa enferma* by Apel.les Mestres. Dedicated to María Más, a student.

W125. **Six Pieces on Spanish Folk Themes (Seis piezas sobre cantos populares españoles). I. Añoranza II. Ecos de la parranda III. Vascongada IV. Marcha oriental V. Zambra VI. Zapateado**

For piano solo. Madrid: UME, 1930. Dedicated to Doña Cecilia Gomez de Condé, daughter of Granados's patron, Eduard Condé. Probable date of composition 1888-90.

W126. **Los soldados de cartón (Marcha)**

For piano solo. Madrid: UME, 1973. Probably written for Granados's children.

W127. **Sonata**

For violin and piano. Madrid: UME (1971). Dedicated to Jacques Thibaud. Photocopy of autograph ms at CDM, 24 pp, 25 x 36 cm. Probable date of composition ca. 1910, not from Madrid period as Tarazona suggests (B304: 24).

W128. **Sonata**

For cello and piano. Unpublished, cited by Iglesias.

W129. **Sonatinas, op. 36, nos. 1-4 by Muzio Clementi. Arranged by Granados for String Trio**

Autograph ms, 8 leaves, 23 cm, at CDM. Signed and dated April 3, 1891, with the note "curso de composición del Sr. Pedrell."

W130. **Suite árabe u oriental**

For orchestra. Unpublished. Autograph ms at CDM, 34 leaves, 36 cm, signed, orchestration incomplete.

W131. **Suite on Gallician Themes (Suite sobre cantos gallegos). I. En la montaña II. Danza gallega III. Morriña IV. Final: Fiesta**

For orchestra. Madrid: UME, n.d. See also W42. Autograph ms at CDM, 4 vols of 35, 17, 12, 38 pp, 37 cm. First performance October 31, 1899, Barcelona.

W132. **Suite vasca, by Father Menesio Otaño. Arranged by Granados**

For piano solo of fourth movement, *Vuelta de la romería*. Ms at CDM, 5 leaves, 32 cm.

W133. **Symphony in E Minor**

Unpublished, incomplete. At CDM: autograph ms of first 17 measures, orchestrated, 18 leaves, 36 cm; miscellaneous autograph sketches, 15 leaves, 36 cm.

See: B109, 190

W134. **Tango of the Green Eyes (Tango de los ojos verdes)**

For piano solo, with indications for orchestral instruments. Unpublished. Sketches for orchestral score at CDM, 4 leaves, 35 cm. First performance February 10, 1916, New York.

See: B15

W135. **Three Preludes. I. La góndola II. El toque de guerra III. Elevación**

For violin and piano. Madrid: UME, 1971.

W136. **Tonadillas in Ancient Style (Tonadillas en estilo antiguo). I. Amor y odio II. Callejeo III. El majo discreto IV. El majo olvidado V. El majo tímido VI. El mirar de la maja VII. El tra la la y el punteado VIII. La maja de Goya IX. La maja dolorosa (numbers 1-3) X. Las currutacas modestas**

For voice and piano. Madrid: UME, 1912; New York: International, 1952. Mss of *La maja dolorosa* no. 2 (1 leaf) and *El majo tímido* (1 leaf) at BOC. First performance June 10, 1914, Barcelona.

See: B17, 79, 151, 222, 263, 288, 316, 319, 383

W137. **Torrijos**

For orchestra. Unpublished. Ms in Nathaniel Schillkret Collection, New York.

W138. **Triana, from Iberia. Albéniz-Granados**

For two pianos, arranged by Granados. Barcelona: Boileau, 1990. Composed 1900-10.

W139. **Trio**

For two violins and viola. Unpublished. Sketches of a slow movement at CDM, 14 pp, 31 cm.

W140. **Trio I. Poco allegro con espressione II. Scherzetto. Vivace molto III. Duetto. Andante con molta espressione IV. Finale. Allegro molto**

For violin, cello, and piano. Madrid: UME n.d., catalogued as op. 50. Ms cited by Iglesias, dated January 2, 1894. First performance February 15, 1895, Madrid.

W141. **Trova**

Arrangement for cello and piano of second movement of the orchestral suite *Elisenda*. See W50. Unpublished. First performance May 2, 1915, Barcelona; New York premiere January 23, 1916.

W142. **Twelve Spanish Dances (Doce danzas españolas). I. Galante II. Orientale III. Fandango IV. Villanesca V. Andaluza (or Playera) VI. Rondalla aragonesa VII. Valenciana (or Calesera) VIII. Sardana IX. Romántica X. Melancólica XI. Arabesca XII. Bolero**

For piano solo. Madrid: UME, 196-?; New York: International, 1973. (Many of the dances were published separately by Casa Dotesio, Barcelona in the early 1890s.) Include dedications to César Cui, Amparo Gal, Julián Martí, Joaquín Vancells, T. Tasso, Alfredo Faria, D. Murillo. Mss of Dances 7 (7 leaves), 8 (7 leaves), 9 (9 leaves), 11 (4 leaves) at BOC. Probable date of composition 1888-90.

First performance April 20, 1890, Barcelona.

See: B64, 94, 151, 227, 265, 388

W143. **Twenty-six Sonatas by Domenico Scarlatti**

Barcelona: Llimona y Vidal, 1905; Madrid: UME, 1967. In two volumes. Foreword by Felip Pedrell. Transcription for piano solo of (Kirkpatrick) 520, 521, 522, 518, 541, 540, 102, 546, 190, 110, 534, 535, 553, 555, 554, 547, 109, 209, 552, 537, 528, 139, 48, 536.

First performance March 1, 1906, Barcelona.

See: B25, 31, 55, 95, 153-54, 228

W144. **Two Impromptus (Dos impromptus). I. Vivo e appassionato II. Impromptu de la codorniz**

For piano solo. Madrid: UME, 1912.

W145. **Two Military Marches (Dos marchas militares). I. Allegretto II. Lento marciale**

For piano duet. Madrid: UME, 1979; Barcelona: Casa Dotesio, 1910.

See: B78

W146. **Valse de concert**

For piano solo. New York: G. Schirmer, 1914, catalogued as op. 35. Dedicated to Mario Calado.

See: B388

W147. **Valses poéticos. Introduction: Vivace molto I. Melódico II. Tempo de Vals noble III. Tempo de Vals lento IV. Allegro humorístico V. Allegretto (Elegante) VI. Quasi ad libitum (Sentimental) VII. Vivo. Presto**

For piano solo. Madrid: UME, 191-?. Dedicated to Joaquím Malats. Probable date of composition 1886-87, although 1893 is often given. First (public) performance February 15, 1895, Madrid; first Barcelona performance December 4, 1899.

See: B10, 105, 332

SELECTED ARRANGEMENTS OF GRANADOS'S WORKS

A1. **A tiempo romántico**

Orchestration of the *Valses poéticos* (W147) by Rafael Ferrer. Madrid: UME, n.d. Ballet commissioned by the Amigos de Granados in 1956 for the fiftieth anniversary of the composer's death.

A2. **Andalucia**

"Sur les motifs de la danse [of *Twelve Spanish Dances*] no. 5/paroles de René Rouzard." Ms at CDM, 1 p, 32 cm, vocal part only; another ms copy, entitled "Andalouse," at BOC, 12 leaves.

A3. **Andaluza**

Vocal transcription of *Spanish Dance* no. 5 (W142), with piano accompaniment. Madrid: UME, n.d. Text by Luis Muñoz Lorente. Later orchestrated, also an Italian translation.

A4. **Canciones amatorias. I. No lloréis ojuelos II. Mañanica era III. Descúbrase el pensamiento de mi secreto cuidado IV. Iban al pinar V. Llorad, corazón VI. Mira que soy niña VII. Gracia mía**

Orchestration and reordering by Rafael Ferrer of the piano/vocal set. Madrid: UME, n.d. See W24.

A5. **Danza aragonesa**

Orchestration by Rafael Ferrer of the second of the *Deux danses caractéristiques* (W45). Madrid: UME, 1961.

A6. **Dedicatoria (Cuentos de la juventud)**

For guitar (W39), arranged by Miquel Llobet. UME: n.d.

A7. **Five Pieces on Spanish Folk Themes (Cinco piezas sobre cantos populares españoles). I. Añoranza II. Ecos de la parranda III. Zapateado IV. Zambra V. Miel de la Alcarria**

Orchestration of selected *Seis piezas sobre cantos populares españoles* (W125) with *Miel de la Alcarria* (W91) by Rafael Ferrer. Madrid: UME n.d.

A8. **Intermezzo (Goyescas)**

For cello and piano, arranged by Gaspar Cassadó. New York: G. Schirmer, 1923. Ms at CDM, 36 cm. See W71.

A9. **La maja de Goya (Tonadillas)**

For guitar, arranged by Miquel Llobet. Madrid: UME, 1958. See W136.

A10. **Marche Militaire no. 4**

The fourth of an incomplete set of military marches arranged for band by Emilio Vega. Ms at CDM, 13 leaves, 36 cm, ms is possibly in Vega's hand, dated Valencia, July 1908. See W82, W145.

A11. **El pelele**

For two pianos, arranged by Frederic Llongás. New York: Schirmer, 1915. See W106.

A12. **Spanish Dance no. 2**

For cello (or viola) and piano, arranged by Milton Kamins. New York: International, 1945. See W142.

A13. **Spanish Dance no. 5**

Arranged for violin and piano by Fritz Kreisler. New York: Carl Fischer, 1915. See W142.

A14. **Spanish Dances nos. 6 and 10**

Arranged for two guitars by Miquel Llobet. Madrid: UME, 1964. See W142.

A15. **Spanish Dances nos. 2, 5, 6**

By Joan Lamote de Grignon. Madrid: UME, n.d. Also a ms at CDM, 37 cm, four orchestra parts. See W142.

See: B107

A16. **Spanish Dance no. 7**

Orchestration in incomplete ms at CDM, 38 pp, 37 cm, in two different hands.

A17. **Tonadillas in Ancient Style (Tonadillas en estilo antiguo).**
I. Callejeo II. El mirar de la maja III. El tra la la y el punteado IV. La maja dolorosa (numbers 1-3) V. El majo discreto VI. Amor y odio VII. El majo tímido

Orchestration by Rafael Ferrer of the piano-vocal score. See W136. Madrid: UME, n.d.

SPURIOUS:

Two Gavottes (Dos Gavotas)

Although published by UME (Madrid, 1973) under Granados's name, these two gavottes are in fact the composer's copy of the two gavottes from J.S. Bach's English Suite in D Minor, BWV 811. This rather grave publisher's error has escaped the notice of several biographers.

Note

Shortly before this study went to press, Douglas Riva was kind enough to inform me of a *Salve regina* for four voices and organ in manuscript (4 pp) in the family archive, dated March 13, 1896. No reference to this *Salve regina* appears in any other source.

4
Discography

D1. **A la cubana**
CRD-1035
Thomas Rajna, piano
Includes his *Aparición*; *Cartas de amor*; *Danza característica*; *Escenas poéticas* (second series); *Quintet in G Minor* (with the Alberti Quartet)
See: W2

D2. **A la cubana**
EDISON BELL 4995
(arranged for orchestra)
Ernest Newman, conductor; orchestra unidentified
Includes his *Marche militaire*
See: W2

D3. **A la pradera**
CRD-1036
Thomas Rajna, piano
Includes his *Moresque y canción árabe*; *Cuentos de la juventud*; *Sardana*; *Bocetos*; *Mazurka (alla polacca)*; *Barcarola*; *Los soldados de cartón*
See: W3

D4. **A la pradera**
Volume 2 of two-volume set, VOX 5484/5
Marylène Dosse, piano
See: W3

D5. **Allegro appassionato**
GRAMOFONO-BARCELONA-AB-602
Several biographers refer to this recording as the only extant example of this piece, whose manuscript is lost.
Performer unidentified
See: W5

D6. **Allegro de concierto**
ADES-OR (HARMONIA MUNDI) 13.207
Rafael Arroyo, piano
Includes his *La maja y el ruiseñor*; works by Albéniz, Falla, Turina
See: W6

D7. **Allegro de concierto**
LONDON 410288-1LH
Alicia de Larrocha, piano
Includes his *Six Pieces on Spanish Folk Themes (Seis piezas sobre cantos populares españoles)*; *Escenas románticas*
See: W6

D8. **Allegro de concierto**
VOX/TURNABOUT 34772
Alicia de Larrocha, piano
Includes his *Valses poéticos*; *Danza lenta*; *El pelele*; *Six Pieces on Spanish Folk Themes (Seis piezas sobre cantos populares españoles)*
See: W6

D9. **Allegro de concierto**
Volume 1 of two-volume set, VOX 5484/5
Marylène Dosse, piano
See: W6

D10. **Allegro de concierto**
BELTER 70915
José Falgarona, piano
Includes his *Spanish Dances 5, 9*; *El pelele*; *Quejas, o La maja y el ruiseñor*
See: W6

D11. **Allegro de concierto**
ANGEL RL-32123 (previously released as S-35628)
José Iturbi, piano
Includes his *Spanish Dances 5, 10, 12*; works by Albéniz
See: W6

D12. **Allegro de concierto**
ASLKAGER CD87024
Dana Protopopesca, piano
Includes his *Valses poéticos*; *Oriental (Canción variada, Intermedio y Final)*; *Capricho español*; *Six Pieces on Spanish Folk Themes (Seis piezas sobre cantos populares españoles)*
See: W6

D13. **Allegro de concierto**
CRD 1023
Thomas Rajna, piano
Includes his *Capricho español*; *Carezza (Valse)*; *Two Impromptus*; *Orientale (Canción variada, Intermedio y Final)*; *Rapsodia aragonesa*; *Valses poéticos*
See: W6

D14. **Allegro de concierto**
BIS 23
Liselotte Weiss, piano
Includes works by Berg, Honegger, Ravel, Schoenberg
See: W6

D15. **Allegro vivace**
CENTAUR CRC 2043
The Unknown Granados
Douglas Riva, piano
Includes his *Azulejos*; *En la aldea*; *Mazurka in E-flat Major*; *Mazurka in E-flat Minor ("Chopin")*; *Romanza*; *Vals*; *Primavera* (*Romanza sin palabras*); *Serenade for Two Violins and Piano*; *Conte*; *Preludio*
See: W7

D16. **Aparición**
Volume 1 of two-volume set, VOX 5484/5
Marylène Dosse, piano
See: W10

D17. **Aparición**
CRD-1035
Thomas Rajna, piano
Includes his *A la cubana*; *Cartas de amor*; *Danza característica*; *Escenas poéticas* (second series); *Quintet in G Minor* (with the Alberti Quartet)
See: W10

D18. **Azulejos**
CENTAUR CRC 2043
The Unknown Granados
Douglas Riva, piano
Includes his *Romanza*; *En la aldea*; *Mazurka in E-flat Major*; *Mazurka in E-flat Minor ("Chopin")*; *Conte*; *Vals*; *Primavera* (*Romanza sin palabras*); *Allegro vivace*; *Serenade for Two Violins and Piano*; *Preludio*
See: W12

D19. **Barcarola**
Volume 1 of two-volume set, VOX 5484/5
Marylène Dosse, piano
See: W14

D20. **Barcarola**
CRD-1036
Thomas Rajna, piano
Includes his *Moresque y canción árabe*; *Cuentos de la juventud*; *Sardana*; *Bocetos*; *Mazurka (alla polacca)*; *Los soldados de cartón*; *A la pradera*
See: W14

D21. **Bocetos**
Volume 1 of two-volume set, VOX 5484/5
Marylène Dosse, piano
See: W16

D22. **Bocetos**
CRD-1036
Thomas Rajna, piano
Includes his *Moresque y canción árabe*; *Cuentos de la juventud*; *Sardana*; *Mazurka (alla polacca)*; *Barcarola*; *Los soldados de cartón*; *A la pradera*
See: W16

D23. **Canciones amatorias**
EVEREST 3237
Conchita Badia, soprano; Alicia de Larrocha, piano
(Homage to Granados)
Includes his *Tonadillas*
See: W24

D24. **Canciones amatorias**
LONDON 26558
Pilar Lorengar, soprano; Alicia de Larrocha, piano
Includes his *Tonadillas*
See: W24

D25. **Canciones amatorias**
RCA LSC 2910-B
(orchestrated by Rafael Ferrer)
Montserrat Caballé, soprano; Rafael Ferrer, conductor; Symphony Orchestra
Includes his *Tonadillas*
See: A4

D26. **Canciones amatorias: Iban al pinar**
ANGEL S-35937
(orchestrated by Rafael Ferrer)
Victoria de los Angeles; Rafael Frübeck de Burgos, conductor; Paris Conservatory Orchestra
Includes his *Llorad corazón*; works by Montsalvatge, Rodrigo, Esplá, Falla
See: A4

D27. **Canciones amatorias: Iban al pinar**
MERIDIAN CDE-84134
(orchestrated by Rafael Ferrer)
Yannula Pappas, mezzo-soprano; Gershom Stern, conductor; Israel Symphony
Includes his *Mañanica era*; *Llorad corazón*; *Mira que soy niña*; works by Esplá, Montsalvatge, Turina
See: A4

D28. **Canciones amatorias: Llorad corazón**
ANGEL 35937
(orchestrated by Rafael Ferrer)
Victoria de los Angeles, soprano; Rafael Frühbeck de Burgos, conductor; Paris Conservatory Orchestra
Includes his *Iban al pinar*; works by Montsalvatge, Rodrigo, Esplá, Falla
See: A4

D29. **Canciones amatorias: Llorad corazón**
MERIDIAN CDE-84134
(orchestrated by Rafael Ferrer)
Yannula Pappas, mezzo-soprano; Gershom Stern, conductor; Israel Symphony
Includes his *Mañanica era*; *Mira que soy niña*; *Iban al pinar*; works by Esplá, Montsalvatge, Turina
See: A4

D30. **Canciones amatorias: Mañanica era**
MERIDIAN CDE-84134
(orchestrated by Rafael Ferrer)
Yannula Pappas, mezzo-soprano; Gershom Stern, conductor; Israel Symphony
Includes his *Llorad corazón*; *Mira que soy niña*; *Iban al pinar*; works by Esplá, Montsalvatge, Turina
See: A4

D31. **Canciones amatorias: Mira que soy niña**
MERIDIAN CDE-84134
(orchestrated by Rafael Ferrer)
Yannula Pappas, mezzo-soprano; Gershom Stern, conductor; Israel Symphony
Includes his *Mañanica era*; *Llorad corazón*; *Iban al pinar*; works by Esplá, Montsalvatge, Turina
See: A4

D32. **Canciones amatorias: No lloréis ojuelos**
EMI EX290946-3 (previously released as OD. 195073)
Ninon Vallin, soprano
Includes his *El majo discreto*; works by Nin, Falla
See: A4 [W24?]

D33. **Canso d'amor**
LONDON OS 26575
Montserrat Caballé, soprano; Miguel Zanetti, piano
Includes his *La maja y el ruiseñor* (*Goyescas*, Act III); *Elegía eterna*; *L'ocell profeta*; works by Falla, Turina
See: W25

D34. **Canto gitano**
CONNAISSEUR MUSIK 394
(for voice and piano)
Anne-Marie Mühle, contralto
See: W29

D35. **Capricho español**
Volume 1 of two-volume set, VOX 5484/5
Marylène Dosse, piano
See: W30

D36. **Capricho español**
ASLKAGER CD87024
Dana Protopopesca, piano
Includes his *Allegro de concierto*; *Valses poéticos*; *Oriental* (*Canción variada, Intermedio y Final*); *Six Pieces on Spanish Folk Themes* (*Seis piezas sobre cantos populares españoles*)
See: W30

D37. **Capricho español**
CRD 1023
Thomas Rajna, piano
Includes his *Allegro de concierto*; *Carezza* (*Valse*); *Two Impromptus*; *Oriental* (*Canción variada, Intermedio y Final*); *Rapsodia aragonesa*; *Valses poéticos*
See: W30

D38. **Capricho español**
CALLIOPE 9204
(arranged for two guitars)
Jean Horreaux; Jean-Marie Trehaud, guitars
Includes his *Spanish Dances 2, 4, 11, 12*; *Serenata del espectro*; *Valses poéticos*; *Deux danses caracteristiques*; *La maja de Goya*
See: W30

D39. **Carezza (Valse)**
Volume 2 of two-volume set, VOX 5484/5
Marylène Dosse, piano
See: W31

D40. **Carezza (Valse)**
CRD 1023
Thomas Rajna, piano
Includes his *Allegro de concierto*; *Capricho español*; *Two Impromptus*; *Oriental* (*Canción variada, Intermedio y Final*); *Rapsodia aragonesa*; *Valses poéticos*
See: W31

D41. **Cartas de amor**
Volume 2 of two-volume set, VOX 5484/5
Marylène Dosse, piano
See: W32

D42. **Cartas de amor**
CRD-1035
Thomas Rajna, piano
Includes his *A la cubana*; *Aparición*; *Danza característica*; *Escenas poéticas* (second series), *Quintet in G Minor* (with the Alberti Quartet)
See: W32

D43. **Conte**
CENTAUR CRC 2043
The Unknown Granados
Douglas Riva, piano
Includes his *Allegro vivace*; *Azulejos*; *En la aldea*; *Mazurka in E-flat Major*; *Mazurka in E-flat Minor ("Chopin")*; *Romanza*; *Primavera* (*Romanza sin palabras*); *Vals*; *Serenade for Two Violins and Piano*; *Preludio*
See: W4

D44. **Cuentos de la juventud**
Volume 1 of two-volume set, VOX 5484/5
Marylène Dosse, piano
See: W39

D45. **Cuentos de la juventud**
CRD-1036
Thomas Rajna, piano
Includes his *Moresque y canción árabe*; *Sardana*; *Bocetos*; *Mazurka* (*alla polacca*); *Barcarola*; *Los soldados de cartón*; *A la pradera*
See: W39

D46. **Cuentos de la juventud: La huérfana**
COLUMBIA 3168X
(arranged for solo guitar)
Vicente Gómez, guitar
Includes his *Spanish Dance 5*
See: W39

D47. **Dante, or La Divina Commedia**
LOUISVILLE 713
Mary Lee Maull, soprano; Jorge Mester, conductor; Louisville Symphony
Includes works by Chávez
See: W40

D48. **Danza característica**
CRD-1035
Thomas Rajna, piano
Includes his *A la cubana*; *Aparición*; *Cartas de amor*; *Escenas poéticas* (second series); *Quintet in G Minor* (with the Alberti Quartet)
See: W41

D49. **Danza lenta**
VOX/TURNABOUT 34772
Alicia de Larrocha, piano
Includes his *Valses poéticos*; *Allegro de concierto*; *El pelele*; *Six Pieces on Spanish Folk Themes (Seis piezas sobre cantos populares españoles)*
See: W44

D50. **Danza lenta**
Volume 1 of two-volume set, VOX 5484/5
Marylène Dosse, piano
See: W44

D51. **Danza lenta**
CRD-1022
Thomas Rajna, piano
Includes his *Escenas románticas*; *Six Pieces on Spanish Folk Themes (Seis piezas sobre cantos populares españoles)*
See: W44

D52. **Dedicatoria**
RCA RCD1-4378
(arranged for guitar by Miguel Llobet)
Julian Bream, guitar
Includes his *La maja de Goya*; *Valses poéticos*; *Spanish Dances 4, 5*; works by Albéniz
See: A6

D53. **Deux danses caracteristiques**
CALLIOPE 9204
(arranged for two guitars)
Jean Horreaux; Jean-Marie Trehaud, guitars
Includes his *Spanish Dances 2, 4, 11, 12*, *Capricho español*; *Serenata del espectro*; *Valses poéticos*; *La maja de Goya*
See: W45

D54. **Elegía eterna**
LONDON OS 26575
Montserrat Caballé, soprano; Miguel Zanetti, piano
Includes his *La maja y el ruiseñor* (*Goyescas*, Act III); *Canso d'amor*; *L'ocell profeta*; works by Falla, Turina
See: W49

D55. **Elegía eterna**
ORFEO A 038 831
Margaret Price, soprano; James Lockhart, piano
Includes his *Tonadillas*; *El majo tímido*; *El tra la la y el punteado*; *La maja dolorosa* (1-3), *El majo discreto*
See: W49

D56. **Elisenda (El jardí d'Elisenda)**
CRC-1037
Thomas Rajna, piano
Includes his *Impromptu, op. 39*; *Six Expressive Studies* (*Seis estudios expresivos*); *Marche militaire*; *Estudio op. Posthumous* (*Andantino espressivo*); *Paisaje*; *Two Military Marches*
See: W75

D57. **En la aldea**
CENTAUR CRC 2043
The Unknown Granados
Douglas Riva; Glen Kirchoff, piano duet
Includes his *Allegro vivace*; *Azulejos*; *Mazurka in E-flat Major*; *Mazurka in E-flat Minor* (*"Chopin"*); *Preludio*; *Vals*, *Romanza*, *Serenade for Two Violins and Piano*, *Conte*, *Primavera* (*Romanza sin palabras*)
See: W52

D58. **Escenas poéticas (first, second series)**
Volume 2 of two-volume set, VOX 5484/5
Marylène Dosse, piano
See: W55, 56

D59. **Escenas poéticas (first series)**
2-CRD 4001/2
Thomas Rajna, piano
Includes his *Libro de horas*; *Goyescas* (Book Two)
See: W55

D60. **Escenas poéticas (second series)**
CRD-1035
Thomas Rajna, piano
Includes his *A la cubana*; *Aparición*; *Cartas de amor*; *Danza característica*; *Quintet in G Minor* (with the Alberti Quartet)
See: W56

D61. **Escenas románticas**
LONDON 410288-1LH
Alicia de Larrocha, piano
Includes his *Allegro de concierto*; *Six Pieces on Spanish Folk Themes* (*Seis piezas sobre cantos populares españoles*)
See: W57

D62. **Escenas románticas**
Volume 2 of two-volume set, VOX 5484/5
Marylène Dosse, piano
See: W57

D63. **Escenas románticas**
CRD-1022
Thomas Rajna, piano
Includes his *Danza lenta*; *Six Pieces on Spanish Folk Themes* (*Seis piezas sobre cantos populares españoles*)
See: W57

D64. **Estudio op. posthumous (Andantino espressivo)**
Volume 1 of two-volume set, VOX 5484/5
Marylène Dosse, piano
See: W58

D65. **Estudio op. posthumous (Andantino espressivo)**
CRC-1037
Thomas Rajna, piano
Includes his *Impromptu, op. 39*; *Six Expressive Studies* (*Seis estudios expresivos*); *Marche militaire*; *Elisenda*; *Paisaje*; *Two Military Marches*
See: W58

D66. **Goyescas: Intermezzo**
COLUMBIA 12547
Enrique Fernández Arbós, conductor; Madrid Symphony
Includes his *Spanish Dance 6*; Albéniz, "El puerto"
See: W71

D67. **Goyescas: Intermezzo**
CAPELLA SMK 73957
Carmen Dragon, conductor; Hollywood Bowl Symphony Orchestra
See: W71

D68. **Goyescas: Intermezzo**
RCA VL 42 061
Arthur Fiedler, conductor; Boston Pops Orchestra
See: W71

D69. **Goyescas: Intermezzo**
DECCA JUBILEE JB 50 (previously released as DECCA SXL 6287)
Rafael Frühbeck de Burgos, conductor; New Philharmonia Orchestra
Includes works by Falla, Ravel
See: W71

D70. **Goyescas: Intermezzo**
VCD-47209
Morton Gould, conductor; London Symphony
Includes works by Ginastera, Ravel, Shostakovich, Turina
See: W71

D71. **Goyescas: Intermezzo**
EMI 037-00 422
Herbert von Karajan, conductor; London Philharmonic
See: W71

D72. **Goyescas: Intermezzo**
PHILIPS LY 839775
Igor Markevitch, conductor; Spanish Radio Orchestra
Includes his *Spanish Dances 8, 9*; *Zapateado* (*Five Pieces on Spanish Folk Themes*)
See: W71

D73. **Goyescas: Intermezzo**
CHESKY RC-9 (previously released as RCA AGL1-1332)
Fritz Reiner, conductor; Chicago Symphony
Includes works by Albéniz, Falla
See: W71

D74. **Goyescas: Intermezzo**
HIS MASTER'S VOICE 6915
Leopold Stokowski, conductor; Philadelphia Symphony
Includes works by Sensemaya
See: W71

D75. **Goyescas: Intermezzo**
LM 2699 RCA Victor
(arranged for cello and piano by Gaspar Cassadó)
Pablo Casals, cello; Nicolai Mednikoff, piano
Includes works by Fauré, (Anton) Rubinstein, Schubert
See: A8

D76. **Goyescas: Intermezzo**
ANGEL 35599
(arranged for cello and piano by Gaspar Cassadó)
Pierre Fournier, cello; Gerald Moore, piano
See: A8

D77. **Goyescas: Intermezzo**
CALLIOPE CAL-9673
(arranged for cello and piano by Gaspar Cassadó)
André Navarra, cello; Erika Kilcher, piano
Includes works by Boccherini, Falla, Locatelli, Nin
See: A8

D78. **Goyescas: Intermezzo**
ODEON 123849
(arranged for cello and piano by Gaspar Cassadó)
André Navarra, cello
Includes his *Spanish Dance 6*
See: A8

D79. **Goyescas: Intermezzo**
PERIOD/NIXA SPL584
(arranged for cello and piano by Gaspar Cassadó)
Janos Starker, cello; Leon Pommers, piano
See: A8

D80. **Goyescas: Intermezzo**
RCA LSC 3257
(arranged for two guitars by Emilio Pujol)
Julian Bream; John Williams, guitars
See: W71

D81. **Goyescas: Intermezzo**
LONDON LS-1187
(arranged for saxophone and piano)
Marcel Mulé, saxophone
Includes works by Debussy, Ibert (Paris Philharmonic), Dubois, Lazarus, Lautier
See: W71

D82. **Goyescas: Intermezzo**
HIS MASTER'S VOICE 602
(arranged for piano, violin, and cello)
Barcelona Trio
Includes his *Trio, op. 50* (first movement)
See: W71

D83. **Goyescas: Intermezzo**
MMG 1146
(arranged for flute, oboe, and guitar)
Trio Sonata
Includes his *Spanish Dance 2*, works by Bach, Villa-Lobos, Wool-ridge, Tompkins, Bender
See: W71

D84. **Goyescas: Opera**
COLUMBIA WL 71322
Ataulfo Argenta, conductor; Orquesta Nacional de España and Coros Cantores de Madrid. With Consuelo Rubio, Ana Maria Iriarte, Manuel Ausens, Gines Torrano
See: W65

D85. **Goyescas (Act III) La maja y el ruiseñor**
LONDON OS 26575
Montserrat Caballé, soprano; Miguel Zanetti, piano
Includes his *L'ocell profeta*; *Elegia eterna*; *Canso d'amor*; works by Falla, Turina
See: W65

D86. **Goyescas: Suite for piano**
RCA RL/RK 35301
Joaquín Achúcarro, piano
Includes his *El pelele*
See: W64

D87. **Goyescas: Suite for piano**
SERAPHIM S-60178
Aldo Ciccolini, piano
See: W64

D88. **Goyescas: Suite for piano**
LONDON 411958-2
Alicia de Larrocha, piano
Includes his *Allegro de concierto*; works by Albéniz, Falla, and Turina
See: W64

D89. **Goyescas: Suite for piano**
LONDON CS/5-7009
Alicia de Larrocha, piano
Includes his *El pelele*
See: W64

D90. **Goyescas: Suite for piano**
LONDON 411958-2 LH
Alicia de Larrocha, piano
See: W64

D91. **Goyescas: Suite for piano**
ERATO DUE 20234
Alicia de Larrocha, piano
See: W64

D92. **Goyescas: Suite for piano (Book Two)**
DECCA DL 9815
Alicia de Larrocha, piano
Includes works by Mompou
See: W64

D93. **Goyescas: Suite for piano**
EPIC LC-3444
Eduardo del Pueyo, piano
Includes his *El pelele*
See: W64

D94. **Goyescas: Suite for piano**
VOX CT-2144 (previously released as VOX 5484/5)
Marylène Dosse, piano
See: W64

D95. **Goyescas: Suite for piano**
WESTMINSTER WLP 5322
José Echániz, piano
See: W64

D96. **Goyescas: Suite for piano**
VOX PL 8580
José Falgarona, piano
See: W64

D97. **Goyescas: Suite for piano (Book One)**
The Welte Legacy of Piano Treasures 669 B11225
Enrique Granados, piano
Includes his *Pièce de Scarlatti* (Scarlatti-Granados); *Spanish Dance 5*; works by Falla
See: W64

D98. **Goyescas: Suite for piano**
RCA VICTOR LM-1925
Amparo Iturbi, piano
See: W64

D99. **Goyescas: Suite for piano**
VOX/TURNABOUT 34247
Rena Kyriakou, piano
See: W64

D100. **Goyescas: Suite for piano**
EMI LZ762523-4
Moura Lympany, piano
See: W64

D101. **Goyescas: Suite for piano**
LONDON LL-954
Nikita Magaloff, piano
See: W64

D102. **Goyescas: Suite for piano**
CLASSICS FOR PLEASURE 4514
John Ogdon, piano
See: W64

D103. **Goyescas: Suite for piano**
TELEFUNKEN TLA-20002
Leopoldo Querol, piano
See: W64

D104. **Goyescas: Suite for piano**
2-CRD 4001/1, 4001/2
Thomas Rajna, piano.
Volume 1 includes his *El pelele*; Volume 2 includes his *Escenas poéticas* (first series); *Libro de horas*
See: W64

D105. **Goyescas: Suite for piano**
HARMONIA MUNDI HM 10032
Eulalia Solé
See: W64

D106. **Goyescas: Suite for piano (Book One)**
REMINGTON R-199-116
Frieda Valenzi, piano
See: W64

D107. **Goyescas: Suite for Piano**
El fandango de candil
COLUMBIA ML4294 (Historical reissue)
Enrique Granados, piano
Includes his *Valses poéticos*; performances by Albéniz, Marshall, de Pachman, Paderewski
See: W64

D108. **Goyescas: Suite for Piano**
El fandango de candil
POLARA CS59876
Kendall Ross Bean, piano
Includes his *Los requiebros*; *Quejas, o La maja y el ruiseñor*; works by Chopin
See: W64

D109. **Goyescas: Suite for Piano**
Quejas, o La maja y el ruiseñor
ADES-OR (HARMONIA MUNDI) 13.207
Rafael Arroyo, piano
Includes his *Allegro de concierto*; works by Albéniz, Falla, Turina
See: W64

D110. **Goyescas: Suite for Piano**
Quejas, o La maja y el ruiseñor
RCA VICTOR 11562
José Iturbi, piano
See: W64

D111. **Goyescas: Suite for Piano**
Quejas, o La maja y el ruiseñor
POLARA CS59876
Kendall Ross Bean, piano
Includes his *Los requiebros*; *El fandango de candil*; works by Chopin
See: W64

D112. **Goyescas: Suite for Piano**
Quejas, o La maja y el ruiseñor
BELTER 70915
José Falgarona, piano
Includes his *Spanish Dances 5, 9*; *El pelele*; *Allegro de concierto*
See: W64

D113. **Goyescas: Suite for Piano**
Quejas, o La maja y el ruiseñor
EVEREST X-909
Enrique Granados, piano
Includes his *Improvisation*; *El pelele*; *Prelude to María del Carmen*; *Reverie-Improvisation*; *Spanish Dances 1, 2, 5, 7, 10*
See: W64

D114. **Goyescas: Suite for Piano**
Quejas, o La maja y el ruiseñor
EMI CDH 7 63787 2
Dame Myra Hess, piano
Includes works by Scarlatti, Beethoven, Mendelssohn, Brahms, Bach-Hess
See: W64

D115. **Goyescas: Suite for Piano**
Quejas, o La maja y el ruiseñor
CENTAUR CRC-2026
Pierre Huybregts, piano
Includes his *Spanish Dance 5*; works by Albéniz, Halffter, Mompou, Turina
See: W64

D116. **Goyescas: Suite for Piano**
Quejas, o La maja y el ruiseñor
VOX/TURNABOUT STV 34372
Beatriz Klein, piano
Includes his *Spanish Dances 1-3, 5*; other Spanish piano music
See: W64

D117. **Goyescas: Suite for Piano**
Quejas, o La maja y el ruiseñor
ALLEGRO 3151
Emilio Osta, piano
Includes works by Albéniz, Soler, Falla, Turina
See: W64

D118. **Goyescas: Suite for Piano**
Quejas, o La maja y el ruiseñor
DELOS DCD-3030
Carol Rosenberger, piano
Includes works by Chopin, Debussy, Fauré, Griffes, Liszt
See: W64

D119. **Goyescas: Suite for Piano**
Quejas, o La maja y el ruiseñor
EMI 027-143555 (was RCA VICTOR 7403)
Artur Rubinstein, piano
RCA disc includes Chopin (Mazurka)
See: W64

D120. **Goyescas: Suite for Piano**
Quejas, o La maja y el ruiseñor
LONDON CS 6202
Gonzalez Soriano, piano
Includes works by Turina, (Ernesto) Halffter
See: W64

D121. **Goyescas: Suite for Piano**
Quejas, o La maja y el ruiseñor
C. DX 1476
(arranged for two pianos by the performers)
Ethel Bartlett; Rae Robertson, pianos
See: W64

D122. **Goyescas: Suite for Piano**
Quejas, o La maja y el ruiseñor
HIS MASTER'S VOICE (SPAIN) 564
(arranged for castanets and orchestra)
Pilar Lopez, castanets; orchestra unidentified
See: W64

D123. **Goyescas: Suite for Piano**
Quejas, o La maja y el ruiseñor
SPANISH COLUMBIA 5254
(arranged for voice, Spanish text)
La Argentina, soprano
See: W64

D124. **Goyescas: Los requiebros**
POLARA CS59876
Kendall Ross Bean, piano
Includes his *La maja y el ruiseñor*; *El fandango de candil*; works by Chopin
See: W64

D125. **Goyescas: Los requiebros**
TELEFUNKEN WE 28000
Enrique Granados, piano
Includes works by Debussy (performed by Debussy)
See: W64

D126. **Goyescas: Serenata del espectro**
CALLIOPE 9204
(arranged for two guitars)
Jean Horreaux; Jean-Marie Trehaud, guitars
Includes his *Spanish Dances 2, 4, 11, 12*; *Capricho español*; *Valses poéticos*; *Deux danses caracteristiques*; *La maja de Goya*
See: W64

D127. **Impromptu, op. 39**
CRC-1037
Thomas Rajna, piano
Includes his *Six Expressive Studies (Seis estudios expresivos)*; *Marche militaire*; *Estudio op. Posthumous (Andantino espressivo)*; *Elisenda*; *Paisaje*; *Two Military Marches*
See: W69

D128. **Improvisation**
EVEREST X-909
Enrique Granados, piano
Includes his *Reverie-Improvisation*; *Prelude to María del Carmen*; *El pelele*; *Quejas, o La maja y el ruiseñor*; *Spanish Dances 1, 2, 5, 7, 10*

D129. **Libro de horas: En el jardín, El invierno, Al suplicio**
Volume 2 of two-volume set, VOX 5484/5
Marylène Dosse, piano
See: W77

D130. **Libro de horas: En el jardín, El invierno, Al suplicio**
CRD 4001/2
Thomas Rajna, piano
Includes his *Escenas poéticas* (first series); *Goyescas* (Book Two)
See: W77

D131. **Marche militaire**
CRC-1037
Thomas Rajna, piano
Includes his *Impromptu, op. 39*; *Six Expressive Studies (Seis estudios expresivos)*; *Estudio op. Posthumous (Andantino espressivo)*; *Elisenda*; *Paisaje*; *Two Military Marches*
See: W82

D132. **Marche militaire**
EDISON BELL 4995
(arranged for orchestra)
Ernest Newman, conductor; orchestra unidentified
Includes his *A la cubana*
See: W82

D133. **Mazurka (alla polacca)**
CRD-1036
Thomas Rajna, piano
Includes his *Moresque y canción árabe*; *Cuentos de la juventud*; *Sardana*; *Bocetos*; *Barcarola*; *Los soldados de cartón*; *A la pradera*
See: W85

D134. **Mazurka in E-flat Major**
CENTAUR CRC 2043
The Unknown Granados
Douglas Riva, piano
Includes his *Allegro vivace*; *Azulejos*; *En la aldea*; *Vals*; *Romanza*; *Mazurka in E-flat Minor ("Chopin")*; *Preludio*; *Conte*; *Serenade for Two Violins and Piano*; *Primavera (Romanza sin palabras)*
See: W4

D135. **Mazurka in E-flat Minor ("Chopin")**
CENTAUR CRC 2043
The Unknown Granados
Douglas Riva, piano
Includes his *Allegro vivace*; *Azulejos*; *En la aldea*; *Vals*; *Romanza*; *Mazurka in E-flat Major*; *Preludio*; *Conte*; *Serenade for Two Violins and Piano*; *Primavera (Romanza sin palabras)*
See: W4

D136. **Moresque y canción árabe**
Volume 2 of two-volume set, VOX 5484/5
Marylène Dosse, piano
See: W95

D137. **Moresque y canción árabe**
CRD-1036
Thomas Rajna, piano
Includes his *Cuentos de la juventud*; *Sardana*; *Bocetos*; *Mazurka (alla polacca)*; *Barcarola*; *Los soldados de cartón*; *A la pradera*
See: W95

D138. **L'ocell profeta**
LONDON OS 26575
Montserrat Caballé, soprano; Miguel Zanetti, piano
Includes his *La maja y el ruiseñor* (*Goyescas*, Act III); *Elegía eterna*; *Canso d'amor*; works by Falla, Turina
See: W100

D139. **Oriental (Canción variada, Intermedio y Final)**
ASLKAGER CD87024
Dana Protopopesca, piano
Includes his *Allegro de concierto*; *Valses poéticos*; *Capricho español*; *Six Pieces on Spanish Folk Themes (Seis piezas sobre cantos populares españoles)*
See: W101

D140. **Oriental (Canción variada, Intermedio y Final)**
CRD 1023
Thomas Rajna, piano
Includes his *Allegro de concierto*; *Capricho español*; *Carezza (Valse)*; *Two Impromptus*; *Rapsodia aragonesa*; *Valses poéticos*
See: W101

D141. **Paisaje**
Volume 2 of two-volume set, VOX 5484/5
Marylène Dosse, piano
See: W104

D142. **Paisaje**
CRC-1037
Thomas Rajna, piano
Includes his *Impromptu, op. 39*; *Six Expressive Studies (Seis estudios expresivos)*; *Marche militaire*; *Estudio op. Posthumous (Andantino espressivo)*; *Paisaje*; *Two Military Marches*
See: W104

D143. **El pelele**
RCA RL-35301
Joaquín Achúcaro, piano
Includes his *Goyescas*
See: W106

D144. **El pelele**
LONDON CS/5-7009
Alicia de Larrocha, piano
Includes his *Goyescas* (complete)
See: W106

D145. **El pelele**
VOX/TURNABOUT 34772
Alicia de Larrocha, piano
Includes his *Valses poéticos*; *Allegro de concierto*; *Danza lenta*; *Six Pieces on Spanish Folk Themes (Seis piezas sobre cantos populares españoles)*
See: W106

D146. **El pelele**
EPIC LC-3444
Eduardo del Pueyo, piano
Includes his *El pelele*
See: W106

D147. **El pelele**
Volume 2 of two-volume set, VOX 5484/5
Marylène Dosse, piano
See: W106

D148. **El pelele**
BELTER 70915
José Falgarona, piano
Includes his *Spanish Dances 5, 9*; *Quejas, o La maja y el ruiseñor*; *Allegro de concierto*
See: W106

D149. **El pelele**
EVEREST X-909
Enrique Granados, piano
Includes his *Improvisation*; *Prelude to María del Carmen*; *Quejas, o La maja y el ruiseñor*; *Reverie-Improvisation*; *Spanish Dances 1, 2, 5, 7, 10*
See: W106

D150. **El pelele**
COLUMBIA 1215
(orchestrated by Sir Henry Wood)
Sir Henry Wood, conductor; Queen's Hall Orchestra
See: W106

D151. **Pièce de Scarlatti** (Scarlatti-Granados)
The Welte Legacy of Piano Treasures 669 B11225
Enrique Granados, piano.
Includes his *Goyescas* (Book One); *Spanish Dance 5*; works by Falla
See: W143

D152. **Prelude to María del Carmen**
EVEREST X-909
Enrique Granados, piano
Includes his *Improvisation*; *El pelele*; *Quejas, o La maja y el ruiseñor*; *Reverie-Improvisation*; *Spanish Dances 1, 2, 5, 7, 10*
See: W84

D153. **Preludio**
CENTAUR CRC 2043
The Unknown Granados
Douglas Riva, piano
Includes his *Allegro vivace*; *Azulejos*; *En la aldea*; *Mazurka in E-flat Major*; *Mazurka in E-flat Minor ("Chopin")*; *Romanza*; *Conte*; *Vals*; *Serenade for Two Violins and Piano*; *Primavera (Romanza sin palabras)*
See: W4

D154. **Primavera (Romanza sin palabras)**
CENTAUR CRC 2043
The Unknown Granados
Douglas Riva, piano
Includes his *Allegro vivace*; *Azulejos*; *En la aldea*; *Mazurka in E-flat Major*; *Mazurka in E-flat Minor ("Chopin")*; *Romanza*; *Conte*; *Vals*; *Serenade for Two Violins and Piano*; *Preludio*
See: W4

D155. **Quintet in G Minor for Piano and Strings**
CRD 1035
Thomas Rajna and the Alberti Quartet
Includes his *A la cubana*; *Aparición*; *Cartas de amor*; *Danza característica*; *Escenas poéticas* (second series)
See: W112

D156. **Rapsodia aragonesa**
Volume 2 of two-volume set, VOX 5484/5
Marylène Dosse, piano
See: W113

D157. **Rapsodia aragonesa**
CRD 1023
Thomas Rajna, piano
Includes his *Allegro de concierto*; *Capricho español*; *Carezza (Valse)*; *Two Impromptus*; *Oriental (Canción variada, Intermedio y Final)*; *Valses poéticos*
See: W113

D158. **Reverie-Improvisation**
EVEREST X-909
Enrique Granados, piano
Includes his *Improvisation*; *Prelude to María del Carmen*; *El pelele*; *Quejas, o La maja y el ruiseñor*; *Spanish Dances 1, 2, 5, 7, 10*
See: W114

D159. **Romanza**
CENTAUR CRC 2043
The Unknown Granados
Ruth Waterman, violin; Douglas Riva, piano
Includes his *Allegro vivace*; *Azulejos*; *En la aldea*; *Mazurka in E-flat Major*; *Mazurka in E-flat Minor ("Chopin")*; *Conte*; *Preludio*; *Serenade for Two Violins and Piano*, *Primavera (Romanza sin palabras)*, *Vals*
See: W115

D160. **Sardana**
CRD-1036
Thomas Rajna, piano
Includes his *Moresque y canción árabe*; *Cuentos de la juventud*; *Bocetos*; *Mazurka (alla polacca)*, *Barcarola*; *Los soldados de cartón*; *A la pradera*
See: W118

D161. **Sardana**
Volume 1 of two-volume set, VOX 5484/5
Marylène Dosse, piano
See: W118

D162. **Serenade (for Two Violins and Piano)**
CENTAUR CRC 2043
The Unknown Granados
Ruth Waterman, violin; Joel Pitchon, violin; Douglas Riva, piano
Includes his *Allegro vivace*; *Azulejos*; *En la aldea*; *Mazurka in E-flat Major*; *Mazurka in E-flat Minor ("Chopin")*; *Romanza*; *Conte*; *Vals*; *Preludio*; *Primavera (Romanza sin palabras)*
See: W119

D163. **Six Expressive Studies (Seis estudios expresivos)**
Volume 1 of two-volume set, VOX 5484/5
Marylène Dosse, piano
See: W124

D164. **Six Expressive Studies (Seis estudios expresivos)**
CRC-1037
Thomas Rajna, piano
Includes his *Impromptu, op. 39*; *Marche militaire*; *Estudio op. Posthumous (Andantino espressivo)*; *Elisenda*; *Paisaje*; *Two Military Marches*
See: W124

D165. **Six Pieces on Spanish Folk Themes (Seis piezas sobre cantos populares españoles)**
LONDON 410288-1LH
Alicia de Larrocha, piano
Includes his Allegro de concierto; *Escenas románticas*
See: W125

D166. **Six Pieces on Spanish Folk Themes (Seis piezas sobre cantos populares españoles)**
VOX/TURNABOUT 34772
Alicia de Larrocha, piano
Includes his *Valses poéticos*; *Allegro de concierto*; *Danza lenta*; *El pelele*
See: W125

D167. **Six Pieces on Spanish Folk Themes (Seis piezas sobre cantos populares españoles)**
Volume 1 of two-volume set, VOX 5484/5
Marylène Dosse, piano
See: W125

D168. **Six Pieces on Spanish Folk Themes (Seis piezas sobre cantos populares españoles)**
CRD-1022
Thomas Rajna, piano
Includes his *Danza lenta*; *Escenas románticas*
See: W125

D169. **Six Pieces on Spanish Folk Themes (Seis piezas sobre cantos populares españoles)**
ASLKAGER CD87024
Dana Protopopesca, piano
Includes his *Allegro de concierto*; *Valses poéticos*; *Oriental (Canción variada, Intermedio y Final)*; *Capricho español*
See: W125

D170. **Six Pieces on Spanish Folk Themes (Seis piezas sobre cantos populares españoles): Zapateado (Six Pieces on Spanish Folk Themes, no. 6)**
PHILIPS LY 839775
(orchestrated by Rafael Ferrer)
Igor Markevitch, conductor; Spanish Radio Orchestra
Includes his *Intermezzo* from *Goyescas*; *Spanish Dances 8,9*
See: A7

D171. **Los soldados de cartón**
CRD-1036
Thomas Rajna, piano
Includes his *Moresque y canción árabe*; *Cuentos de la juventud*; *Sardana*; *Bocetos*; *Mazurka (alla polacca)*; *Barcarola, A la pradera*
See: W126

D172. **Los soldados de cartón**
Volume 2 of two-volume set, VOX 5484/5
Marylène Dosse, piano
See: W126

D173. **Spanish Dances (complete)**
LONDON 414557-2 LH
Alicia de Larrocha, piano
See: W142

D174. **Spanish Dances (complete)**
VOX/TURNABOUT CT-4771
Alicia de Larrocha, piano
See: W142

D175. **Spanish Dances (complete)**
EPIC LC-3423
Eduardo del Pueyo, piano
See: W142

D176. **Spanish Dances (complete)**
PROMISE CD 88 001
Nadine Delsaux, piano
See: W142

D177. **Spanish Dances (complete)**
Volume 2 of two-volume set, VOX 5484/5
Marylène Dosse, piano
See: W142

D178. **Spanish Dances (complete)**
WESTMINSTER WLP 5181
José Echániz, piano
See: W142

D179. **Spanish Dances (complete)**
CRD-4021
Thomas Rajna, piano
See: W142

D180. **Spanish Dances (complete)**
TRIANON TRX6131
Magda Tagliaferro, piano
See: W142

D181. **Spanish Dance no. 1**
EVEREST X-909
Enrique Granados, piano
Includes his *Spanish Dances 2, 5, 7, 10*; *Improvisation*; *Reverie-Improvisation*; *El pelele*; *Prelude to María del Carmen*; *Quejas, o La maja y el ruiseñor*
See: W142

D182. **Spanish Dance no. 1**
VOX/TURNABOUT STV 34372
Beatriz Klein, piano
Includes his Spanish Dances 2, *3*, *5*; *Quejas, o La maja y el ruiseñor*; other Spanish piano music
See: W142

D183. **Spanish Dance no. 1**
VOX/TURNABOUT CT-2247
(arranged for guitar)
Manuel Barrueco, guitar
Includes his *Spanish Dances 3, 4, 5, 12*; works by Albéniz
See: W142

D184. **Spanish Dance no. 1**
EMI 1067-270216-1
(arranged for guitar)
Elliot Fisk, guitar
Includes his *Spanish Dances 3, 4, 5, 6, 10*; *La maja de Goya*
See: W142

D185. **Spanish Dance no. 1**
OTTAVO OTR-C48710
(arranged for two guitars by the performers)
Groningen Guitar Duo
Includes his *Spanish Dances 4, 6, 11*; works by Albéniz, Falla, Turina
See: W142

D186. **Spanish Dance no. 2**
PIANISSIME MAG-2018
Gérard Gahnassia, piano
Includes his *Spanish Dance 5*; works by Albéniz, Falla, Turina, Longas
See: W142

D187. **Spanish Dance no. 2**
EVEREST X-909
Enrique Granados, piano
Includes his *Spanish Dances 1, 5, 7, 10*; *Improvisation*; *Reverie-Improvisation*; *El pelele*; *Prelude to María del Carmen*; *Quejas, o La maja y el ruiseñor*
See: W142

D188. **Spanish Dance no. 2**
NIMBUS 5130
Youra Guller, piano
Includes his *Spanish Dance 5*; works by Albéniz, Bach, Liszt
See: W142

D189. **Spanish Dance no. 2**
VOX/TURNABOUT STV 34372
Beatriz Klein, piano
Includes his *Spanish Dances 1, 3, 5*; *Quejas, o La maja y el ruiseñor;* other Spanish piano music
See: W142

D190. **Spanish Dance no. 2**
COLUMBIA 63
(arranged for cello and piano)
Grigor Piatigorsky, cello; Valentin Pavlovsky, piano
Includes works by Prokofiev
See: A12

D191. **Spanish Dance no. 2**
ODEON 121036
(orchestrated by Joan Lamote de Grignon)
Banda Municipal de Madrid
See: A15

D192. **Spanish Dance no. 2**
RCA Victor 35977
(orchestrated by Joan Lamote de Grignon)
Eugene Goossens, conductor; New Light Symphony
Includes his *Spanish Dance 5*
See: A15

D193. **Spanish Dance no. 2**
URANIA 7144
(orchestrated by Joan Lamote de Grignon)
Georges Sebastian, conductor; Orchestre de l'Association des Concerts Colonne
Includes his *Spanish Dances 5, 6*; works by Respighi, Chávez
See: A15

D194. **Spanish Dance no. 2**
MGM E-3018
(orchestrated by Joan Lamote de Grignon)
Wilhelm Schüchter, conductor; Philadelphia Orchestra
Includes his *Spanish Dances 5, 6*; works by Turina
See: A15

D195. **Spanish Dance no. 2**
PHILLIPS 6514 182
(arranged for guitar by Pepe Romero)
Pepe Romero; Celín Romero, guitars
Includes his *Spanish Dances 4, 5, 10*
See: W142

D196. **Spanish Dance no. 2**
FONO SCHALLPLATTEN 68 7 06
(arranged for two guitars)
Albéniz Guitar Duo
See: W142

D197. **Spanish Dance no. 2**
SOL 1181/82
(arranged for two guitars)
Frankfurter Guitarrenduo
See: W142

D198. **Spanish Dance no. 2**
CALLIOPE 9204
(arranged for two guitars)
Jean Horreaux; Jean-Marie Trehaud, guitars
Includes his *Spanish Dances 4, 11, 12*; *Capricho español*; *Serenata del espectro*; *Valses poéticos*; *Deux danses caracteristiques*; *La maja de Goya*
See: W142

D199. **Spanish Dance no. 2**
MMG 1146
(arranged for flute, oboe, and guitar)
Trio Sonata
Includes his *Intermezzo* from Goyescas; works by Bach, Villa-Lobos, Woolridge, Bender, Tompkins
See: W142

D200. **Spanish Dance no. 3**
VOX/TURNABOUT STV 34372
Beatriz Klein, piano
Includes his *Spanish Dances 1, 2, 5*; *Quejas, o La maja y el ruiseñor*; other Spanish piano music
See: W142

D201. **Spanish Dance no. 3**
VOX/TURNABOUT CT-2247
(arranged for guitar)
Manuel Barrueco, guitar
Includes his *Spanish Dances 1, 4, 5, 12*; works by Albéniz
See: W142

D202. **Spanish Dance no. 3**
EMI 1067-270216-1
(arranged for guitar)
Elliot Fisk, guitar
Includes his *Spanish Dances 1, 4, 5, 6, 10*; *La maja de Goya*
See: W142

D203. **Spanish Dance no. 4**
VOX/TURNABOUT CT-2247
(arranged for guitar)
Manuel Barrueco, guitar
Includes his *Spanish Dances 1, 3, 5, 12*; works by Albéniz
See: W142

D204. **Spanish Dance no. 4**
EMI 1067-270216-1
(arranged for guitar)
Elliot Fisk, guitar
Includes his *Spanish Dances 1, 3, 5, 6, 10*; *La maja de Goya*
See: W142

D205. **Spanish Dance no. 4**
PHILLIPS 6514 182
(arranged for guitar by Pepe Romero)
Pepe Romero; Celín Romero, guitars
Includes his *Spanish Dances 2, 5, 10*
See: W142

D206. **Spanish Dance no. 4**
DEUTSCHE GRAMMOPHON 2530159
(arranged for guitar)
Narciso Yepes, guitar
See: W142

D207. **Spanish Dance no. 4**
OTTAVO OTR-C48710
(arranged for two guitars by the performers)
Groningen Guitar Duo
Also includes his *Spanish Dances 1, 6, 11*
See: W142

D208. **Spanish Dance no. 4**
CALLIOPE 9204
(arranged for two guitars)
Jean Horreaux; Jean-Marie Trehaud, guitars
Includes his *Spanish Dances 2, 11, 12*; *Capricho español*; *Serenata del espectro*; *Valses poéticos*; *Deux danses caractéristiques*; *La maja de Goya*
See: W142

D209. **Spanish Dance no. 4**
DECCA 180
(orchestrated by Sir Henry Wood)
Sir Henry Wood, conductor; Queen's Hall Orchestra
Includes his *Spanish Dance 6*
See: W142

D210. **Spanish Dance no. 4**
RCA RCD1-4378
(arranged for guitar)
Julian Bream, guitar
Includes his *Spanish Dance 5*; *Dedicatoria*; *La maja de Goya*; *Valses poéticos*; works by Albéniz
See: W142

D211. **Spanish Dance no. 5**
MGM E87
George Copeland, piano
Includes works by Albéniz, Infanta, Nin, Mompou
See: W142

D212. **Spanish Dance no. 5**
BELTER 70915
José Falgarona, piano
Includes his *Spanish Dance 9*; *Allegro de concierto*; *El pelele*; *Quejas, o La maja y el ruiseñor*
See: W142

D213. **Spanish Dance no. 5**
PIANISSIME MAG-2018
Gérard Gahnassia, piano
Includes his *Spanish Dance 2*; works by Albéniz, Falla, Turina, Longas
See: W142

D214. **Spanish Dance no. 5**
The Welte Legacy of Piano Treasures 669 B11225
Enrique Granados, piano.
Includes his *Goyescas* (Book One), *Pièce de Scarlatti* (Scarlatti-Granados); works by Falla
See: W142

D215. **Spanish Dance no. 5**
EVEREST X-909
Enrique Granados, piano
Includes his *Spanish Dances 1, 2, 7, 10*; *Improvisation*; *Reverie-Improvisation*; *El pelele*; *Prelude to María del Carmen*; *Quejas, o La maja y el ruiseñor*
See: W142

D216. **Spanish Dance no. 5**
ASCO A-119
Enrique Granados, piano
Includes performances by Sauer, Carreño, Debussy, Saint-Saëns, Dohnanyi, Rachmaninoff
See: W142

D217. **Spanish Dance no. 5**
TELEFUNKEN (from Welte-Mignon)
Enrique Granados, Piano
Includes performances by Strauss, Reger, Humperdinck, Mahler, Leoncavallo, Fauré, Glazunov, Scriabin
See: W142

D218. **Spanish Dance no. 5**
NIMBUS 5130
Youra Guller, piano
Includes his *Spanish Dance 2*; works by Albéniz, Bach, Liszt
See: W142

D219. **Spanish Dance no. 5**
CENTAUR CRC-2026
Pierre Huybregts, piano
Includes his *Quejas, o La maja y el ruiseñor*; works by Albéniz, Halffter, Mompou, Turina
See: W142

D220. **Spanish Dance no. 5**
ANGEL RL-32123 (previously released as S-35628)
José Iturbi, piano
Includes his *Spanish Dances 10, 12*; *Allegro de concierto*; works by Albéniz
See: W142

D221. **Spanish Dance no. 5**
VOX/TURNABOUT STV 34372
Beatriz Klein, piano
Includes his *Spanish Dances 1, 2, 3*; *Quejas, o La maja y el ruiseñor*; other Spanish piano music
See: W142

D222. **Spanish Dance no. 5**
HIS MASTER'S VOICE 3170 (also, VICTOR 12-0736)
Arturo Benedetti Michelangeli, piano
Includes Albéniz ("Malagueña")
See: W142

D223. **Spanish Dance no. 5**
APR7003 (reissue of a 1925 recording)
Benno Moiséiwitsch, piano
Includes his *Spanish Dance 6*
See: W142

D224. **Spanish Dance no. 5**
ANGEL S-36064
(arranged for guitar)
Laurindo Almeida, guitar
Includes works by Debussy, Ravel, Falla, Albéniz, Villa-Lobos
See: W142

D225. **Spanish Dance no. 5**
VOX/TURNABOUT CT-2247
(arranged for guitar)
Manuel Barrueco, guitar
Includes his *Spanish Dances 1, 3, 4, 12*; works by Albéniz
See: W142

D226. **Spanish Dance no. 5**
RCA RCD1-4378
(arranged for guitar)
Julian Bream, guitar
Includes his *Spanish Dance 4*; *Dedicatoria*; *La maja de Goya*; *Valses poéticos*; works by Albéniz
See: W142

D227. **Spanish Dance no. 5**
EMI 1067-270216-1
(arranged for guitar)
Elliot Fisk, guitar
Includes his *Spanish Dances 1, 3, 4, 6, 10*; *La maja de Goya*
See: W142

D228. **Spanish Dance no. 5**
PHILLIPS 6514 182
(arranged for guitar by Pepe Romero)
Pepe Romero, Celín Romero, guitars
Includes his *Spanish Dances 2, 4, 10*
See: W142

D229. **Spanish Dance no. 5**
ERATO ECD-55028
(arranged for guitar)
Turibio Santos, guitar
Includes his *Spanish Dance 10*; *La maja de Goya*; works by Albéniz, Rodrigo, Sanz, Turina, Villa-Lobos
See: W142

D230. **Spanish Dance no. 5**
AMERICANA DECCA DU40068
(arranged for guitar by Andres Segovia)
Andres Segovia, guitar
Includes works by Albéniz
See: W142

D231. **Spanish Dance no. 5**
CBS 78 268
(arranged for guitar)
John Williams, guitar
Includes his *Valses poéticos*
See: W142

D232. **Spanish Dance no. 5**
RCA VICTOR LM 1742
(arranged for violin and piano by Fritz Kreisler)
Yehudi Menuhin, violin; Gerald Moore, piano
Includes works by Kreisler, Dvorak, Ravel
See: A13

D233. **Spanish Dance no. 5**
G. DB 1498
(arranged for violin and piano by Fritz Kreisler)
Jacques Thibaud, violin; T. Janopoulo, piano
See: A13

D234. **Spanish Dance no. 5**
EMI 063-03426
(arranged for violin and piano by Fritz Kreisler)
Itzak Perlman, violin; Samuel Sanders, piano
See: A13

D235. **Spanish Dance no. 5**
EURO XK 80578
(arranged for cello and piano)
Mstislaw Rostropovitch, cello; Alexander Dedjuchin, piano
See: W142

D236. **Spanish Dance no. 5**
ODEON 188923
(arranged for cello and piano)
André Navarra, cello; pianist unidentified
Includes Glazounov (*Sérénade espagnol*)
See: W142

D237. **Spanish Dance no. 5**
RCA VICTOR 1311
(arranged for cello and piano)
Pablo Casals, cello; Nicolai Mednikoff, piano
See: W142

D238. **Spanish Dance no. 5**
PARLOPHONE 10838
(arranged for cello and piano)
Emmanuel Feurmann, cello
See: W142

D239. **Spanish Dance no. 5**
DECCA (GREAT BRITAIN) 15008
(arranged for saxophone and piano)
Marcel Mulé, saxophone
See: W142

D240. **Spanish Dance no. 5**
COLUMBIA ML4260
(arranged for clarinet and orchestra)
Artie Shaw, clarinet; New Music String Quartet
Includes works by Débussy, Gershwin, Milhaud
See: W142

D241. **Spanish Dance no. 5**
DEUTSCHE GRAMMOPHON 2530230
(arranged for harp)
Nicanor Zabaletta, harp
Includes works by Albéniz, Falla, Turina
See: W142

D242. **Spanish Dance no. 5**
LONDON STS5-15601
(orchestrated by Rafael Ferrer)
Ataulfo Argenta, conductor; London Symphony
Includes works by Chabrier, Moskowski, Rimsky-Korsakov
See: W142

D243. **Spanish Dance no. 5**
RCA Victor 35977
(orchestrated by Joan Lamote de Grignon)
Eugene Goossens, conductor; New Light Symphony
Includes his *Spanish Dance 2*
See: A15

D244. **Spanish Dance no. 5**
URANIA 7144
(orchestrated by Joan Lamote de Grignon)
Georges Sebastian, conductor; Orchestre de l'Association des Concerts Colonne
Includes his *Spanish Dances 2*, *6*; works by Respighi, Chávez
See: A15

D245. **Spanish Dance no. 5**
MGM E-3018
(orchestrated by Joan Lamote de Grignon)
Wilhelm Schüchter, conductor; Philadelphia Orchestra
Includes his *Spanish Dances 2*, *6*; works by Turina
See: A15

D246. **Spanish Dance no. 5**
DECCA 181
(orchestrated by Sir Henry Wood)
Sir Henry Wood, conductor; Queen's Hall Orchestra
See: W142

D247. **Spanish Dance no. 5 (Andaluza)**
RCA VICTOR 1421
(arranged for voice, Spanish text)
Tito Schipa, tenor
See: A3

D248. **Spanish Dance no. 5 (Andaluza)**
ODEON 1211146
(arranged for voice, Spanish text)
Conchita Supervia, mezzo-soprano
See: A3

D249. **Spanish Dance no. 5**
HIS MASTER'S VOICE 540
(arranged for voice, Italian text)
Margherita Carioso, soprano; orchestra unidentified
Includes works by Calleja
See: A3

D250. **Spanish Dance no. 6**
APR7003 (reissue of a 1925 recording)
Benno Moiséiwitsch, piano
Includes his *Spanish Dance 5*
See: W142

D251. **Spanish Dance no. 6**
COLUMBIA (GREAT BRITAIN) 2521
(arranged for two pianos)
Rawicz and Landauer Piano Duo
See: W142

D252. **Spanish Dance no. 6**
COLUMBIA 12547
(orchestrated by Joan Lamote de Grignon)
Enrique Fernández Arbós, conductor; Madrid Symphony
Includes his *Intermezzo* from *Goyescas*; Albéniz ("El puerto")
See: A15

D253. **Spanish Dance no. 6**
URANIA 7144
(orchestrated by Joan Lamote de Grignon)
Georges Sebastian, conductor; Orchestre de l'Association des Concerts Colonne
Includes *Spanish Dances 2*, *5*; works by Respighi, Chávez
See: A15

D254. **Spanish Dance no. 6**
MGM E-3018
(orchestrated by Joan Lamote de Grignon)
Wilhelm Schüchter, conductor; Philadelphia Orchestra
Includes his *Spanish Dances 2*, *5*; works by Turina
See: A15

D255. **Spanish Dance no. 6**
DECCA 180
(orchestrated by Sir Henry Wood)
Sir Henry Wood, conductor; Queen's Hall Orchestra
Includes his *Spanish Dance 4*
See: W142

D256. **Spanish Dance no. 6**
RCA VICTOR 7250
(arranged for piano and violin)
Jacques Thibaud, violin
See: W142

D257. **Spanish Dance no. 6**
ODEON 123849
(arranged for cello and piano by Gaspar Cassadó)
André Navarra, cello
Includes his *Intermezzo* from *Goyescas*
See: W142

D258. **Spanish Dance no. 6**
EMI 1067-270216-1
(arranged for guitar)
Elliot Fisk, guitar
Includes his *Spanish Dances 1*, *3*, *4*, *5*, *10*; *La maja de Goya*
See: W142

D259. **Spanish Dance no. 6**
RCA 26.41 229AW
(arranged for two guitars)
Julian Bream, John Williams, guitars
Includes his *Spanish Dance 10*
See: A14

D260. **Spanish Dance no. 6**
OTTAVO OTR-C48710
(arranged for two guitars by the performers)
Groningen Guitar Duo
Also includes his *Spanish Dances 1, 4, 11*
See: A14

D261. **Spanish Dance no. 7**
EVEREST X-909
Enrique Granados, piano
Includes his *Spanish Dances 1, 2, 5, 10*; *Improvisation*; *Reverie-Improvisation*; *El pelele*; *Prelude to María del Carmen*; *Quejas, o La maja y el ruiseñor*
See: W142

D262. **Spanish Dance no. 8**
PHILIPS LY 839775
(orchestrated by Rafael Ferrer)
Igor Markevitch, conductor; Spanish Radio Orchestra
Includes his *Spanish Dance 9*; *Intermezzo* from *Goyescas*; *Zapateado* (*Six Pieces on Spanish Folk Themes*, no. *6*)
See: W142

D263. **Spanish Dance no. 9**
BELTER 70915
José Falgarona, piano
Includes his *Spanish Dance 5*; *Allegro de concierto*; *El pelele*; *Quejas, o La maja y el ruiseñor*
See: W142

D264. **Spanish Dance no. 9**
PHILIPS LY 839775
(orchestrated by Rafael Ferrer)
Igor Markevitch, conductor; Spanish Radio Orchestra
Includes his *Spanish Dance 8*; *Intermezzo* from *Goyescas*; *Zapateado* (*Six Pieces on Spanish Folk Themes*, no. *6*)
See: W142

D265. **Spanish Dance no. 9**
DECCA (SPAIN) 40127
(arranged for castanets and piano)
L'Argentinita, castanets
See: W142

D266. **Spanish Dance no. 10**
EVEREST X-909
Enrique Granados, piano
Includes his *Spanish Dances 1, 2, 5, 7*; *Improvisation*; *Reverie-Improvisation*; *El pelele*; *Prelude to María del Carmen*; *Quejas, o La maja y el ruiseñor*
See: W142

D267. **Spanish Dance no. 10**
ANGEL RL-32123 (previously released as S-35628)
José Iturbi, piano
Includes his *Spanish Dances 5, 12*; *Allegro de concierto*; works by Albéniz
See: W142

D268. **Spanish Dance no. 10**
EMI 1067-270216-1
(arranged for guitar)
Elliot Fisk, guitar
Includes his *Spanish Dances 1, 3, 4, 5, 6*; *La maja de Goya*
See: W142

D269. **Spanish Dance no. 10**
PHILLIPS 6514 182
(arranged for guitar by Pepe Romero)
Pepe Romero; Celín Romero, guitars
Includes his *Spanish Dances 2, 4, 5*
See: W142

D270. **Spanish Dance no. 10**
ERATO ECD-55028
(arranged for guitar)
Turibio Santos, guitar
Includes his *Spanish Dance 5*; *La maja de Goya*; works by Albéniz, Rodrigo, Sanz, Turina, Villa-Lobos
See: W142

D271. **Spanish Dance no. 10**
DECCA SMD 1306
(arranged for guitar)
Narcisco Yepes, guitar
See: W142

D272. **Spanish Dance no. 10**
RCA 26.41 229AW
(arranged for two guitars)
Julian Bream, John Williams, guitars
Includes his *Spanish Dance 6*
See: A14

D273. **Spanish Dance no. 11**
OTTAVO OTR-C48710
(arranged for two guitars by the performers)
Groningen Guitar Duo
Also includes his *Spanish Dances 1, 4, 6*
See: W142

D274. **Spanish Dance no. 11**
CALLIOPE 9204
(arranged for two guitars)
Jean Horreaux, Jean-Marie Trehaud, guitars
Includes his *Spanish Dances 2, 4, 12*; *Capricho español*; *Serenata del espectro*; *Valses poéticos*; *Deux danses caracteristiques*; *La maja de Goya*
See: W142

D275. **Spanish Dance no. 11**
PETERS - PLE 029
(arranged for harp)
Susanna Mildonian, harp
Includes works by Albéniz
See: W142

D276. **Spanish Dance no. 12**
ANGEL RL-32123 (previously released as S-35628)
José Iturbi, piano
Includes his *Spanish Dances 5, 10*; *Allegro de concierto*; works by Albéniz
See: W142

D277. **Spanish Dance no. 12**
VOX/TURNABOUT CT-2247
(arranged for guitar)
Manuel Barrueco, guitar
Includes his *Spanish Dances 1, 3, 4, 5*; works by Albéniz
See: W142

D278. **Spanish Dance no. 12**
CALLIOPE 9204
(arranged for two guitars)
Jean Horreaux, Jean-Marie Trehaud, guitars
Includes his *Spanish Dances 2, 4, 11*; *Capricho español*; *Serenata del espectro*; *Valses poéticos*; *Deux danses caractéristiques*; *La maja de Goya*
See: W142

D279. **Tonadillas**
EVEREST 3237
Conchita Badia, soprano; Alicia de Larrocha, piano
(Homage to Granados)
Includes his *Canciones amatorias*
See: W136

D280. **Tonadillas**
RCA LSC 2910-B
(orchestrated by Rafael Ferrer)
Montserrat Caballé, soprano; Rafael Ferrer, conductor; Symphony Orchestra
Includes his *Canciones amatorias*
See: A17

D281. **Tonadillas**
DENON C37-7539
Susan Daniel, soprano; Richard Amner, piano
Includes works by Falla and Nin
See: W136

D282. **Tonadillas**
ANGEL S-3672
Victoria de los Angeles, soprano; Gonzalo Soriano, piano
Includes works by Falla
See: W136

D283. **Tonadillas**
LONDON 26558
Pilar Lorengar, soprano; Alicia de Larrocha, piano
Includes his *Canciones amatorias*
See: W136

D284. **Tonadillas**
SERAPHIM 6029 (was PARLOPHONE 161/2)
Conchita Supervia, mezzo-soprano; Frank Marshall, piano
Includes his *El majo discreto*; *El tra la la y el punteado*; *El majo tímido*; *La maja dolorosa (1-3)*; *El mirar de la maja*; *Amor y odio*; *Callejeo*; *Las currutacas modestas*
See: W136

D285. **Tonadillas**
EMI EL270307
(arranged for guitar by Russ)
Kathleen Battle, soprano; John Williams, guitar
See: W136

D286. **Tonadillas: Amor y odio**
RCA GL89904
(arranged for guitar by Julian Bream)
Julian Bream, guitar
Includes his *El majo discreto*; *El tra la la y el punteado*; *El majo tímido*; *El mirar de la maja*; *La maja de Goya*; *Callejeo*
See: W136

D287. **Tonadillas: Callejeo**
RCA GL89904
(arranged for guitar by Julian Bream)
Julian Bream, guitar
Includes his *El majo discreto*; *El tra la la y el punteado*; *El majo tímido*; *El mirar de la maja*; *La maja de Goya*; *Amor y odio*
See: W136

D288. **Tonadillas: Las currutacas modestas**
HYPERION CD 66 176 WY
Ann Murray, mezzo-soprano; Graham Johnson, piano
Includes his *La maja dolorosa (1-3)*; *El majo discreto*; *El majo olvidado*; *El mirar de la maja*
See: W136

D289. **Tonadillas: La maja de Goya**
RCA RCD1-4378
(arranged for guitar by Andres Segovia)
Julian Bream, guitar
Includes his *Dedicatoria*; *Valses poéticos*; *Spanish Dances 4, 5*; works by Albéniz
See: A9

D290. **Tonadillas: La maja de Goya**
RCA GL89904
(arranged for guitar by Julian Bream)
Includes his *El majo discreto*; *El tra la la y el punteado*; *El majo tímido*; *El mirar de la maja*; *Amor y odio*; *Callejeo*
See: W136

D291. **Tonadillas: La maja de Goya**
EMI 1067-270216-1
(arranged for guitar)
Elliot Fisk, guitar
Includes his *Spanish Dances 1, 3, 4, 5, 6, 10*
See: A9

D292. **Tonadillas: La maja de Goya**
CALLIOPE 9204
(arranged for two guitars)
Jean Horreaux, Jean-Marie Trehaud, guitars
Includes his *Spanish Dances 2, 4, 11, 12*; *Capricho español*; *Serenata del espectro*; *Valses poéticos*; *Deux danses caracteristiques*
See: W136

D293. **Tonadillas: La maja de Goya**
VOX/TURNABOUT PVT-7135
(arranged for guitar by Andres Segovia)
Konrad Ragossnig, guitar
Includes works by Albéniz, Falla, Fasch, Turina
See: W136

D294. **Tonadillas: La maja de Goya**
ANGEL CDC-47192
(arranged for guitar by Andres Segovia)
Angel Romero, guitar
Includes works by Albéniz, Bolling, Tárrega, Turina
See: W136

D295. **Tonadillas: La maja de Goya**
ERATO ECD-55028
(arranged for guitar by Andres Segovia)
Turibio Santos, guitar
Includes his *Spanish Dances 5, 10*; works by Albéniz, Rodrigo, Sanz, Turina, Villa-Lobos
See: W136

D296. **Tonadillas: La maja de Goya**
BRUNSWICK 04394
(arranged for guitar by Andres Segovia)
Andres Segovia, guitar
Includes works by Albéniz
See: W136

D297. **Tonadillas: La maja dolorosa (1-3)**
CLAVES 8 704
Teresa Berganza, mezzo-soprano; Juan Antonio Alvarez-Parejo, piano
Includes his *El majo discreto*
See: W136

D298. **Tonadillas: La maja dolorosa (1-3)**
CBS 74 105
Marilyn Horne, soprano; Martin Katz, piano
See: W136

D299. **Tonadillas: La maja dolorosa (1-3)**
ETCETERA 1041
Nelly Miricioiu, soprano; David Harper, piano
See: W136

D300. **Tonadillas: La maja dolorosa (1-3)**
HYPERION CD 66 176 WY
Ann Murray, mezzo-soprano; Graham Johnson, piano
Includes his *Las currutacas modestas*; *El majo discreto*; *El majo olvidado*; *El mirar de la maja*
See: W136

D301. **Tonadillas: La maja dolorosa (1-3)**
ORFEO A 038 831
Margaret Price, soprano; James Lockhart, piano
Includes his *Tonadillas*; *El majo tímido*; *El tra la la y el punteado*; *El majo discreto*; *Elegia eterna*
See: W136

D302. **Tonadillas: La maja dolorosa (1-3)**
LSC 2776
Shirley Verrett, mezzo-soprano
Includes his *El mirar de la maja*
See: W136

D303. **Tonadillas: La maja dolorosa no. 3**
DEUTSCHE GRAMMOPHON 2530 598 (previously released as DECCA SMD 1166)
Teresa Berganza, mezzo-soprano; Felix Lavilla, piano
Includes his *El majo tímido*; *El tra la la y el punteado*
See: W136

D304. **Tonadillas: La maja dolorosa no. 3**
ANGEL S-35775
(arranged for voice, piano, English horn)
Victoria de los Angeles, soprano; Gonzalo Soriano, piano; M. Sagu, English horn
See: W136

D305. **Tonadillas: La maja dolorosa no. 3**
REMINGTON R-199-139
Lydia Ibarrondo, mezzo-soprano; Miguel Sandoval, piano
Includes works by Turina, Nin, Obradors, Molandrón
See: W136

D306. **Tonadillas: El majo discreto**
RCA VICTOR 4464
Conchita Badia, soprano
Includes works by Falla, Galvés, Turina, Vives
See: W136

D307. **Tonadillas: El majo discreto**
CLAVES 8 704
Teresa Berganza, mezzo-soprano; Juan Antonio Alvarez-Parejo, piano
Includes his *La maja dolorosa*
See: W136

D308. **Tonadillas: El majo discreto**
HYPERION CD 66 176 WY
Ann Murray, mezzo-soprano; Graham Johnson, piano
Includes his *Las currutacas modestas*; *La maja dolorosa (1-3)*; *El majo olvidado*; *El mirar de la maja*
See: W136

D309. **Tonadillas: El majo discreto**
ORFEO A 038 831
Margaret Price, soprano; James Lockhart, piano
Includes his *Tonadillas*; *El majo tímido*; *El tra la la y el punteado*; *La maja dolorosa (1-3)*; *Elegía eterna*
See: W136

D310. **Tonadillas: El majo discreto**
FONO SCHALLPLATTEN PD 07175
Benita Valente, soprano; David Effron, piano
Includes his *El mirar de la maja*
See: W136

D311. **Tonadillas: El majo discreto**
EMI EX290946-3 (previously released as ODEON 195073)
Ninon Vallin, soprano
Includes his *No lloréis ojuelos*; works by Nin, Falla
See: W136

D312. **Tonadillas: El majo discreto**
RCA GL89904
(arranged for guitar by Julian Bream)
Includes his *La maja de Goya*; *El tra la la y el punteado*; *El majo tímido*; *El mirar de la maja*; *Amor y odio*; *Callejeo*
See: W136

D313. **Tonadillas: El majo discreto**
FONO SCHALLPLATTEN PD 07175
(orchestrated by Rafael Ferrer)
Benita Valente, soprano; Eastman Chamber Ensemble
Includes his *El mirar de la maja*
See: A17

D314. **Tonadillas: El majo olvidado**
HYPERION CD 66 176 WY
Ann Murray, mezzo-soprano; Graham Johnson, piano
Includes his *Las currutacas modestas*; *La maja dolorosa (1-3)*; *El majo discreto*; *El mirar de la maja*
See: W136

D315. **Tonadillas: El majo tímido**
RCA VICTOR 4465
Conchita Badia, soprano
Includes his *Mañanica era*; Falla (Jota)
See: W136

D316. **Tonadillas: El majo tímido**
DEUTSCHE GRAMMOPHON 2530 598 (previously released as DECCA SMD 1166)
Teresa Berganza, mezzo-soprano; Felix Lavilla, piano
Includes his *La maja dolorosa no. 3*; *El tra la la y el punteado*
See: W136

D317. **Tonadillas: El majo tímido**
ORFEO A 038 831
Margaret Price, soprano; James Lockhart, piano
Includes his *Tonadillas*; *El tra la la y el punteado*; *La maja dolorosa (1-3)*; *El majo discreto*; *Elegía eterna*
See: W136

D318. **Tonadillas: El majo tímido**
RCA GL89904
(arranged for guitar by Julian Bream)
Includes his *La maja de Goya*; *El tra la la y el punteado*; *El majo discreto*; *El mirar de la maja*; *Amor y odio*; *Callejeo*
See: W136

D319. **Tonadillas: El mirar de la maja**
SERAPHIM 60044
Victoria de los Angeles, soprano; Gerald Moore, piano
Includes works by Haydn, Wolf, Mendelssohn, Bizet, Liszt, Verdi, Brahms, Schumann, Schubert
See: W136

D320. **Tonadillas: El mirar de la maja**
HYPERION CD 66 176 WY
Ann Murray, mezzo-soprano; Graham Johnson, piano
Includes his *Las currutacas modestas*; *La maja dolorosa (1-3)*; *El majo discreto*; *El majo olvidado*
See: W136

D321. **Tonadillas: El mirar de la maja**
FONO SCHALLPLATTEN PD 07175
Benita Valente, soprano; David Effron, piano
Includes his *El majo discreto*
See: W136

D322. **Tonadillas: El mirar de la maja**
LSC 2776
Shirley Verrett, mezzo-soprano
Includes his *La maja dolorosa (1-3)*
See: W136

D323. **Tonadillas: El mirar de la maja**
RCA GL89904
(arranged for guitar by Julian Bream)
Includes his *La maja de Goya*; *El tra la la y el punteado*; *El majo discreto*; *El majo tímido*; *Amor y odio*; *Callejeo*
See: W136

D324. **Tonadillas: El mirar de la maja**
FONO SCHALLPLATTEN PD 07175
(orchestrated by Rafael Ferrer)
Benita Valente, soprano; Eastman Chamber Ensemble
Includes his *El majo discreto*
See: A17

D325. **Tonadillas: El tra la la y el punteado**
DEUTSCHE GRAMMOPHON 2530 598 (previously released as DECCA SMD 1166)
Teresa Berganza, mezzo-soprano; Felix Lavilla, piano
Includes his *El majo tímido*; *La maja dolorosa no. 3*
See: W136

D326. **Tonadillas: El tra la la y el punteado**
ORFEO A 038 831
Margaret Price, soprano; James Lockhart, piano
Includes his *Tonadillas*; *El majo tímido*, *La maja dolorosa* (*1-3*); *El majo discreto*; *Elegía eterna*
See: W136

D327. **Tonadillas: El tra la la y el punteado**
RCA GL89904
(arranged for guitar by Julian Bream)
Julian Bream, guitar
Includes his *La maja de Goya*; *El mirar de la maja*; *El majo discreto*; *El majo tímido*; *Amor y odio*; *Callejeo*
See: W136

D328. **Trio for Violin, Cello, and Piano, op. 50**
ORION 83447
Thomas Rajna, piano with members of Gotham Trio
Includes works by Martinu
See: W140

D329. **Trio for Violin, Cello, and Piano, op. 50**
MUNDIMUSICA (1987)
Trio Mompou: Luciano González-Sarmiento, piano; Joan-Lluís Jordá, violin; Pilar Serrano, cello
See: W140

D330. **Trio, op. 50 (first movement)**
HIS MASTER'S VOICE 602
Barcelona Trio
Includes his *Intermezzo* from *Goyescas* (arranged for piano, violin, and cello)
See: W140

D331. **Two Impromptus (Dos impromptus)**
Volume 1 of two-volume set, VOX 5484/5
Marylène Dosse, piano
See: W144

D332. **Two Impromptus (Dos impromptus)**
CRD 1023
Thomas Rajna, piano
Includes his *Allegro de concierto*; *Capricho español*; *Carezza* (*Valse*); *Oriental* (*Canción variada, Intermedio y Final*); *Rapsodia aragonesa*; *Valses poéticos*
See: W144

D333. **Two Military Marches (Dos marchas militares)**
CRC-1037
Thomas Rajna, piano
Includes his *Impromptu, op. 39*; *Six Expressive Studies* (*Seis estudios expresivos*); *Marche militaire*; *Estudio op. Posthumous* (*Andantino espressivo*); *Elisenda*; *Paisaje*
See: W145

D334. **Vals**
CENTAUR CRC 2043
The Unknown Granados
Douglas Riva, piano
Includes his *Allegro vivace*; *Azulejos*; *En la aldea*; *Mazurka in E-flat Major*; *Mazurka in E-flat Minor ("Chopin")*; *Romanza*; *Conte*; *Preludio*; *Serenade for Two Violins and Piano*; *Primavera* (*Romanza sin palabras*)
See: W4

D335. **Valses poéticos**
Antología Històrica de la Música Catalana
EDITA PDI E-30.1069
Antoni Besses, piano
Includes works by Mompou, Gerhardt, Viñes, Montsalvatge, del Pueyo
See: W147

D336. **Valses poéticos**
VOX/TURNABOUT 34772
Alicia de Larrocha, piano
Includes his *Six Pieces on Spanish Folk Themes* (*Seis piezas sobre cantos populares españoles*); *Allegro de concierto*; *Danza lenta*; *El pelele*
See: W147

D337. **Valses poéticos**
Volume 2 of two-volume set, VOX 5484/5
Marylène Dosse, piano
See: W147

D338. **Valses poéticos**
COLUMBIA ML4294 (Historical reissue)
Enrique Granados, piano
Includes his *Goyescas: El fandango de candil*; performances by Albéniz, Marshall, de Pachman, Paderewski
See: W147

D339. **Valses poéticos**
ASLKAGER CD87024
Dana Protopopesca, piano
Includes his *Allegro de concierto*; *Oriental* (*Canción variada, Intermedio y Final*); *Capricho español*; *Six Pieces on Spanish Folk Themes* (*Seis piezas sobre cantos populares españoles*)
See: W147

D340. **Valses poéticos**
CRD 1023
Thomas Rajna, piano
Includes his *Allegro de concierto*; *Capricho español*; *Carezza* (*Valse*); *Two Impromptus*; *Oriental* (*Canción árabe*, Intermedio y Final); *Rapsodia aragonesa*
See: W147

D341. **Valses poéticos**
RCA RCD1-4378
(arranged for guitar)
Julian Bream, guitar
Includes his *Dedicatoria*; *La maja de Goya*; *Spanish Dances 4*, *5*; works by Albéniz
See: W147

D342. **Valses poéticos**
CALLIOPE 9204
(arranged for two guitars)
Jean Horreaux; Jean-Marie Trehaud, guitars
Includes his *Spanish Dances 2*, *4*, *11*, *12*; *Capricho español*; *Serenata del espectro*; *Deux danses caracteristiques*; *La maja de Goya*
See: W147

D343. **Valses poéticos**
CBS 78 268
(arranged by John Williams for guitar)
John Williams, guitar
Includes his *Spanish Dance 5*
See: W147

Appendix 1
Listing of Original Works by Scoring

Piano solo

A la antigua (incomplete)
A la cubana
A la pradera
Album: Paris, 1888
Allegro appassionato
Allegro de concierto
Allegro vivace
El amor de la vírgin (incomplete)
Aparición
Arabesca
Azulejos
Balada
Barcarola
Bocetos
Canción árabe
Canción y danza
Canción morisca
Capricho español
Carezza
Cartas de amor
Clothilde
Cuentos de la juventud
Danza característica
Danza lenta
Deux danses caractéristiques
Dificultades especiales del piano (incomplete)
Dolora en La menor
Elvira
Escenas infantiles
Escenas poéticas (first series)
Escenas poéticas (second series)
Escenas románticas
Estudio (Andantino espressivo)
Exquise (Vals tzigane)
Goyescas
Goyescas (Crepúsculo) [Sérénade goyesca?]
Impresiones de viaje (incomplete)
Impromptu (Allegro assai)
Impromptu (Prestissimo)
Intermezzo (Goyescas)
Jácara
El jardí d'Elisenda
Libro de horas
Marche militaire
María del Carmen. Prelude
Mazurka (alla polacca)
Mazurka (alla polacca)
Mazurka in E-flat Major

Minuetto
Minuetto de la felicidad
Moresque y canción árabe
Ni así la distingue
Obras fáciles para la educación del sentimiento
Oriental (Canción variada, Intermedio y Final)
Paisaje
El pelele
Prelude in D
Preludio
Rapsodia aragonesa
Reverie-Improvisation
Romeo y Julieta
Sardana
Serenata española
La sirena (Valse Mignone)
Six Expressive Studies in the Form of Easy Pieces
Six Pieces on Spanish Folk Themes
Los soldados de cartón
Tango de los ojos verdes
Twelve Spanish Dances
Two Impromptus
Valse de concert
Valses poéticos

Piano ensemble

En la aldea (duet)
"Triana" from Albéniz's *Iberia* (two pianos)
Two Military Marches

Chamber ensemble

Andante (violin and piano)
Danza gallega (cello and piano)
Elisenda (piano, voice, harp, string quintet, flute, oboe, clarinet)
Escena religiosa (piano, organ, violin, timbales)
Intermezzos for the Wedding Mass of Dionisio Condé (string quartet, harp, organ)
Madrigal (cello and piano)
Melodía (violin and piano)
Pequeña romanza (string quartet)
Quintet in G Minor (string quartet and piano)
Romanza (violin and piano)
Serenade (two violins and piano)
Sonata (cello and piano)
Sonata (violin and piano)
Sonatinas (Clementi) arranged for String Trio
Three Preludes (violin and piano)
Trio (two violins and viola--incomplete))
Trio (violin, cello, piano)
Trova (cello and piano)

Lyric dramas

Blancaflor
La cieguecita de Belén
Follet

Gaziel
Goyescas
Liliana
María del Carmen
Melopea (incomplete)
Ovillejos o La gallina ciega (incomplete)
Petrarca
Picarol
Rosamor (incomplete)

Solo songs

La boira (with piano)
Canciones amatorias (with orchestra)
Canciones amatorias (with piano)
Canso d'amor (with piano)
Canso de Janer (with piano)
Cansonetta: El rey y el juglar (with piano)
Canción del postillón (with piano)
Canto gitano (with piano)
La diosa en el jardín (with piano)
Elegía eterna (with orchestra)
Elegía eterna (with piano)
L'ocell profeta (with piano)
Si al Retiro me llevas (with piano)
Tonadillas (with orchestra)
Tonadillas (with piano)

Choral

Cant de les estrelles
L'herba de amor (Pregaría en estil gregoriá)
Salve regina (see p. 132)

Orchestral

Boires baixes
Concerto for cello and orchestra (incomplete)
Concerto for piano and orchestra (incomplete)
Dante
Danza gitana
L'himne dels morts
Intermezzo (Goyescas)
Llegenda de la fada (incomplete)
Marcha de los vencidos
Miel de la Alcarria
Navidad. Finale
La nit del mort (incomplete)
Suite árabe u oriental (incomplete)
Suite on Gallician Themes
Symphony in E Minor (First movement only)
Torrijos

Arrangements and transcriptions

Chorale of J. S. Bach (string orchestra)
Concerto no. 2 in F Minor (Chopin. Re-orchestration of first movement)

Fugue in C-sharp Minor (J. S. Bach. For string orchestra, flute, oboe, clarinet, bassoon, trumpet, trombone)
Jota aragonesa (A. Noguéra. For piano solo, for orchestra)
Moment musical (Schubert-Granados. For piano solo)
Suite vasca (Father Menesio Otaño. Transcription for piano solo of fourth movement)
Twenty-six Sonatas by Domenico Scarlatti (arranged, transcribed for piano)

Pedagogical writings

Breves consideraciones sobre el ligado
Método teórico práctico para el uso de los pedales del piano
Ornamentos
El pedal

Appendix 2
Chronology of Important Events During Granados's Lifetime

1867

Enrique Granados born on July 27 in Lleida.

A new constitution is adopted in Spain at the end of the Third Carlist War (a conflict over the claim to the throne), which remains in effect until 1923.

1877

The Catalan poet-priest Jacint Verdaguer (1843-1902) writes the epic poem "L'Atlántida," which later served as the subject of a symphonic poem by Enric Morera (1865-1942) and as text for a cantata by Manuel de Falla (1876-1946).

Joan Baptiste Parés (1847-1926) opens Barcelona's first major art gallery.

1879

Valentí Almirall (1841-1904) founds the first daily newspaper in Catalan, *El Diari Català*. Other new publications include the journal *L'Avenç*, the liberal Castilian-language newspaper *La Vanguardia*, and the anarchist weekly *La Tramontana*.

Catalan painter Ramon Casas (1866-1932) goes to Paris to study.

1882

Wagner's *Lohengrin* has its first performance at Barcelona's Liceu opera house on May 17.

Catalan composer Antoní Nicolau (1858-1933) premieres his symphonic poem, *El Triunfo de Venus*, in Paris.

1883

Architect Antoní Gaudí (1852-1926) begins his first significant works: the Casa Vicens in Barcelona (completed 1885) and the stables and estate at Pedralbes for Count Eusebi Güell, an important patron. In November Gaudí is appointed architect of his best-known project, the yet unfinished Sagrada Familia cathedral.

Menéndez Pelayo (1856-1912) writes *Historia de las ideas estéticas en España*.

Isaac Albéniz (1860-1909) studies composition with Felip Pedrell (1841-1922) in Barcelona.

1884

Catalan painter Santiago Rusiñol (1861-1931) holds his first exhibits. Clarín (1852-1901) writes *La regenta*.

1885

Catalan industrialists ally themselves with intellectuals to present King Alfonso XII with demands to recognize Catalonia's unique position in Spain in terms of economy, language, and culture.

With Alfonso's death in November, Queen María Cristina's regency begins.

The original Cau Ferrat (Den of Iron) is founded in Barcelona by Rusiñol and the sculptor Enric Clarasó (1857-1941) as a studio and meeting place for Catalan artists and intellectuals.

Wagner's *Der Fliegende Holländer* is performed at the Liceu.

1886

César Franck (1822-1890) composes his Violin Sonata.

1887

Wagner's *Tannhäuser* is performed at the Liceu.

1888

The Universal Exposition of Barcelona is inaugurated with a performance of *Lohengrin* and a series of piano recitals by Albéniz.

A monument to Anselm Clavé (1824-74), founder of the workers' choral movement, is unveiled. Choral singing continues to increase in popularity among the working classes.

The Spanish Socialist Party (PSOE) holds its first Congress in Barcelona.

César Franck composes his Symphony in D minor.

Erik Satie (1866-1925) composes his *Gymnopédies*.

Vincent van Gogh (1853-1900) paints *The Sunflowers*.

Under the influence of Dukas (1865-1935), d'Indy (1851-1931), and Bordes (1863-1909), Albéniz initiates a new period in his development, composing the complex, polyphonic piano piece *La Vega*.

Auguste Rodin (1840-1917) completes *The Thinker*.

1890

Rusiñol, Casas, and Clarasó have their first joint show at the Sala Parés, and the modernist school of painting and sculpture is critiqued as "pictorial, anarchist, and anti-historical."

From Paris, where Rusiñol now resides as correspondent to *La Vanguardia*, descriptions of Parisian café life reach Spain.

Felip Pedrell begins work on his Wagnerian trilogy, *Els Pirineus*.

Claude Debussy (1862-1918) composes *Suite Bergamasque* for piano.

1891

Felip Pedrell publishes *Por nuestra música*, a series of essays to awaken Spanish musical identity.

Founding ceremony of the Orfeó Català.

Fourteen-year-old cellist Pablo Casals (1876-1973) makes his Barcelona debut.

1892

The first Festa Modernista, consisting of a painting exhibition by Rusiñol and Casas, takes place in Sitges.

1893

The second Festa Modernista, also at Sitges, features a performance in Catalan translation of Maeterlinck's *L'Intruse*. Includes a concert of works by Enric Morera and César Franck.

Provoked by the execution of a fellow anarchist, Santiago Salvador drops two bombs from the balcony of the Liceu, killing twenty people.

Claude Debussy composes his String Quartet.

Albéniz settles permanently in Paris.

1894

The third Festa Modernista, an art exhibit, is held at Sitges.

Debussy composes *Prélude à l'après-midi d'un faune*.

1895

Insurrection in Cuba (still a Spanish colony) turns into a guerilla war.

Morera founds a workers' choral society, Catalunya Nova.

Vincent d'Indy gives a cycle of concerts under the auspices of the Catalan Concert Society.

Pablo Picasso (1881-1973) moves to Barcelona.

1896

Felip Pedrell is named professor at the Madrid Conservatory.

Albéniz's operas *The Magic Opal* and *San Antonio de la Florida* are presented at Madrid's Apolo theater.

Giacomo Puccini (1858-1924) composes *La Bohème*.

1897

The fourth Festa Modernista features Morera's opera, *La Fada* (libretto by Massó i Torrents) and a reading of Apel.les Mestres's poetry cycle, "Cants Intims."

The tavern Els Quatre Gats is founded by Pere Romeu (1862-1908) and artists Casas, Rusiñol, and Utrillo.

Vincent d'Indy composes *Ferval*.

Angel Ganivet (1865-1898) writes *Ideario español*.

1898

The United States declares war on Spain after the explosion of the American warship the *Maine* in Havana harbor. Spain suffers a humiliating defeat and ceases to be a colonial power.

Rusiñol's drama *L'Alegria que passa* (with music by Morera) is given at the Teatre Líric.

1899

Wagner's *Die Walküre* performed at the Liceu.

Picasso frequents Els Quatre Gats and the café begins to publish a journal, *Els Quatre Gats*, later replaced by another publication, *Pel & Ploma*.

The fifth and final Festa Modernista takes place on July 5, consisting of a piano recital by Joaquín Nin (1879-1949) and a performance of Rusiñol's *L'Alegria que passa*.

Arnold Schoenberg (1874-1951) composes *Verklärte Nacht*.

1900

Picasso's first one-man show takes place at Els Quatre Gats.

Wagner's *Götterdämmerung* is performed at the Liceu.

The Wagner Association is founded to promote, publish, and translate into Catalan Wagner's music-dramas.

1902

Alfonso XIII assumes the throne.

Debussy composes *Pélleas et Mélisande*.

Ramón María del Valle Inclán (1866-1936) writes *Sonata del otoño*.

1904

Manuel de Falla composes *La Vida Breve*.

Maurice Ravel (1875-1937) composes his String Quartet.

1905

The foundation stone for Barcelona's Palau de la Música Catalana is laid.

Pianist Ricardo Viñes (1875-1943) gives a four-concert series, "Keyboard Music from its Origins to the Present," at Paris's Salle Erard, presenting repertory ranging from Byrd and Cabezón to Debussy's *L'Isle joyeuse*, composed the previous year.

Albéniz begins the piano suite *Iberia*.

1907

The Institute of Catalan Studies is founded by Prat de la Riba to research Catalan history and language and publish Catalan-language studies in various disciplines.

In Paris, Pablo Picasso paints *Les Demoiselles d'Avignon*.

Manuel de Falla moves to Paris.

1908

Inaugural concerts celebrate the completion of the Palau de la Música Catalana.

1909

To protest mobilization of troops in Morocco, violent demonstrations rage through Barcelona, culminating in a general strike. Churches, convents, and Catholic schools are burned by demonstrators. After a week of unrest, later known as Tragic Week (Setmana Tràgica), dead and wounded exceed four hundred.

Arnold Schoenberg composes his Piano Pieces, op. 11.

Violinist Mateu Crickboom (1871-1947), a leading figure in musical Barcelona, returns to his native Belgium.

Igor Stravinsky (1882-1971) composes *The Fire Bird*, which is premiered in Paris by the Ballets Russes.

Debussy composes his first book of Preludes for solo piano. (The second book is completed in 1913.)

1912

Picasso exhibits his "Blue Period" works at the Galeries Dalmau. This show is immediately followed by an exhibition of Cubist art.

Joan Miró (1893-1983) takes up painting in Barcelona.

Schoenberg composes *Pierrot Lunaire*.

Azorín (1873-1967) writes *Castilla*.

1913

Wagner's Parsifal is performed at the Liceu in commemoration of the hundredth anniversary of the composer's birth.

Miguel de Unamuno (1846-1936) writes *Del sentimiento trágico de la vida.*

La Vida Breve is performed at Paris's Opéra-Comique.

Stravinksy's *Le Sacre du Printemps* is premiered in Paris.

1914

World War I is declared. Although Spain remains neutral, the Spanish political right supports Germany.

José Ortega y Gasset (1883-1955) writes *Meditaciones del Quijote.*

Unamuno writes *Niebla.*

Manuel de Falla composes *Siete canciones populares.*

1915

Due to World War I, many Spanish artists leave Paris and return to Spain.

Manuel de Falla's ballet, *El Amor Brujo*, is given at Madrid's Teatro Lara. The National Society of Music, based in Madrid to promote Spanish works, holds its first concert consisting of chamber music by Turina and songs by Falla.

Debussy composes the Etudes, his last major piano work.

Charles Ives (1874-1954) composes his *Concord* Sonata.

Index

B=Bibliography; W=Works; D=Discography; unprefixed numbers=pages

A la antigua, W1
A la cubana, W2, D1, D2
A la pradera, W3, D3, D4
Abbado, Michelangelo, B4
Aeolian Hall, B6, B12, B57, B86, B119, B131, B134, B288-89, B351-52
Alaveda, Joan, B8
Albéniz, Isaac, 1, 6, 8, 9, 11, 14, 19, 22, 23, 25, 26, 34, 35, W12, W121, W138, D107
Albéniz, Rosina, 25, B381
Albet, Montserrat, B9
Album: Paris, 1888, 8, W4, W52, W87, W111
Aldrich, Richard, 29, B10
Alfonso XIII (Spain), 33, B5, B320
Alier, Roger, B11
Allegro appassionato, W5, D5
Allegro de concierto, 23-24, 26, 31, W6, D6-14
Allegro vivace, W7, D15
El amor de la Virgen, W8
Andante, W9
Andreu i Grau, Salvador, 22, 27, B207, B270, B314, B366
Anglès, Higini, B13
Aparición, W10, D16-17
Arabesca, 9, B64, W11
Astor, Mrs. Vincent, 30
Athenaeum (Barcelona), 7, B33, B330
Athenaeum (Madrid), 28, B255
Auberge du Clou, 19
Aviñoa, José, B22
Azulejos, 25, 26, W12, D18
Bach, Johann Sebastian, 19, 20, B24, B314
Badia, Conchita, 2, 18, 23, 28, 33, B1, B8, B17, B139, B162, B174, B180, B316, B323, D23, D279, D306, D315
Balada, 11, W13
Bannard, Joshua, B23
Barbieri, Francisco Asenjo, 12
Barcarola, W14, D19-20
Barrientos, María, 29, 33, B41, B80, B168, W49
Barrueco, Manuel, D183, D201, D203, D225, D277
Bauer, Harold, 25, W64
Bavagnoli, Gaetano, 30, B116
Beecham, Sir Thomas, 33, B318
Beethoven, Ludwig van, 9, 11, 17, 20, 22, 24, 25, 33, B52, B80, B314, B317, B329, B338, B368
Benko, George, B26
Berganza, Teresa, D297, D303, D307, D316, D325
Bertran, Marcos Jesús, B27
Biblioteca de l'Orfeó Català (Barcelona), W20, W28, W31, W49-50, W64, W67, W104, W136, W142, A2
Bizet, Georges, 9, 13, 24
Blancaflor, 14, W15
Bliss, Robert, 31, B79, B402
Boas, Robert, B28
Bocetos, W16, D21-22
Bohle, Bruce, B29
La boira, 17, W17
Boires baixes, B215, W18, W25
Boladeres Ibern, Guillermo, B30
Bonet y Cembrano, B31

Bori, Lucrezia, 30, B41
Borowski, Felix, B32
Brahms, Johannes, 24, B24
Braslau, Sophie, 29, B32
Bream, Julian, D52, D80, D210, D226, D259, D272, D286-87, D289-90, D312, D318, D323, D327, D341
Breitkopf and Härtel, W12
Bretón, Tomás, 12, 23, B188, B255
Brody, Elaine, 7n.7, B34-35
Broekhoven, J. van, B36
Buenos Aires, 34, B82, B171

Caballé, Montserrat, D25, D33, D54, D85, D138, D280
Café de las Delicias, 6
Cambó-les-Bains, 25
Camps, Josep, W82
Camuto, Alessandro, B37
Canción árabe, W20
Canción y danza, W21
Canción morisca, W22
Canción del postillón, W23
Canciones amatorias, 23, W24, A4, D23-25
  Mañanica era, D30
  Llorad, corazón, D28-29
  Mira que soy niña, D31
  No lloréis, ojuelos, D32
  Iban al pinar, D26-27
Canso d'amor, W18, W25, D33
Canso de Janer, W26
Cansonetta: El rey y el juglar, W27
Cant de las estrelles, 10, 26, W28
Canto gitano, W29, D34
Capricho español, W30, D35-38
Cardona, Rodolfo, B38
Carezza, W31, D39-40
Carreras i Granados, Antoní, B39
Cartas de amor, W32, D41-42
Casa Dotesio, 9, 26, B78, B122, W25, W75, W142, W145
Casals, Pablo, 2, 11, 12, 20, 29, 30, 33, 34, B10, B40-41, B58, B80, B130, B192, B216, B233, B273, B298, W42, W65, W71, W75, W80, D75, D237
Casas, Ramón, 1
Cassadó, Gaspar, 20n.41, 28, B223, A8, D75-79, D257
Cassadó, Joaquím, 20
Castilla, Alfonso de, B41
Catalan Concert Society, 11, 19
Catalunya Nova, 11, B331
Cau Ferrat, 19, B89
Céligny, 28, B384, B401

Centre de Documentació Musical (Barcelona), W12, W15, W24, W25, W33-34, W37, W40, W43, W50, W53, W60-61, W65, W71, W73, W76, W78-79, W81-83, W91, W96, W98, W100, W103, W112, W127, W129-34, W139, A2, A8, A10, A15-16
Chabrier, Emmanuel, 24, B53
Chamber Music Association of Barcelona (Associació de Música da Camera), 21
Chase, Gilbert, B42
Chase, William B., B43
Chausson, Ernest, 19, B89
Chavarri, Eduard L., B44
Chicago Grand Opera, 27, B399
Chicago Symphony, 29, B32, B126, B226, B343, W40
Chopin, Fryderyk, 9, 19, 21, 24, 25, 31, 33, B19-20, B64, B170, B187, B203, B259, B274, B279, B296, B314, B333, B338, B358
Chorale (J. S. Bach), W33
Ciccolini, Aldo, D87
La cieguecita de Belén, W34
Círculo de Bellas Artes, 24, B319
Clark, Walter, W83n.1
Clarín [Leopoldo Alas], 12, B268
Clothilde, W35
Collet, Henri, B45-46
Comellas, Jaume, B47
Concerto (cello), W36
Concerto (piano), W37
Concerto no. 2 in F Minor (Chopin), 20, W38
Condé, Eduard, 7, W30-31, W73, W125
Cooke, James E., B56
Copeland, George, 29, B57, D211
Corredor, J., B58
Cortot, Alfred, W64
Crickboom, Mathieu, 11, 19, 24, B40, B52-53, B208, B272, B287, B336
Crutchfield, Will, B61
Cuentos de la juventud, W39, A6, D44-46, D52
Cui, César, 9, B227
Culmell, Rosa, 29
Culp, Julia, 31, 33, B62, B80, B376
Curet, Francesc, B63
Cuspinera, C., B64

Dalcroze, Emile-Jacques, 22, B166
Damrosch, Walter, 33
Dante, 25, 27, 29, W40, D47

Danza característica, W41, D48
Danza gallega, W42
Danza gitana, W43
Danza lenta, W44, D49-51
Davis, Peter G., B66
de Bériot, Charles Auguste, 7
de Bériot, Charles Wilfrid, 7, 8, B35
Debussy, Claude, 8, B108, B255
de Larrocha, Alicia, 2, 23, B66, B69-71, B87, B111, B120, B140, B182, B282, B294, D7-8, D23-24, D49, D61, D88-92, D144-45, D165-66, D173-74, D279, D283, D336
Del Campo, Angel, B72
Delclós, Tomás, B73
de los Angeles, Victoria, D26, D28, D282, D304, D319
de Luca, Guiseppe, 30
Demarquez, Suzanne, B75
de Musset, Alfred, 15, B2
Deux danses caractéristiques, W45, A5, D53
Diémer, Louis, 7, B98, B209, B312
Dificultades especiales del piano, W46
d'Indy, Vincent, 8, 11, B255
La diosa en el jardín, W47
Dolora en La menor, W48
Domènech i Muntaner, Lluis, 23

Eames, Emma, B79
Ecole Niedermeyer, 7
Elegía eterna (orchestra), 28-29, W49
Elegía eterna (piano), W49, D54-55
Elisenda, 27, 33, W75, W50, W141
Elvira (mazurka), W51
En la aldea, W4, W52, D57
Ericson, Raymond A., B87
Escena religiosa, W53
Escenas infantiles, W54
Escenas poéticas (first series), W55, D58-59
Escenas poéticas (second series), W56, D58, D60
Escenas románticas, 24, W57, D61-63
Escolanía de la Mercé, 5
Escoles modernes, 22
La Esquella de la Torratxa, 13, B60, B269
Esteban, Julio, B94
Ester-Sala, María, B95
Esteve, Vincent, W44
Estudio, W58, D64-65
Exquise (*Vals tzigane*), W59

Falla, Manuel de, 1, 6, 8, 23, 35, B34, B66, B75, B152, B178, B200, B255, B282
Fasolt, Rémy, B98
Fauré, Gabriel, 20, 25, B255, B305, B312
Feliu y Codina, Josep, 12, B63, B110, B268, W45, W83, W91, W103
Fernández-Cid, Antonio, B101
Ferrer, Rafael, 9, B109, B190, A1, A4-5, A7, A17
Festes modernistes, 18-19
Feuermann, Emmanuel, D238
Finck, H. T., B103
Fiol Gonzalez, E., B104
Fisk, Elliot, D184, D202, D204, D227, D258, D268, D291
Fitziu, Anna, 30-31, B43, B86, B131, B134, B346, B351
Follet, 17, 24, 34, B307, W60
Fournier, Pierre, D76
Franck, César, 1, 8, 19, B273, B317
Franco, Francisco, 35, B120
Friends of Music, 29, B10, B105, B129, B246
Fugue (J. S. Bach), 19, W61

Gal, Francesc, 10
Gal y Lloberas, Amparo, 10, 29, 31, 32, B85, B99, B125, B184, B304, B391, W64, W142
Gandara, Francisco, B108
García, Manuel, 30n.65
Garriga, Carlotta, W64
Gatti-Casazza, Giulio, 27, 30, B400
Gaudí, Antoní, 1, 18
Gay, Joan, 1
Gaziel, 18, W62
Gelatt, Roland, B109
Gerhardt, Roberto, 23
Goodfriend, James, B111
Gorgoza, Emilio, 27, 29, B79, B288
Gottschalk, Louis Moreau, 7
Goya, Francisco, 25, B65, B70, B133, B157, B238, B276, B278, B282, B292
Goyescas (*Crepúsculo*), W63
Goyescas (opera), 6, 14, 25-32, W65, D84, D85
Goyescas (piano suite), 6, 24, 25-31, W64, D86-106
  Los requiebros, D124-25
  Coloquio en la reja, 26
  El fandango de candil, D107-8

Quejas, o La maja y el ruiseñor, D109-23
Epílogo: Serenata del espectro, D126
Grainger, Percy, 29, B119
Granados, Eduardo, 10, 33, 34, B13, B186, B195, B405, B407-8, W25, W39, W96
Granados, Enrique
youth, 5-8
early career, 9-11
stage works, 12-19
teacher, 22-23
pedagogical writings, 22, W19, W90, W102, W105
maturity, 23-28
in America, 29-31
death, 32-33
recordings, D97, D107, D113, D125, D216-17
Granados, Solita, 10, 28, 34, W55
Granados, Victor, 5n.1, 10
Granados Academy, 22, 23, 27, 34, B1, B2, B8, B16, B163, B166, B207, B210, B230, B260, B270, B274, B314-15, B321, B407
Granados de Carreras, Natalia, 10, B68, B101, B124, B167, B196, B217, B264, B283, W51
Granados Trio (Trío Granados), 23, B210
Greely-Smith, Nixola, B133
Grieg, Edvard, 9, 15, 19, 20, 24, 25, 29, B2, B18, B203, B227, B296
Gual, Adrià, 14, B2, B63, B135, B261, B327, B363, W15
Guillemot, Jules, B136
Gurina, Marina, 12, B198

Hackett, Karleton, B137
Halperson, M. von, B138
Hammond-Brake, Mavis, B139
Hansen, Mark, B140
Heine, Heinrich, 15, W28
L'Herba de amor, W66
Hess, Carol A., B141
Hess, Dame Myra, D114
L'Himne dels morts, B44, W67
Hindenburg, Field Marshall Paul von, 32
Hispanic Society of America, 31, B97, B121, B144, B169
Horne, Marilyn, D298
Horszowski, Mieczyslaw, 24, B338
Hotel de Cologne et d'Espagne, 7
Hull, A. Eaglefield, B146

Ibsen, Henryk, 14
Iglesias, Antonio, 8n.10, B147, W1, W5, W8-9, W16-18, W27, W32, W36, W51, W54-55, W59, W68, W82, W93, W94, W99, W140
Impresiones de viaje, W68
Impressionism, French, 8
Impromptu (*Allegro assai*), 11, W69, D127
Impromptu (*Prestissimo*), 11, W70
Intermezzo (*Goyescas*), cello, A8, D75-79
Intermezzo (*Goyescas*), orchestra, 30, W71, D66-74
Intermezzo (*Goyescas*), piano, W72
Intermezzos for the Wedding Mass of Dionisio Condé, W73
Iturbi, Amparo, D98
Iturbi, José, D11, D110, D220, D267, D276

Jácara, W74
El jardí d'Elisenda, 27, 33, W50, W75, D56
Jardí, Enric, B149
Jean-Aubry, G., B150-52
Jones, J. Barrie, B153
Jota aragonesa, W76
Joventut, 15, B31, B230-36, B327
Junqueda, José, 5
Jurnet, Francesc, 5

Kahn, Otto, 31, B402
Katz, Martin, D298
Kehler, George, B154
Kirchoff, Glen, W119
Kobbé, Gustave, B155
Konstantin, Rozensil'd, B156-57
Kreisler, Fritz, 31, 33, B80, B402, A13

Lamote de Grignon, Joan, 9, 11, 17, 26, B107, B174, A15, D191-94, D243-45, D252-54
Langhi, Ugo Ramellini, B158
Larrad, Mark, B159-60, B251
Legion of Honor, French, 28
Lekeu, Guillaume, 11, B220, B272
Libro de horas, W77, D129-30
Liceu Conservatory, 23, 55, B106
Liceu (opera house), 15, 17, 21, 25, 35, B120, B189, B193
Liliana, 18, W78
Liszt, Franz, 24, 26, B83, B170, B194, B197, B314
Livermore, Ann, B161-62
Llates, Rosendo, B163
Llegenda de la fada, W79

Lleget, Mario, B164
Lleida (Lérida), 5, 7, 26, B106
Lliurat, F., B165
Llobet, Miquel, A6, A9, A14
Llongás, Frederic, A11
Llongueras, Joan, B166
Llopis, Arturo, B167
London, 27, 29, 32, 33, B5, B90, B168, B214, B242, B318, B395, B397
Longland, Jean Rogers, B169
Lopez, Rosa Angelica, B170
Lorengar, Pilar, D24, D283
Lowenberg, Alfred, B171
Lympany, Moura, D100

McCormack, John, 33
McGrigor, Albert, B182
Madrid Conservatory, 11, 23, B59, B181
Madrid Philharmonic, 33, B322
Madrid Symphony, 25, B284
Madrigal, 28, 29, W80
Madriguera, Paquita, B172
Maeterlinck, Maurice, 14, 19
Malats, Joaquím, 1, 6, 14, 19, 20, 25, 26, B14, B50-51, B149, B182, B205, B245, B269, B379, B381, W6-7, W147
Malibran, María, 7
Mallorca, 18, B224
Manegat, Julio, B173
Maner, Mercedes, 33
Marcha de los vencidos, 11, 34, W81
Marche militaire, W82, D131-32
María del Carmen (opera), 12-14, 19, 23, 30, 35, W83
María del Carmen (piano prelude), W84, D152
María Cristina, Regent (Spain), 13
Marquez Villanueva, Francisco, 12n.20, 15, 18, B175
Marshall, Frank, 2, 23, 34, B21, B75, B101, B140, B176-77, B182, B262, B273, W64, W69, D107, D284
Marshall Academy (see Granados Academy), B260, W35, W46, W50, W60, W64, W69, W89, W116-17
Martinelli, Giovanni, 30
Martinotti, Sergio, B178
Mas-López, Edita, B179
Mason, A. L., B181
Massenet, Jules, 8n.11, 9, B48, W14
Mataró, 23
Matthay, Tobias, 22
Maxine Elliot Theater, B15
Mazurka (alla polacca), W85, D133
Mazurka (alla polacca), W86
Mazurka in E-flat Major, W4, W87, D134
Meléndez, Lluis, B183
Melodía, 24, W88
Melopea, W89
Mendelssohn, Felix, 9, B187
Menhuin, Yehudi, D232
Mestres, Apel.les, 15, 17, 18, 34, B16, B63, B110, B159, B179, B184, B218-19, B251, B253, B261, B308, B311, B363, B371, W49-50, W60, W62, W78, W108-9, W124
Método teórico práctico para el uso de los pedales del piano, 22, B140, W90
Metropolitan Opera, 27, 29, 30, 31, 33, B41, B43, B85, B116, B118, B124, B252, B290, B362, B378, B400, B404
Michelangeli, Arturo Benedetti, D222
Miel de la Alcarria, 8, 12, W45, W91, A7
Millet, Lluís, 10, 17, B102, B185, B255
Minuetto, W92
Minuetto de la felicidad, W93
Miró, Gabriel, B186
Moment musical, W94
Monteux, Pierre, 28, B243
Montoliu, Manuel de, B187
Montsalvatge, Xavier, B188-90
Montserrat (Abbey), W66
Moore, Gerald, D76, D232, D319
Moragas, Rafael, 17, 26, B191-94
Moreau, Leon, 20, 34n.78
Morera, Enric, 1, 10, 11, 15, 16, 19, B11, B89, B235-36, B245, B331, B363
Moresque y canción árabe, W95, D136-37
Morgades, Lourdes, B195-96
Morrison, Bryce, B197
Moszkowski, Moritz, 25
Mozart, Wolfgang Amadeus, 9, 20, 24, 33, B53, B269, B298, B314, B318, B338
Municipal Band (Banda Municipal), 22, B250
Muñoz, Eduardo, B198
Murcia, 12, B110
Musical Association of Barcelona (Associació Musical de Barcelona), 17, 25, 26, B19, B316

Musical Society of Barcelona
(Societat Musical de Barcelona), 11

Nagin, Carl, B199
Neufert, Kurt, B200
Newman, Ernest, B204, D2, D132
Ni así la distingue, W97
Nicolau, Antoní, 1, 9, 11, 17, B102, B245
Nin, Joaquín, 1, 19, 22, B45, B205-6
Nin-Culmell, Joaquín, 3
La nit del mort, W98

Obras fáciles para la educación del sentimiento, W99
Ogdon, John, D102
L'ocell profeta, W100, D138
Oller, Narcís, 6
Olot, 5
Orfeó Català, 9, 10, 22, 26, 29, 96, 106, B107, B168, B185, B213, B337, B393
Oriental, W101, D139-40
Orrey, Leslie, B214
Ors, Eugeni, B215
Ovillejos o La gallina ciega, W103

Packard, Dorothy Ream, B217
Paderewski, Ignaz, 20, 31, 33, B48, B80, B402, D107
Pahissa, Jaime, 1, 18, B253
Paisaje, W104, D141-42
Palacio de Bellas Artes, 18, B253
Palau, Enric, B219
Palau de la Música Catalana, 23, 25, 26, 27, 28, B17-18, B49, B54, B107, B213, B220-23, B225, B247, B295, B299, B313, B325, B341, B380
Paricio, Assumpció, 18, B308
Paris Conservatory, 5, 7, 25, B48, B98, B142, B209
Paris Opera, 28, B101, B169, B171, B398
Parsons, Armand, B226
El pedal, W105
Pedrell, Felip, 1, 2, 6, 22, 34, B84, B95, B111, B152, B227-29, B321, W4, W129, W143
Pel & Ploma, 17, B89, B193, B215
El pelele, 29, 31, B222, W106, A11, D143-50
Pena, Joaquím, 15, 16, 20, 21, 26, B13, B194, B230-36
Pequeña romanza, W107
Perini, Flora, 30
Periquet, Fernando, 27, 28, 29, B189, B237, B238, B255, B292, B319, B347, B368, B405, B408
Perlman, Itzak, D234
Peter II (Brazil), 5, B374
Petrarca, 15, W108
Peyser, Herbert F., B239
Pfeifer, Ellen, B240
Philharmonic Society (Barcelona), 11, 14, 19, 34, B24, B269, B287, B332
Phillips, Harvey E., B241
Piatigorsky, Grigor, D190
Picarol, 15, 16, W109
Picasso, Pablo, 1, 18
Pillois, Jacques, 28, B243
Pomés Pont, Antonio, B244
Powell, Linton E., B245
Prado Museum, 25
Prelude in D, W110
Price, Margaret, D55, D301, D309, D317, D326
Puaux, René, B249
Pujol, Joan Baptista, 5, 6, 22, B13, B182, B245, B330, W4

Els Quatre Gats, 19, B149
Queen's Hall Orchestra, 27, B90, B242, B395
Quintet in G Minor, 11, W112, D155

Rajna, Thomas, D1, D3, D13, D17, D20, D22, D37, D40, D42, D45, D48, D51, D56, D59-60, D63, D65, D104, D127, D130-31, D133, D137, D140, D142, D155, D157, D160, D164, D168, D171, D179, D328, D332-33, D340
Rapsodia aragonesa, W113, D156, D157
Ravel, Maurice, 7, 8, B35, B199
Reiner, Fritz, D73
Renaixança, 9, B11, B159
Reverie-Improvisation, W114, D158
Ricarts i Matas, Josep, B256
Riera, Juan, B257
Rinaldi, Antonio, B258
Risler, Eduard, 22, 23, 24, B53, B259, W64
Ritz-Carlton Hotel, 29, B105, B129-30, B246, B350
Riva, Douglas, 3, 34, B196, B260-64, W32, D15, D18, D43, D57, D134-35, D153-54, D159, D162, D334
Rodriguez, Santiago, B265
Romanza, W115, D159

Romeo y Julieta, W116
Rosamor, W117
Rosenthal, Moritz, 25
Rosetti, Dante Gabriel, 25, B305
Rostand, Claude, B266
Rostropovich, Mstislaw, D235
Rubinstein, Artur, B69, D119
Ruiz-Pipó, Antonio, B267
Rusiñol, Santiago, 1, 15, B236

Sagardia, Angel, B268
Saint-Saëns, Camille, 9, 11, 20, 24, 25, B19, B48, B53, B222, B255, B269, B298, B320, B332, W37
Sala, Estela, 11, B269, B332
Sala Granados, 22, 27, 28, B223, B270-74
Salabert, 17, 34, B195
Salazar, Adolfo, B275
Salle des Agricultures, 25, B136
Salle Pleyel, 24, 28, B81, B208
Salón Romero, 11
Salvador, Miguel, B276
Salvat, Joan, B277
Samulski-Parekh, Mary M. V., B278
San Sebastian, 24, B189
Santa Cruz de Tenerife, 5
Santpere, Josep, 18
Sardana, 6, W118, D160-61
Sauer, Emil von, W64
Scarlatti, Domenico, 24, 26, 31, B25, B31, B55, B86, B95, B147, B153-54, B208, B228, B259, B297, B324
Schelling, Ernest, 27, 28, 29, 31, 33, 34, B12, B48, B56, B90-91, B132, B203, B212, B242, B258, B279-80, B340, B383-90, B392-B402, B404-8, W104, W118
Schelling, Lucie (Mrs. Ernest), B391, W65
Schillkret, Nathaniel, W28, W116, W137
Schirmer, G., 27, 33, B385-87, B390, B392, B394, B398, B406-7, W2, W40, W44, W47, W65, W69, W71-72, W82, W106, W110, W118, W120, W146, A8, A11
Schirmer, Rudolph, B384, B389, B400
Schoenberg, Harold, B281-82
Schola Cantorum, 8
Schubert, Franz, 9, B78, B164, B187, B314, W94
Schumann, Robert, 6, 9, 21, 24, B13, B21, B53, B170, B187, B314, B332
Segovia, Andres, D230, D289, D293-96
Serenade, 28, W119, D162
Sérénade goyesca, W120
Serenata española, 9, B64, W121
Setmana Trágica (Tragic Week), 25, B38, B379
Si al Retiro me llevas, W122
La sirena, W123
Sitges, 18-19, B89
Six Expressive Studies in the Form of Easy Pieces, W124, D163-64
Six Pieces on Spanish Folk Themes, W125, A7, D165-70
Slonimsky, Nicholas, B285-86
Smith, Ismael, 32
Society of Classical Concerts (Societat de Concerts Clàssics), 19, 21, 34, B22, B231-34, B296, B298, B333
Los soldados de cartón, W126, D171-72
Sonata (cello and piano), W128
Sonata (violin and piano), W127
Sonatinas, op. 36 (Clementi), W129
Spanish Civil War, 34-35
Starker, Janos, D79
Starkie, Walter, B293
Stevens, Denis, B294
Stokowski, Leopold, D74
Stravinsky, Igor, 28, B243
Suarez Bravo, F., 19, B295-99
Subirá, José, B300-302
Suite árabe u oriental, W130
Suite on Gallician Themes, 11, 34, W131
Suite vasca, W132
Supervia, Conchita, D248, D284
S.S. *Sussex*, 31, 32, B3, B5, B12, B67, B74, B106, B123, B125, B137, B163, B173, B183-84, B249, B291, B303, B353
Symphony in E Minor, 34, W133

Tagliaferro, Magda, D180
Tango de los ojos verdes, W134
Tarazona, Andres Ruiz, 5n.4, B304, W93-94, W97, W127
Teatre Bosch, 18, B307
Teatre de Catalunya, 24,
Teatre Intim, 14, B2, B135, B309
Teatre Líric (Teatro Lírico), 9, 14, 19, 20, B64, B298, B309
Teatre Líric Catalá, 15, B63, B311

Teatre de Novetats, 14, 20, 21, B50-51, B269, B337
Teatre Principal, 14, 17, 18, 24, 27, B25, B31, B52-53, B93, B297, B308, B336, B338
Teatre Tívoli, 13, 14, B27, B310
Teatro Parish, 12, 13, B198, B300
Teatro Real, 28, B198, B320
Thibaud, Jacques, 25, 27, B54, B136, B317, W127, D233, D256
Three Preludes, W135
Tintorer, Emili, B327
Tonadillas, 23, 27, 28, 29, W136, A17, D279-85
  Amor y odio, D286
  Callejeo, D287
  El majo discreto, D306-13
  El majo olvidado, D314
  El mirar de la maja, D319-24
  El tra la la y el punteado, D325-27
  La maja de Goya, A9, D289-96
  La maja dolorosa, D297-305
  Las currutacas modestas, D288
  El majo tímido, D315-18
Torrijos, W137
Triana (Albéniz), W138
Trio (violin, cello, piano), W140, D328-30
Trio (two violins, viola), W139
Trova, 28, 29, W50, W141
Turner, J. Rigbie, B328
Twelve Spanish Dances, 6, 8, 9, 11, 26, 28, 29, 31, W142, D173-80
  Galante, D181-85
  Orientale, 26, A12, A15, D186-99
  Fandango, 9, D200-202
  Villanesca, D203-10
  Andaluza, 26, A2, A3, A13, A15, D211-49
  Rondalla aragonesa, 26, A14, A15, D250-60
  Valenciana, 26, 29, 31, A16, D261
  Sardana, D262
  Romántica, D263-65
  Melancólica, A14, D266-72
  Arabesca, D273-75
  Bolero, D276-78
Twenty-six Sonatas by Domenico Scarlatti, arr. by Granados, 24, 26, 31, W143, D151
Two Impromptus, W144, D331-32
Two Military Marches, W145, D333

Unión Musical Española, W3, W6, W10, W14, W16, W20, W24, W29-32, W39, W41-42, W44, W49, W55-58, W64, W66-67, W71, W74-75, W80, W85, W90, W95, W100-101, W104, W107, W112-13, W115, W122, W124-27, W131, W135-36, W140, W142-45, W147, A1, A3, A4-7, A9, A14-15, A17
Ureña, Pedro Henriques, B357

Valencia, 24
Valls i Gorina, Manuel, B358-60
Valse de concert, W146
Valses poéticos, 11, 26, 29, W147, A1, D335-43
Van Vechten, Carl, B361
Vernon, Grenville, B362
Vidiella, Carles, 6, 20, B333
Vila San-Juan, Pablo, B364-65
Villalba, P. Luis, B366
Villar, Rogelio, B367-69
Viñas, Francisco, 7, B222
Viñes, Ricardo, 1, 7n.7, 7-8, 26, B34-35, B370, W64
Vives, Amadeu, 1, 10, 17, 35, B255, B371
Vives, Ricart, 28, B55, B271, B315
von Karajan, Herbert, D71

Wagner Association (Associació Wagneriana), 19, 21, 24, B20-21
Wagner, Isolde, 26, B194
Wagner, Richard, 1, 6, 13, 15, 16, 19, 21, 24, B149, B187, B198, B236, B314, B359
Walthew, Richard H., B372
Weinstock, Herbert, B373
Williams, John, D80, D231, D259, D272, D285, D343
Wilson, Charles, B375
Wilson, Margaret, 31, B62, B376
Wilson, Woodrow, 31, 32, B62, B249, B376
Wirth, Helmut, B377
Wood, Sir Henry, 27, B397, D150, D209, D246, D255
World War I, 28, B183

Ysaye, Eugène, 24, B24

About the Author

CAROL A. HESS is Affiliate Professor of Music at Holy Names College, Oakland, Calif. She holds Masters' degrees in piano and piano pedagogy and is completing a Ph.D. in musicology at the University of California at Davis. She has written several articles on Spanish music.

Recent Titles in
Bio-Bibliographies in Music

Peggy Glanville-Hicks: A Bio-Bibliography
Deborah Hayes

Francis Poulenc: A Bio-Bibliography
George R. Keck, compiler

Robert Russell Bennett: A Bio-Bibliography
George J. Ferencz

György Ligeti: A Bio-Bibliography
Robert W. Richart

Karel Husa: A Bio-Bibliography
Susan Hayes Hitchens

Ferruccio Busoni: A Bio-Bibliography
Marc-André Roberge

Frank Bridge: A Bio-Bibliography
Karen R. Little

Otto Luening: A Bio-Bibliography
Ralph Hartsock

John McCabe: A Bio-Bibliography
Stewart R. Craggs

Lukas Foss: A Bio-Bibliography
Karen L. Perone

Henri Sauguet: A Bio-Bibliography
David L. Austin

Randall Thompson: A Bio-Bibliography
Caroline Cepin Benser and David Francis Urrows

André Messager: A Bio-Bibliography
John Wagstaff

Roy Harris: A Bio-Bibliography
Dan Stehman

Violet Archer: A Bio-Bibliography
Linda Hartig